W9-BZV-876

Spreading The Gospel Of Grace!

A Sermonic Commentary of the Acts of the Apostles

Dr. Norman P. Anderson

This book is not a critical commentary, so don't expect a verse by verse, and word for word exposition of the Book of Acts. It is a preaching commentary, based on a series of messages developed and preached to a congregation that I pastored. I have added a lot of extra supportive data and updated much of the material to today.

All Bible references are quoted from the New King James Version, unless otherwise stated.

Dedication page

I dedicate this book to all of the beloved people of Elk Grove Baptist Church of Elk Grove Village, Illinois that were part of the congregation while I served as their pastor. I was privileged to be their pastor from September of 1985 through June of 2000.

I preached this series of sermons on the Acts of the Apostles during 1995 and 1996. For all that the Lord accomplished in His church and in our lives during those years of serving the Lord Jesus Christ together, we give all glory to our gracious Almighty God. Many souls were rescued from the kingdom of darkness and were transformed by the power of the gospel.

Thanks for the privilege of learning to walk more closely with our Lord Jesus Christ. We trust that there was a miniature 'grace revolution' in each of our lives that will bear eternal fruit for His glory.

Table of Contents

Introduction to the Book of
The Acts of the Apostles

Dr. Luke wrote two of the twenty seven New Testament books, the Gospel after his name, and this book of the Acts of the Apostles. He was a companion of the Apostle Paul for some of his travels, as attested by certain passages where the author of the Acts of the Apostles switches to the pronoun 'we', instead of pronouns that indicate he is simply relating events as reported to him.

Most scholars believe that Luke was a Gentile although there are a few who believe he was a Hellenist Jew.

The author of the Third Gospel and Acts writes to someone named "Theophilus" (Luke 1:3; Acts 1:1). He writes an *"orderly account"* (Luke 1:3) of the life of Jesus, after having had *"a perfect understanding of all things from the very first"* according to what the original eyewitnesses and servants of the word handed down to Luke. Luke 1:2. With this information, one can gather that the author was not an eyewitness of the events of Jesus's life. But, the author had close access to those who were eye-witnesses.

Some fishermen loved to fly into the north woods of Canada for their annual fishing trip. They had to take all their supplies in as there was no lodge on the lake. They had built a rugged fishing shack to accommodate them with some modem of comfort. They were settling in for their week of fun, when they remembered that they had forgotten to pack any cooking oil to use in their fry pan. Then one of them discovered the fry pan on the stove. He delightfully called to his buddies, "Hey, we are OK. The oil is in the pan yet from last year!"

Don't use the oil in the pan from last year or last week, or even from yesterday. Let the Holy Spirit keep you fresh in His presence and power! It is my prayer that this book will contribute to the fresh oil of the Holy Spirit in your life.

As we begin these studies in the book of Acts, we see the foundation laid for a world-wide spiritual revolution. The Lord of the church reveals His plan for His church and establishes His power for His church. It is my prayer that these sermons that I have put into this written form will be a great blessing to your life. May our Lord inspire you and enrich your walk of obedience to Him. I implore you to yield your life to the service of our Lord that will impact your community and our world with the gospel of salvation. It is the gospel of God's grace.

Chapter One
Are You Ready For A Revolution?
Scripture: Acts 1:1-26

We live in a revolutionary world. Some revolutions are political and are often carried out by military force. Democracies are replaced by oligarchies and dictators. Socialism, and its twin, communism, takes over and government controls everything. Government doles out free stuff and citizens soon discover that there is never a free lunch.

When George Orwell wrote his novel 'Nineteen Eighty Four!' in the year of 1949, most people regarded it as an extreme speculation of the future, not dreaming that much of the speculation would become actual reality of our day. Big Brother is watching almost everything you do and nothing is personal and protected information. Surveys done without our knowledge even predict with amazing accuracy what you may purchase this week as you do your grocery shopping. The thought police are seeking more forcefully to control what you think and what you may express in public. We call it political correctness and anyone who dares to speak his mind is in danger of being accused of 'hate speech'.

One of the major revolutions of the last seventy years is the technological revolution with unbelievable rapid change in our way of living. Our security and our privacy is threatened on every hand. My son and his wife shared with me an incident that happened recently as they were sitting in their kitchen with both their cell phones turned on but not actively involved in a telephone call or a search on the internet. They were talking about recipes for preparing rutabagas. Within a couple of minutes they received several e-mailed recipes for cooking rutabagas. This shows how we are constantly being monitored through surveillance.

Chuck Swindoll wrote this a few years ago. "Soon many recent innovations will be commonplace. At the touch of a button, we'll have unlimited access to libraries of information. Shopping malls will be condensed to a home video disk for our televisions. Our cars will be rolling offices equipped with FAX machines, mini-microwaves, and video maps to guide us around traffic jams." . . . "Scientists are even forecasting a society based on artificial intelligence, robotics, and genetic engineering. What will it be like to program a computer to think the way you do, or swallow a micro-robot that doctors can guide to perform surgery, or wipe out genetic diseases like cystic fibrosis and Down's syndrome? These are all possibilities as we careen toward the year 2000 and beyond.[1]

With all these revolutions going on in our world, there is one revolution that is absolutely essential to every individual. It is the spiritual revolution that comes through Jesus Christ, a revolution of grace. Christ talked about it to Nicodemus in John 3 when he said, *"Except a man be born again, he cannot see the kingdom of heaven."* We are all dead in our sins and we must be made alive spiritually by the Holy Spirit of God or we are all doomed to an eternity totally separated from God.

Are you ready for a revolution? When you come to trust Christ as your Savior and Lord, the revolution begins in your life. Jesus Christ continues to radically change you as you submit yourself to His rule and control. When you are personally revolutionized by Christ, you then have one goal in life; that is to be part of the world wide revolution by being an effective and fruitful witness for Christ.

Let's consider **The Power for the Revolution.** There are three foci of the power for the revolution.

---

[1]   Charles Swindoll, Acts, Volume 1, page 9.

1. First, there is resurrection power. Verses 1-3.

"The former account I made, O Theophilus, of all that Jesus began both to do and teach, until the day in which He was taken up, after He through the Holy Spirit had given commandments to the apostles whom He had chosen, to whom He also presented Himself alive after His suffering by many infallible proofs, being seen by them during forty days and speaking of the things pertaining to the kingdom of God."

One constant theme of the apostles in their recorded preaching in the book of Acts is the resurrection of Christ. What power! Christ overcame the power of death and walked forth from the grave, victorious forever over the power of death. When you receive Christ as your Savior, you also receive new life that not even the grave can end.

We have the assurance that to be absent from the body is to be present with the Lord and we shall also be raised in Christ Jesus with new bodies that are no longer mortal. It is resurrection power that is revolutionary. This is dynamic power of energy and the ability to transform a life.

2. Secondly there is ascension power. Verses 9-11.

In the Christian church, there is very little emphasis upon the ascension of Christ, but there ought to be. Here is where the power of authority is focused. The power of authority is the power of the policeman who is directing traffic. When he puts up his hand to stop you in traffic, he does not have the physical strength and power to actually stop your car. But he has a uniform and a badge that gives him the authority to order you to stop your car.

Ephesians 1:16-23 says, *"Therefore I also, after I heard of your faith in the Lord Jesus and your love for all the saints, do not cease to give thanks for you, making mention of you in my prayers: that the God of our Lord Jesus Christ, the Father of glory, may give to you the spirit of wisdom and revelation in the knowledge of Him, the eyes of your understanding being enlightened; that you may know what is the hope of His calling, what are the riches of the glory of His inheritance in the saints, and what is the exceeding greatness of His power toward us who believe, according to the working of His mighty power which He worked in Christ when He raised Him from the dead and seated Him at His right hand in the heavenly places, far above all principality and power and might and dominion, and every name that is named, not only in this age but also in that which is to come. And He put all things under His feet, and gave Him to be head over all things to the church, which is His body, the fullness of Him who fills all in all."* Other translations make it clear that there is a difference between the power of the resurrection and the power of the ascension.[2]

Jesus Christ ascended to the Father and all authority was given to Christ Jesus over every other authority that exists anywhere in all of creation. Christ's authority is active in our behalf as believers. He is interceding for us constantly at the right hand of the Father, where He is given Sovereign authority.

3. Thirdly, there is Holy Spirit power. Verses 4-5, 8.

Christ promised the Holy Spirit to us and told his disciples that *"It is to your advantage that I go away; for if I do not go away, the Helper will not come to you; but if I depart, I will send Him to you."* John 16:7. In Acts 1:8, Luke records the words of Jesus just before He ascended to the Father. *"You shall receive power"* ('dunamis' or ability) *"when the Holy Spirit has come*

---

[2]   The Greek words used for the power of the resurrection are 'dunamis' (dynamic energy or power) and 'isxuos' (strength). The Greek word used for the power of the ascension is 'exousias' (authority).

upon you . . ." This is the source of the ability to live and speak as witnesses for the Savior. Are you trusting the Holy Spirit for power? Are you committed to being godly and Christ like? If not, you are quenching and grieving the Holy Spirit.

Now let's give our attention to **The Plan for the Revolution.**

1. There is reality, not just a symbol. Verses 4-5.

- Acts 1:4 -5 says, *". . . being assembled together with them, He commanded them not to depart from Jerusalem, but to wait for the Promise of the Father, which, He said, you have heard from Me; for John truly baptized with water, but you shall be baptized with the Holy Spirit not many days from now."*

Water baptism is the symbol; the baptism of the Holy Spirit is the reality. Water baptism is an important symbol commanded by Christ. However, if you are not born again by the Spirit, water baptism means nothing and does nothing. Water baptism is the outward symbol of the reality of the Holy Spirit.

I am convinced that a whole lot of professing Christians, including those who have been baptized by immersion as professing believers, are merely cultural Christians and have never experienced the reality of being born again by the Holy Spirit. I say this because there is no evidence of the reality of Christ in their lives. Nothing seems to have changed and there is no fruit of righteousness in their behavior.

2. There is power, not just a program. Verse 8.

Acts 1:8 says, *"But you shall receive power when the Holy Spirit has come upon you; and you shall be witnesses to Me in Jerusalem, and in all Judea and Samaria, and to the end of the earth."*

Churches need programs and ministries, but we can end up just running the machinery of our programs without the power of the Holy Spirit. Sometimes we seem to forget why we do programs!

For example, we do an outreach friendship day every September to launch our fall ministries. This requires a lot of planning, and a whole lot of effort to make it happen. But it can become just a lot of work and activity if we lose our dependence upon the Holy Spirit for His supernatural power. The Lord doesn't want us to use a bag of tricks and gimmicks to influence people; it is the power of the gospel, the word of God that changes people's lives as it brings them to repentance and to saving faith in Jesus Christ. Romans 1:16 expresses this well. *"I am not ashamed of the gospel of Christ, for it is the power of God to salvation of everyone who believes, for the Jew first, and also for the Greek."*

3. We are to be witnesses, not just promoters. Verse 8.

A witness is one who shares what he knows to be true. A witness for Christ is one who knows Him personally and has been changed by His personal relationship with Him.

The modern day churches have often fallen into the trap of promoting the church rather than witnessing of Christ. George Barna said, "Jesus Christ was a marketing specialist." Really? It seems to me that the Gospels reveal that he said such things that often upset the religious leaders. His teachings drove people away. John 6:66-68 tells us, *"From that time many of His disciples went back and walked with Him no more. Then Jesus said to the twelve, "Do you also want to go away?" But Simon Peter answered Him, "Lord, to whom shall we go? You have the words of eternal life."*

Karl Barth once wrote, "The word of God is not for sale; and therefore it has no need of shrewd salesmen. The word of God is not seeking patrons; therefore it refuses price cutting and bargaining; therefore it has no need of middlemen. The word of God does not compete with other commodities which are being offered to men on the bargain counter of life. It does not care to be sold at any price. It only desires to be its own genuine self, without being compelled to suffer alterations and modifications . . . It will, however, not stoop to overcome resistance with bargain counter methods. Promoters' success are sham victories; their crowded churches and the breathlessness of their audiences have nothing in common with the word of God."

The evangelical churches, in my analysis, are becoming continually weaker and more ineffective, because we are succumbing to being merely promoters rather than witnesses. The message is often being compromised because the bottom line is more numbers at any cost. We are not promoters to get people to join some religious club; we are witnesses to bring sinners into encounter with Jesus Christ.

4. The plan is universal, not just local. Verse 8.

It is clear that the Lord's plan was that the witness of His people would be world-wide, and not just confined to the Jews in Jerusalem or even in Palestine.

Many churches actually have almost no involvement in world-wide missions. Many of the new churches that are focusing on "user friendly approaches" will openly say, "We are going to just focus here in our community and we do not have any intention of supporting missionaries in Ivory Coast or Thailand."

Now let us take a look at **The People for the Revolution.**

1. They were failing, often faithless people. Verses 12-15.

When you read the list of those who were present in the upper room, you see that it was just a small group. The eleven disciples are named, Jesus's brothers, the women and Mary, the mother of Jesus. There were about 120 in all. Not an impressive lot and from their past failures, not a very likely lot to leave the task of spreading the gospel in their hands. However they are a transformed group of people after the resurrection, and after Pentecost. This is clearly seen in the book of Acts.

2. They were praying people. Verse 14.

"They all continued with one accord in prayer and supplication . . ." They were waiting for the coming of the Holy Spirit as the Lord had commanded them to do. Verse 4.

Today, we do not need to wait for the H.S. to come or persevere in prayer to get the Holy Spirit. Pentecost has already happened. The Holy Spirit is here and indwells every true believer. However we need to be people of prayer so that we are filled or controlled constantly by the Holy Spirit. If our lives are dirty or cluttered, the Holy Spirit cannot fill us.

3. They were committed people. Verse 15 ff.

Here you find Peter leading the people to select another to take Judas Iscariot's place among the twelve. He had to be one who was a first-hand witness of Christ and His resurrection. Verses 21 - 22. There is a great debate among Bible scholars as to whether Peter was acting unwisely on his own or if this was really according to God's will. G. Campbell Morgan and others believe that Peter jumped the gun and was simply following his own impulses. They taught that Saul of Tarsus, (renamed

Paul after his conversion on the Damascus Road) was God's intended replacement for Judas. Some also question their method of casting lots to make their choice. However, this was basically their voting system. Their hearts were right and they were depending upon the Lord to guide their vote. Verses 24 - 26. These common every day variety people were committed to following through on the Lord's commands, to be his witnesses to the whole world.

Kenneth Gangel once wrote, "In 1903, Bolshevism was born with seventeen supporters. By the mid-1980's, Communism controlled over 1 billion people, almost one-fourth of the population of the entire world. American Communists, not a dominant force on the political scene in the United States, reportedly contribute 38 percent of their gross annual income for the cause of Communism. American Christians, by contrast, give less than 1 percent."

What we need in the modern day evangelical church, including our local assembly, is a revival in our lives to lead us to commitment to Christ and His kingdom's work.

4. They were expectant people. Verses 4, 14.

The Lord commanded them to stay in Jerusalem and wait; and they were praying constantly, expecting the promise of the Holy Spirit to be fulfilled. They were not disappointed; God answered their prayers as He had promised.

How about us? Do we pray? When we pray, do we expect anything from the Lord?

Thomas A. Kinsey, a pastor in Salem, New Hampshire, tells about a birthday card he sent his dad. It was his father's 75th birthday. Kinsey was looking for "that perfect card." Standing there in the card shop, his eyes kept going back to one card, one that had a drawing of two boats tied to a dock in what appeared to be a New England town.

Although Kinsey lives in New England, his parents live in the hills of West Virginia. His parents had never owned a boat or even shown any interest in boating. His dad had a childhood experience that caused him to fear the water. He had never learned how to swim. But, Kinsey continued to look at the card - there was something about it that was meaningful.

You see, Kinsey describes his father as a very simple man. If you drew a line through the pilgrimage of life, his father would not vary from that line one bit. He believes in simplicity. His style is uncomplicated.

As Kinsey continued to look at the card, he noticed that one boat was a sailboat, the other a rowboat. He wondered, if his father had to make the choice of which boat he would prefer to cross that body of water, which would he choose? Kinsey bought the card, and in a note to his Dad shared the thoughts he had in the card shop. Then he asked his father this question, "In your simple style of living, and with your ability to decide things that make the most sense, which boat would you choose?"

Several weeks later, he received this response from his father, "I noticed that the rowboat had no engine, but that the sailboat had a sail. My question, before making a decision, is there any wind?"[3]

The question we want to ask is, is there any wind? Must we spend the rest of our days rowing-dependent only on our own power alone - or might we put up our sails and catch the wind of God?

---

[3] Dynamic Preaching Magazine, May, 1993.

Is there any wind? The answer is yes, there is the wind of the Holy Spirit for all believers. Another probing question: Are you in a place with the Lord where you are catching the wind? Let's confess our sins, and ask the Lord to cleanse us so that His Holy Spirit might control us. Let's catch the wind in our sails.

"Spirit of the Living God"
(Daniel Iverson, lyrics and tune)

Spirit of the living God, fall afresh on me!
Spirit of the living God, fall afresh on me!
Melt me, mold me, fill me, use me.
Spirit of the living God, fall afresh on me!

Chapter 2
The Shot Heard Around The World!
Scripture: Acts 2:1-47

"Don't fire unless fired upon; but if they mean to have a war, let it begin here," were the words uttered, April 19, 1775 by John Parker, commander of the force of the Minutemen at the Battle of Lexington, Massachusetts. Someone did fire the first shot, no one knows who, and the war began that ultimately led to the Declaration of Independence of the colonies and the formation of a democracy in the United States of America. It was Ralph Waldo Emerson in his 1836 writing "The Concord Hymn" that called this first shot of the Revolutionary War "the shot heard around the world".

The Revolution of Grace was launched officially by another shot that has been heard around the world for almost two millennia now. Pentecost is the historic day when the Holy Spirit came in fulfillment of the promised gift of God, the Father. Acts 1:4, 5. The historic coming of the H.S. is the power of God for the revolutionary work of Christ in building His church.

It is crucial to understand and interpret this second chapter of Acts properly. We must not read into the text certain phenomena that have arisen in recent decades of church history. It is also crucial to realize that we cannot and should not try to repeat Pentecost. Pentecost is not to be repeated any more than the crucifixion of Christ is to be repeated. Rather believers are to seek the constant control of the Holy Spirit, making use of the available resource of the Holy Spirit to be Christ's witnesses every day. Our lives need to be consistently Christ-like and our tongues need to be consistently inflamed by the Holy Spirit to speak forth the gospel. For every true believer this can be so and ought to be so because of Pentecost.

Vance Havner once cryptically said, "We are not going to move this world by criticism of it nor by conformity to it, but by combustion within it of lives ignited by the Spirit of God."[4]

First, let's take a look at **The Event of Pentecost. Verse 1.**

Pentecost is the term we associate with the coming of the Holy Spirit ten days after Christ ascended into heaven. However, the day of Pentecost was a feast celebrated by the Jews every year. F. F. Bruce describes the Day of Pentecost. "The day of Pentecost was so called because it was celebrated on the fiftieth (Greek - pentekostos) day after the presentation of the first harvested sheaf of the barley harvest, i.e. the fiftieth day from the first Sunday after Passover (cf. Leviticus 23:15f.). It was known among Hebrew speaking people as the "feast of weeks" . . . and also as "the day when "the first-fruits of wheat harvest" (Exodus 34:22a) were presented to God."[5] Pentecost took place fifty days after Passover and was like an annual 'Thanksgiving Day' for the Jews.

Therefore the occasion of Pentecost was not new; what happened on that particular "Day of Pentecost" was new. The Holy Spirit came in Old Testament times upon specific people, enabling them to accomplish specific God-assigned tasks. The Holy Spirit came in a new way at Pentecost. The Holy Spirit came to indwell all true believers and to constantly work in the hearts of unbelievers, drawing them to the Savior. Pentecost is the first occasion where all believers were baptized by the Spirit and were also immediately indwelt permanently by the Holy Spirit. From Pentecost onward until today, every person who comes to repentance and faith in Jesus Christ, at that

---

[4] Vance Havner quoted by Warren Wiersbe, The Bible Exposition Commentary, Volume 1, Victor Books, Wheaton, IL, 1989, page 406.

[5] F.F. Bruce, Commentary. On Acts, New International Commentary, Eerdman's Publishing Co, Grand Rapids, MI., pages 53-54.

moment is baptized with the Spirit of God. That is the occasion of the new birth.

Now let's consider **The Evidence or Signs of the Baptism of the Holy Spirit. Verses 2-11.**

The evidence was heard by all gathered in the house. Two notable things are heard by all in the house: a sound of a mighty wind and the speaking in tongues or other languages.

1. There was *"a sound from heaven, as of a rushing mighty wind"* Verses 2 or as the NIV expresses it, *"the sound like the blowing of a violent wind."* We read that this wind came from heaven. This wind was spectacular and a noticeably loud sound, like the roar of a jumbo jet as the pilot begins his take off.

My wife and I remember when we were pastoring and living in Elk River, Minnesota in 1965. Tornadoes hit Fridley, Minnesota around five in the evening of May 6th. About 13 or 14 people were killed and 425 homes were totally destroyed. As we stood outside our home, we heard the distant roar like a jet in the distance, at our home in Elk River, about 30 miles away. We are certain it was the sound of the tornadoes passing by that thankfully didn't touch down in our community.

Noisy tornadoes are devastating, destructive winds. The Pentecost wind was not a destructive wind but it was a revolutionary, constructive wind that got everyone's attention as they waited prayerfully in that upper room,

2. On the day of Pentecost, *"they were all filled with the Holy Spirit and began to speak with other tongues, as the Spirit gave them utterance."* Verse 4.

The following explanation in verses 5-11 makes it abundantly clear that the '*tongues*' spoken was not some sort of heavenly language but rather the various languages spoken by Jews that were gathered there in Jerusalem from other parts of the civilized world. Even though those speaking were Galileans, they were speaking in other languages of Jews who had been born in other parts of the Roman Empire and were in Jerusalem on business or because they were on some religious pilgrimage for certain holy days, Passover and the Feast of Weeks, (Pentecost), for example. In verses 8, they are expressing their amazement that they heard these Galilean followers of Jesus speaking *"our own language in which we were born. . ."* [6]

They heard them *"speaking in our own tongues,"* (languages) *"the wonderful works of God."* Verse 11.

It was the sound of the violent wind that brought other people to the location of this house where the 120 were gathered. Verse 6 says, *"And when this sound occurred, the multitude came together. . ."* The evidence that they saw (verse 3) was the appearance of tongues of fire that came and settled upon the apostles who were gathered there. Many assume that the tongues of fire fell on all one hundred twenty believers who were gathered together. However, verse 14 leads me to believe that only the twelve apostles spoke in tongues and it was only upon the apostles that the tongues of fire descended. According to the last part of verse 3, one tongue of fire sat upon each of them.

As they saw this, they no doubt thought of the words of John, the Baptist, at the baptism of Jesus. *"I indeed baptize you with water unto repentance, but He who is coming after me is*

---

[6] In Greek, the word "dialectos" is used in Acts 2:6 and 8; and the word "glossa" is used in Acts 2:4 and 11.

mightier than I, whose sandals I am not worthy to carry. He will baptize you with the Holy Spirit and fire."

Our brothers and sisters in Christ, of the charismatic persuasion, make the mistake of still seeking for the repetition of Pentecost, asking for the baptism of the Holy Spirit. They interpret that believers must wait or tarry until the Spirit baptizes them, usually also adding that receiving the gift of speaking in tongues is the sign of the baptism of the Spirit.

The historical baptism of the Holy Spirit happened once and for all time, never to be repeated. Joel's prophecy has been fulfilled once for all time. Therefore, for born-again believers to be seeking for the same signs of the original coming of the Holy Spirit that occurred at Pentecost is unwarranted and improper. Pentecost's signs are not to be repeated, even as the resurrection of Christ needs not to be repeated, or the post resurrection appearances of Christ need not to be repeated.

The baptism of the Holy Spirit of each true believer takes place at the time of his true repentance and new birth. 1 Corinthians 12:13 clearly states *"For by one Spirit we were all baptized into one body . . . and have all been made to drink into one Spirit."* These signs were necessary at Pentecost to confirm the fulfilled promise of Jesus in John 16:7-11, regarding the special outpouring of the Holy Spirit historically. *"Nevertheless I tell you the truth. It is to your advantage that I go away; for if I do not go away, the Helper will not come to you; but if I depart, I will send Him to you. And when He has come, He will convict the world of sin, and of righteousness, and of judgment: of sin, because they do not believe in Me; of righteousness, because I go to My Father and you see Me no more; of judgment, because the ruler of this world is judged."* In Acts 1:4-5, Jesus had also told them before His ascension that they would be baptized by the Spirit *"not many days from now."* Acts 1:4-5.

Next we see **The Explanation of the Coming of the Holy Spirit. Verses 12-21.**

The reaction amongst the Jews gathered there in Jerusalem is amazement and perplexity as to what they heard. Verse 12. *"Whatever could this mean?"* is the significant question that they are asking.

If you can get every unbeliever to the point of asking this question about Christ, about the cross, the resurrection and the working of God, the Holy Spirit, they are well on their way to believing in Christ.

This first question often leads a person through the investigation stage to the next question in verse 37, *"Brothers, what shall we do?"* or, in essence, "How can I be saved?"

First we see the explanation given by the scoffers or the mockers. Verse 13. *"Others mocking said, "They are full of new wine.""* They are drunk, they've just had too much to drink! It is interesting that Paul refers to wine in Ephesians 5:18. *"And do not be drunk with wine, in which is dissipation; but be filled with the Spirit . . ."*

Then Peter steps up and gives the explanation as he speaks for the twelve apostles. Verses 14-21. First, he states that they are not drunk; you don't expect that all twelve men are going to be drunk at nine in the morning. Warren Wiersbe says that orthodox Jews did not eat food or drink wine before 9 A.M. on a Sabbath or holy day. Peter continues that this is the fulfillment of the prophecy, spoken by Joel. Verses 17-21. *'And it shall come to pass in the last days, says God, that I will pour out of My Spirit on all flesh; . . . Your sons and your daughters shall prophesy, your young men shall see visions, your old men shall dream dreams. And on My menservants and on My maidservants I will pour out My Spirit in those days; and they shall prophesy. I will show wonders in heaven above and signs in the earth beneath: Blood and fire and vapor of smoke. The sun shall be turned into darkness, and the moon into blood, before the coming of the great and awesome day of the Lord. And it shall come to pass that whoever calls on the name of the Lord shall be saved.'"*

When you read Joel's prophecy, he obviously refers significantly to the end time judgment when Messiah returns a second time, but Peter says, this is the fulfillment of the Holy Spirit coming to launch the period of the "last days". From Pentecost until Christ comes back again is the "last days", the period of time that we call the 'age of grace' in which all people everywhere have time to be saved.

Here we have a clue as to who it was that spoke in tongues on the day of Pentecost. In verse 14, we read, *"Peter standing up with the eleven"* (the twelve apostles) *"raised his voice and said to them . . ." In verse* 15, Peter said *"These men* ('outoi' in Greek) *are not drunk...."* Obviously he is referring to the other disciples, not to the entire 120 which included many women. So I conclude that it is not the entire 3000 who were saved on the day of Pentecost, as many Charismatic Christians assume, that spoke in the other languages of the Jews that had gathered in Jerusalem from other lands.

Now we come to the **The Exposition at Pentecost. Verses 22-36.**

Peter preaches under the power and anointing of the Holy Spirit. Chuck Swindoll comments that Peter's sermon probably took no more than 4 minutes, but he overlooked verse 40 which says, *"with many other words he testified and exhorted them, saying "Be saved from this perverse generation.""* Luke's recorded content of Peter's sermon is simply the condensed version.

Here Peter the coward is gone and the bold preacher has arrived. He pulls no punches. He doesn't worry about political correctness, nor is he concerned about winning a popularity contest with his Jewish audience. He accuses them of participating in the crucifixion of the Messiah. Verses 22-24, 36. *"Men of Israel, hear these words: Jesus of Nazareth, a Man attested by God to you by miracles, wonders, and signs which God did through Him in your midst, as you yourselves also know - Him, being delivered by the determined purpose and foreknowledge of God, you have taken by lawless hands, have crucified, and put to death; whom God raised up, having loosed the pains of death, because it was not possible that He should be held by it. . . . Therefore let all the house of Israel know assuredly that God has made this Jesus, whom you crucified, both Lord and Christ."*

Peter was not concerned about them saying to him after he finished preaching, "Oh, Pastor, that was a wonderful sermon." Peter's exposition holds forth Jesus Christ and causes every Jew listening to examine who Christ Jesus is. They were all waiting for the promised Messiah (Hebrew), the Christ (Greek), the Anointed One of God.

Peter emphasizes four points about Christ.

1. The historic basis: Verse 22. *"Men of Israel, hear these words: Jesus of Nazareth, a Man attested by God to you by miracles, wonders, and signs which God did through Him in your midst, as you yourselves also know . . ."*

2. He appeals to King David's prophecy in Psalm 16:8-11 as he declares that Jesus's resurrection is the fulfillment of that prophetic Psalm. David wasn't speaking about himself because his tomb was there in their city, Jerusalem. Verses 25-31.

3. The apostles were all eye witnesses of the resurrected Christ. Verse 32. They were not present to see Him come forth from the grave, but they had seen Jesus in His new resurrected body. They had conversed with Him, had eaten with Him and had touched the nail-scarred hands and feet.

4. God the Father had taken Christ Jesus and exalted Him to his right hand. The Father gave Him the promised Holy Spirit who was now poured out upon them by Christ Jesus that very day. Verse 33.

It was a very simple message with profound power, the power of God unto salvation.

Finally we see **The Effects of Pentecost. Verses 37-47.**

1. The Holy Spirit induced conviction. Verse 37. *"Now when they heard this, they were cut to the heart, and said to Peter and the rest of the apostles, "Men and brethren, what shall we do?"*

This is what we need today, sinners "cut to the heart." When the word of God is preached, we need the Holy Spirit moving upon people's consciences, making them deeply aware and bothered about their sins. Preaching is not supposed to just comfort the afflicted but to afflict the comfortable. We do not come to church just to feel good, but to hear the word of God and respond properly to it. When we repent and believe in Jesus Christ, we will then feel wonderful because of what God has done in changing our hearts and lives. This is where the 'seeker-sensitive' methodology goes astray. The purpose of preaching the gospel is not to make non-repentant sinners feel good so they will come to church again. The intended result is that the gospel will cut them to the heart, showing them that they are hopelessly lost without a Savior.

2. The Holy Spirit inspired instruction. Verses 38-40.

"Then Peter said to them, "Repent, and let every one of you be baptized in the name of Jesus Christ for the remission of sins; and you shall receive the gift of the Holy Spirit. For the promise is to you and to your children, and to all who are afar off, as many as the Lord our God will call." And with many other words he testified and exhorted them, saying, "Be saved from this perverse generation."

a. Repent!

The word 'repent' is from a Greek word, 'metanoia' which means to "change your mind", not just to feel sorry for your sins. It means that you change your mind about yourself, recognizing that you are a hopelessly lost sinner, undeserving of any mercy from God. It means you change your mind about who Jesus really is. It means that you now accept who Christ really is and what He has done for you on the cross. Like these Jewish people gathered there in Jerusalem, many of whom probably were mocking Him and crying out "Crucify Him." Now they see that He is the Messiah Savior, God, the Son, the Lamb of God sacrificed on the divine altar of a Roman cross.

b. Be baptized!

Water baptism does not save you, the baptism of the Holy Spirit does! Clearly from other Scriptures, baptism is for those who have repented and believed and have experienced the new birth by the Holy Spirit. Even in context here, we see that it is those who believed who were baptized and added to the church membership. Verse 41. *"Then those who gladly received his word were baptized; and that day about three thousand souls were added to them."*

c. Don't delay - do it now! Verse 40. *"And with many other words he testified and exhorted them, saying, "Be saved from this perverse generation."*

"Be saved from this perverse generation" is not an exhortation to do something that will add in any way to their salvation. Peter is warning them that as long as they delay their repentance and faith, they are still under the judgment of God that will come upon this corrupt generation. *"This perverse generation"* is an apt description of our generation also, and of every generation.

3. The Holy Spirit generated new life. Verses 41-45.

These believers gave evidence of genuine new birth. They had not just gone through a formality, but they had genuinely met the Savior and been made alive spiritually by the Holy Spirit. Notice the changes that we observe in verses 42-45. They didn't have to be begged to come to church every week, to sit under the teaching of the word of God, or to pray and fellowship with other believers. They devoted themselves to the doctrine or teaching of the apostles, to the observance of the Lord's Supper in true worship of the Savior, to prayer and to fellowship!

4. The Holy Spirit gave power for further witness. Verses 46-47.

It wasn't just a "Sunday go to meetin" kind of religion; it was an every-day experience. If your professed experience with Christ Jesus allows you for six days of the week to live differently than you do on Sunday, you don't have the real new birth. The result of such dynamically alive believers is that people are saved daily and added to the church.

It was Pastor Chuck Swindoll who told the story of Craig Barnes. It went something like this.

"After my parents got divorced and went their separate ways, my older brother and I spent a lot of time trying to figure out what had happened to our family. I was confused, hurt and furious at the turns life had taken. Eventually, I took to the road and began traveling around, trying to "find myself." But no matter how far I roamed, I couldn't escape the "why" questions. Why wasn't it working out at school? Why did I have no goals, no family, and no future? And where in the world was God?

One Sunday afternoon, I was hitchhiking somewhere in Oklahoma. An older black couple pulled over in their battered pickup truck and offered me a ride. The driver introduced himself as Stanley Samuels. He told me that he and his wife were on their way to the Ebenezer Baptist Church, where he was a deacon. Everybody always showed up for "Fifth Sunday - All Day Singing - Dinner on the Ground." They asked me to go with them. I started to say I was in a hurry, but the excuse sounded dumb before it even left my mouth.

As we made our way down the country road, Deacon Samuels and I got to know each other pretty well. He asked me what I was up to, and I told him I didn't have a clue. He told me he had just lost his job at the cooperative grain mill, and he really didn't know why. Things were hard, but he really believed God knew that.

When we arrived, Deacon Samuels just walked around smiling, joking with friends. After a while I saw him stand tall and begin to hum "Amazing Grace". By the time he got to the end of the first line, everyone had joined in singing, "I once was lost, but now am found . . ." I started to cry. It was the first time I had cried since my mother had left. Now the tears wouldn't stop. They felt warm and reassuring.

Through the fears, the pain and the hard questions, a glimmer of faith emerged, reminding me of the searching hands of the Father, I am found."

You may be a successful but frustrated business person; a frazzled, disappointed single parent; a confused, love-hungry teenager. The message is still the same: repent, believe in the Lord Jesus Christ and you will be saved! Find God through Jesus Christ! Better yet, let God find you!

I Surrender All!
(Lyrics by Judson W. Van DeVenter, 1896)

All to Jesus I surrender,
All to Him I freely give;
I will ever love and trust Him,
In His presence daily live.

Refrain:
I surrender all,
I surrender all;
All to Thee, my blessed Savior,
I surrender all.

All to Jesus I surrender,
Humbly at His feet I bow;
Worldly pleasures all forsaken,
Take me, Jesus, take me now.

All to Jesus I surrender,
Make me, Savior, wholly Thine;
Let me feel the Holy Spirit,

Truly know that Thou art mine.

All to Jesus I surrender,
Lord, I give myself to Thee;
Fill me with Thy love and power,
Let Thy blessing fall on me.

All to Jesus I surrender,
Now I feel the sacred flame;
Oh, the joy of full salvation!
Glory, glory, to His Name!

Chapter 3
The Revolution Explodes!
Scripture: Acts 3:1-26

Some people overcome their obstacles and handicaps through discipline and hard work. Booker T. Washington was born a slave, but had a deep desire for an education in spite of his family's desperate poverty. After much effort and study, he graduated from college, became the president of Tuskagee Institute, and is now considered by the New Encyclopedia Britannica to be "the most influential spokesman for black Americans" of his day.

Sometimes some ingenuity and creativity will work in your favor if you are up against a big disadvantage. One man faced a Goliath-sized problem when developers built a gleaming supermarket and a gigantic discount house on either side of his tiny general store. Undaunted, he scraped together his savings and purchased an eye-catching neon sign. Placed right over his storefront between the two mammoth competitors, it read: 'Main Entrance Here!'[7]

In Acts 3, we have the account of a man who could not help himself out of his predicament by any amount of positive thinking or creativity. It took the Lord's touch to heal him and revolutionize his life. It is God's plan and will to work through His people to revolutionize the world by changing the lives of people. Such obvious workings by God's Spirit plainly show forth the transforming power of Jesus Christ and glorify Him.

In this third chapter of Acts, we see **The Demonstration of Divine Power. Verses 1-10.**

---

[7] Dale E. Galloway, Rebuild Your Life , Tyndale House Publ., Wheaton, IL, 1987, pages 116-17.

1. Through faithfulness in the routine calendar. Verse 1.

The new founded church of Christ was still very much tied to the Jewish traditions and continued to keep the customary hours of prayer at the temple. They kept the tradition of prayer at 9 A.M., at noon and at 3 P.M.; however their praying was now no longer just a tradition. They were coming to the Heavenly Father, through their mediator, Jesus Christ.

It was as Peter and John were faithful in their routine calendar that they found themselves in the place where the Lord could work through them. Habits of worship are good for us. We need to discipline ourselves to come to corporate worship every Sunday. My parents taught us kids that there were certain times that we were to always be in the Lord's house; Sunday morning for worship and Sunday School, Sunday evening for the service and Wednesday evening for Bible study and prayer. In those by-gone days, all evangelical churches had Sunday evening services and mid-week prayer meetings. The writer of Hebrews makes this point in Hebrews 10:24-25. *"And let us consider one another in order to stir up love and good works, not forsaking the assembling of ourselves together, as is the manner of some, but exhorting one another and so much the more as you see the Day approaching."*

The demonstration of Divine Power often comes as we are faithful in the routine disciplines of believers. Peter and John had no premonition that God was going to do a special work that day at the temple gate. There is a much greater opportunity for you to experience the moving of the Holy Spirit of God in your life as you faithfully come to worship and study the word of God, than if you stay home to watch a football game, or bury your head in the Sunday newspaper, or seek to catch up on some duty around your home.

2. Through availability in the daily contacts. Verses 2-3.

Many were the beggars around the temple and on the streets. The temple was the favorite place to beg because people coming to the temple were in a mood to be generous in their alms giving. In verse 2, we read of one beggar being carried to his spot by relatives or friends, so he could ply worshipers for pity, so that they might give him some money.

The timing of it is God's doing, not just a happenstance. His friends had carried him and got him there at the precise time when Peter and John are coming, and he asks them for money.

Do you pray each morning about the Lord's leading you in the circumstances of your day? Do you view your contacts as divine appointments? Are you alert and available to be a witness for Christ?

Chapter 3 poses a real contrast to chapter 2. Peter preached to a massive crowd and 3000 were saved, but the encounter with this crippled beggar is personal work with just one lost sinner. But it is this work of the Lord's power in the life of the one person that causes the revolution of grace to explode. We never know what God will start when we become the instrument to reach just one crippled sinner.

When Dwight L. Moody, as a teen-age boy, went to work for his uncle in his shoe store, he was, according to agreement, enrolled in the Young Men's Bible Class at Mount Vernon Church, which was taught by Edward Kimball. Kimball was one Sunday school teacher who felt the importance of his work. He went to the store, hunted up the newcomer, put his hand on Dwight's shoulder and said, "I'm concerned for you." His lips trembled and he could say no more, but when he was gone Moody said to himself, "Now this is strange! Here is a man who has known me only two weeks, and he is concerned about my soul! I guess it's time I was concerned about myself." Young Moody went down into the basement, knelt behind some empty boxes, and gave himself to Christ. So easy was it to win this princely soul winner to Jesus.[8]

3. Through usability of Spirit-filled channels. Verses 4-6.

Peter and John do not simply ignore the crippled man and seek to brush him aside. Typical of many preachers, and other Christians also, they didn't have money to give to him. Verses 4-6 tell us, *". . . fixing his eyes on him, with John, Peter said, "Look at us." So he gave them his attention, expecting to receive something from them. Then Peter said, "Silver and gold I do not have, but what I do have I give you: In the name of Jesus Christ of Nazareth, rise up and walk."* The gift that Peter and John bestowed upon this despairing crippled man was more than he could have expected. To be able to walk, to leap, and to praise God, was a phenomenal gift in the name of Jesus of Nazareth.

If we have possessions to give, we ought to give to legitimate needs, but not to those who just do not want to work. The apostle Paul clearly says in 2 Thessalonians 3:10, *"if anyone will not work, neither shall he eat."* Even if we do not have money to give, we must not turn away without displaying a compassionate heart.

Even when we have the resources to give to the needs of another, just our giving of alms does not completely fulfill our responsibility as Christians. There is a much deeper need in every human life than merely the meeting of the temporal and physical needs. If they had been able to give him enough for a meal, he would be forced to beg come another day. So Peter and John, filled with the Holy Spirit, gave the cripple what he

---

[8] Encyclopedia of Illustrations, Tan, page 1319.

really needed, "*in the name of Jesus Christ of Nazareth*". They give him his health and salvation.

Are we as Spirit-filled Christians supposed to be going around healing people in the name of Christ, as Peter did? No! Signs and wonders were done by the apostles and their close associates as a means of authenticating the message of the risen Christ. John McArthur comments ". . . contrary to the teaching of many today, the early church was not a miracle-working church. Rather, they were a church with miracle-working apostles."[9]

We still see God performing occasional miracles of healing at times. However, it is not God's will to heal everyone from every disease and affliction whenever we pray for healing. All are going to die someday and that is established fact. The truth is that ultimate healing for the follower of Jesus is when we go home to heaven and someday receive our new bodies like unto Christ's resurrected body. This subject requires a further exploration at some other time. We need to remember that even false prophets, according to Christ, will do signs and wonders in an effort to lead people astray. Mark 13:22 says, *"For false christs and false prophets will rise and show signs and wonders to deceive, if possible, even the elect."*

Spirit filled believers, while helping with physical needs whenever possible, need to keep in mind that the main need of any human being is to know Christ personally as Savior and Lord.

4. Through transformation of helpless cripples. Verses 7-10.

---

[9] John Macarthur, Commentary on Acts, Volume 1, Moody Publishers, Chicago, IL,

In this account, we see the wonderful healing of a physical cripple, crippled from birth. He had never known what it was to walk, to run, and to leap. Now he walks, jumps and praises God all over the temple courts. Not only was his physical body healed, but he is transformed inwardly through Jesus Christ. This cripple is such a marvelous example of what Christ came to do - to make men whole spiritually.

Warren Wiersbe says, "It is easy to see in this man an illustration of what salvation is like. He was born lame, and all of us are born unable to walk so as to please God. Our father Adam had a fall and passed his lameness on to all of his descendants (Rom. 5:12-21). The man was also poor, and we as sinners are bankrupt before God, unable to pay the tremendous debt that we owe Him (Luke 7:36-50). He was "outside the temple," and all sinners are separated from God, no matter how near to the door they might be. The man was healed wholly by the grace of God, and the healing was immediate (Eph. 2:8-9). He gave evidence of what God had done by "walking, and leaping and praising God" (Acts 3:8) and by publicly identifying himself with the Apostles, both in the temple (Acts 3:11) and in their arrest (Acts 4:14). Now that he could stand, there was no question where this man stood!"[10]

Verse 11 tells us that the healed man held on to Peter and John, and that is a good thing for a new believer to do - hold on to believers. John Phillips comments, "We can picture the man as he walked out of the Temple, right past the Gate Beautiful. He must have cast a passing glance at the spot where that morning he had sat, a prisoner of his misery and woe. Do you think he said to Peter, "Thanks for everything, Peter, but I'm going back now to my old ways of life. I have a sentimental attachment to the spot over there. All I know is begging. Say

---

[10] Warren Wiersbe, The Bible Exposition Commentary, Volume 1, Victor Books, Wheaton, IL, page 412.

hello to me when you come back again"? Not he! He hung on to Peter and John until he was well past that benighted spot haunted by so many bitter memories of his past."[11]

As a believer, are you laying hold of the power of Christ in your life? Or are you still limping from some old enslaving habit, or some old associations that keep you from experiencing the deliverance and healing that Christ offers?

Now let's consider **The Explanation of Divine Power. Verses 11-26.**

1. The power is in Christ, not the channel. Verses 11-16.

Here is the pattern for us from the beginning. In all that the Lord does, take no glory to yourself. In verses 12-13, Peter clearly proclaims that it is not by their power or godliness that they had made this man to walk. *"So when Peter saw it, he responded to the people: "Men of Israel, why do you marvel at this? Or why look so intently at us, as though by our own power or godliness we had made this man walk? The God of Abraham, Isaac, and Jacob, the God of our fathers, glorified His Servant Jesus, whom you delivered up and denied in the presence of Pilate, when he was determined to let Him go."* Peter makes it crystal clear that this miracle was only possible through the Savior, Jesus Christ, exalted by the Heavenly Father.

Peter and John do not exalt or promote the healed man either. In some of our churches today we would immediately rush him up on to the platform and we would promote him on television, or get him on the Christian banquet circuit, and probably stunt his growth. This would happen especially if he is considered a

---

[11] John Phillips, Exploring Acts, Commentary on Acts, Kregel Publications, Grand Rapids, MI, page 70

celebrity, a sports star or a well-known person in our secular society.

Then Peter jumps at the opportunity to once again preach Christ. Verses 14-16. He is not "politically correct" nor is he particularly tactful. In fact, he would be considered down-right rude. Such an insensitive preacher could never be allowed to pastor our church. He would run-off all of our good givers. In the last part of verse 13, Peter says, *". . . whom you delivered up and denied in the presence of Pilate, when he was determined to let Him go."* Then in verse 15, he boldly declares that they *"killed the Prince of life, whom God raised from the dead, of which we are witnesses."*

His message is designed to bring conviction because conviction must precede conversion. Sinners must be preached lost, and be convicted of their desperate need of forgiveness and salvation, before they can ever be saved.

Whatever you see God do through you, make sure you remember to give Him the glory, because the power is in Christ, not in you. Whatever we do, we do in *"His name"* for all power and all authority is in Christ Jesus, not in us. If the president of the United States sends out a letter, the power of his authority in that office is behind his letter. The power of Christ Jesus is His authority over Satan, over sin and over death. That authority is given to Him by God, the Father, who exalted Him above every name and every authority that exists in all creation. Paul, the apostle prays that we may know *". . . what is the exceeding greatness of His power toward us who believe, according to the working of His mighty power which He worked in Christ when He raised Him from the dead and seated Him at His right hand in the heavenly places, far above all principality and power and might and dominion, and every name that is named, not only in this age but also in that which is to come. And He put all things under His feet, and gave Him to be head over all things to the church, which is His body, the fullness of Him who fills all in all."* Ephesians 1:19-23.

2. The power is in Christ, not in religion. Verses 17-26.

These are religious Jews to whom Peter is preaching; people who were religious but rejected the Messiah. Many are the Christian churches where the pastors reject the Christ, claiming that he is not virgin born, that he is merely a good teacher and a good man. Peter declares that these religious Jews acted in ignorance. Verse 17.

Peter calls for repentance and turning to God, so that their sins might be blotted out before God. Verse 19 - 21 says, *"Repent therefore and be converted, that your sins may be blotted out, so that times of refreshing may come from the presence of the Lord, and that He may send Jesus Christ, who was preached to you before, whom heaven must receive until the times of restoration of all things, which God has spoken by the mouth of all His holy prophets since the world began."*

Remember that the transformed life, like this cripple who was completely healed, has the strongest impact in our witness for Christ Jesus. You need much more than religion, even if your religion flies the Christian flag. You need a personal relationship with Christ Jesus, who died for your sins and rose again from the dead. You need the living Christ to come into your life and touch your life with His Holy Spirit, so that you are born again by His saving power and authority.

At Calvary!
(William R. Newell, published in 1895)

Years I spent in vanity and pride,
Caring not my Lord was crucified,
Knowing not it was for me He died

On Calvary.

Refrain:
Mercy there was great, and grace was free;
Pardon there was multiplied to me;
There my burdened soul found liberty,
At Calvary.

By God's Word at last my sin I learned;
Then I trembled at the law I'd spurned,
Till my guilty soul imploring turned
To Calvary.

Now I've giv'n to Jesus everything,
Now I gladly own Him as my King,
Now my raptured soul can only sing
Of Calvary.

Oh, the love that drew salvation's plan!
Oh, the grace that brought it down to man!
Oh, the mighty gulf that God did span
At Calvary!

Chapter 4
The Revolution Opposed!
Scripture: Acts 4:1-31

You cannot avoid attracting a crowd when a well-known beggar at the temple gate Beautiful is now seen walking, and running, and leaping and praising God. He had been a fixture at the entrance to the temple for years. No longer!

It didn't take long for the opposition to come on strongly, and it came from the religious establishment! Isn't it amazing how opposition to Christ's real work often comes from the power-brokers within the religious realm?

The words of Christ prophetically given before he went to the cross were rapidly coming to pass. John 15:18-20 give us the prophetic word of our Master. *"If the world hates you, you know that it hated Me before it hated you. If you were of the world, the world would love its own. Yet because you are not of the world, but I chose you out of the world, therefore the world hates you. Remember the word that I said to you, 'A servant is not greater than his master.' If they persecuted Me, they will also persecute you. If they kept My word, they will keep yours also."* Jesus also said, (John 16:2) *"They will put you out of the synagogues; yes, the time is coming that whoever kills you will think that he offers God service."*

History tells us about the apostles' deaths, by being thrown to the lions, burned at the stake, or crucified. They suffered many other countless means of torture. The early church father, Tertullian, said, "The blood of the martyrs is the seed of the church."

Whenever God is dynamically working by His Holy Spirit, His people must be prepared to handle opposition, for it will surely come. Often it comes from the religious establishment. This religious establishment in Acts 4 is the same one that crucified Jesus of Nazareth. Verse 1 lists the priests, the captain of the temple guard and the Sadducees. Verses 5-6 more specifically refers to the Council that met to consider what to do about Peter and John. This was the same Council that had condemned Jesus of Nazareth to death only two or three months before. There was nepotism of the most detestable kind going on in the succession to the high priest's office. Warren Wiersbe comments, "When Annas was deposed from the priesthood, Caiaphas, his son-in-law was appointed. In fact, five of Annas' sons held the office at one time or another. Someone has defined a "nepotist" as "a man who, being evil, knows how to give good gifts to his children."

First, let's discover **What It Is That Disturbs The Religious Establishment. Verses 1-2.**

1. The disruption of the status-quo.

Verse 2 tells us that they were *"greatly disturbed."* The status quo meant that the Jewish people looked to their rabbis and to the Sanhedrin for guidance of their spiritual lives. The Council, chaired by the high priest, operated as judge and jury in religious and in political or criminal matters. They were under the Roman jurisdiction, and in capital cases seeking the death penalty, they needed the Roman authority's approval. Therefore they had brought Jesus unto Pilate.

They thought that they were rid of Jesus of Nazareth for they had put him to death. But here they are confronted, not with the miracle worker, Jesus, but with a couple of His associates, who now had raised up a crippled man. When the Council interrogated Peter and John, they responded in such fashion that the Council took note of the *"courage"* of these unschooled and ordinary men. Verse 13 tells us, *"Now when they saw the boldness of Peter and John, and perceived that they were uneducated and untrained men, they marveled. And they realized that they had been with Jesus. "*

There was a remarkable difference from the time that Peter and John had denied Jesus at His trial. They noted that they had been with Jesus or they had been His followers. Now those who had been accustomed to being the leaders of the Jews felt their control slipping away. Things were quickly getting out of hand. These unschooled fishermen were having an impact upon the crowds and many were becoming followers of this new movement. This gathering of the followers of Jesus was a growing group that were still gathering in the temple courts to worship Jesus. Besides all this there stood in their midst one who obviously had been healed and no one could deny it.

2. The rejection of false theology.

The apostles were preaching the resurrection of the dead in Jesus. This contradicted the teaching of the Sadducees who did not believe in a future resurrection from the dead; that is why they were "Sad-U-See!"

Peter and John were teaching that this Jesus Christ (the Messiah) of Nazareth whom they had crucified just a couple of months before had been raised from the dead by God. Verses 2, 10. It is in the name of the resurrected Jesus Christ, who is the long expected Messiah that this man stands before you healed or saved. *'Healed'* of verse 8 and *'saved'* of verse 12 are from the same root Greek word. 'Saved' means to be whole or healthy spiritually.

We are to handle false teaching, false doctrine, by teaching the truth. Note that Peter and John spent no time talking about the false teaching of the Sadducees, but they just preached the truth about Christ being raised from the dead. If it is true that Christ was raised from the dead and is alive, then obviously their teaching was false.

All that the Council needed to do to contradict the teaching of Peter was to produce the dead body of Jesus. They knew that they could not do so because the tomb had been empty since that first Sunday morning after Passover. This is one of the great proofs of the resurrection, that the Jewish rulers could not produce a body to refute the teaching of the resurrection. The risen Christ had also appeared alive to many eye witnesses.

3. The enthusiasm of new leaders.

These revolutionized apostles could not be refuted. They were powerful witnesses of the risen Christ. These unschooled fishermen were impressive in their knowledge of the Hebrew Scriptures and their knowledge of the Messianic prophecies.

These transformed apostles were enthusiastic, filled with convincing authenticity, as they spoke of the living Christ. They were courageous in the face of opposition, even after having spent the night in jail. These men were not up there just droning on about some dry philosophical point. That is very disturbing to the dead religious establishment that is just presiding over the relics of the past.

What happens in an old main line church that has lost its message of the living Christ and even denies the truths of Scripture when one of their dead members suddenly is born again through the witness of some obedient follower of Christ? The enthusiastic witness of this changed life will either ignite a revival or he will be opposed by the dead leaders of this so-called church. More than likely, he will be ostracized and forced to find another church that preaches the truth of the resurrection.

Now let's investigate **The Form That Their Opposition Takes. Verses 3:5-7, 18-22.**

1. They use all available political power. Verse 3.

The Jewish leaders detain them in jail until the next day. They could get away with this in spite of the fact that the crowds had seen this miracle. They would bring them before the Council the next day. As you go through the book of Acts, you find that jails were the homes of many of the Christians, especially the leaders of the church, on frequent occasions.

Warren Wiersbe comments, "The early church had none of the "advantages" that some ministries boast of and depend on today. They did not have big budgets provided by wealthy donors. Their pastors lacked credentials from the accepted schools, nor did they have the endorsement of the influential political leaders of that day. Most of their ministers had jail records and would probably have a hard time today joining our churches, let alone leading them."[12]

2. They use tactics of intimidation. Verses 5-7.

Here you see the establishment pulling rank on these upstart apostles. Here the question is one of authority! Verse 5-7 gives us the picture. Imagine these Jewish priests in their finest official robes confronting these poorly dressed, even scruffy apostles. "*. . .it came to pass, on the next day, that their rulers, elders, and scribes, as well as Annas the high*

---

[12] Warren Wiersbe, The Bible Expository Commentary, Volume 1, Victor Books, Wheaton, IL, 1989, page 415

priest, Caiaphas, John, and Alexander, and as many as were
of the family of the high priest, were gathered together at
Jerusalem. And when they had set them in the midst, they
asked, "By what power or by what name have you done
this?"

Imagine being dragged before these power leaders who
claimed their authority for God over the people! "Who are
you to be infringing upon our authority?" How intimidating
it would be for a young fledgling pastor to be dragged before
a council of Seminary presidents and profesors to be
interrogated about what he was teaching!

3. They use the pressure of verbal threats. Verses 18-22.

The Jewish leaders are in turmoil because they cannot refute
Peter and John. Verses 16 - 17. *"What shall we do to these*
men? For, indeed, that a notable miracle has been done
through them is evident to all who dwell in Jerusalem, and
we cannot deny it. But so that it spreads no further among
the people, let us severely threaten them - that from now on
they speak to no man in this name." So they command them
not to speak any further in the name of Jesus. Verse 18. Then
verse 21 tells us that they *"threaten"* them further."

4. They use physical violence and even death when
possible.

As we go through Acts, we find physical violence and even
death inflicted upon followers of Christ Jesus. This was done
whenever they thought that they could get away with it. They
feared the crowd's reaction and often were detained from
physical punishment, only because the crowd would have
rebelled. We find that to be the case here. The crowd had a
miracle man standing in their midst as evidence. Verses 21-

22 declares that this is the only reason, they did not physically punish the apostles.

Now let's consider **The Ways That God's Servants Respond. Verses 8-12, 18-20, 23-31.**

1. An uncompromising stand for the exclusive gospel. Verses 8-12.

Peter boldly proclaims Jesus Christ and His name as the means by which the lame man was healed and clearly states that there is only one name by which anyone can be saved. Hear again verses 8-12. *"Then Peter, filled with the Holy Spirit, said to them, "Rulers of the people and elders of Israel: If we this day are judged for a good deed done to a helpless man, by what means he has been made well, let it be known to you all, and to all the people of Israel, that by the name of Jesus Christ of Nazareth, whom you crucified, whom God raised from the dead, by Him this man stands here before you whole. This is the 'stone which was rejected by you builders, which has become the chief cornerstone.' Nor is there salvation in any other, for there is no other name under heaven given among men by which we must be saved."*

This is the most troubling part of the gospel for many people today, even for many who claim to be Christians. You will hear many people respond somewhat like this, if you dialogue with them about the exclusive Christ. "Well, you're into Christ; I'm into Buddha or Mohammed; That's OK, whatever religion is best for you!" Or "I love Jesus as much as you do, but I believe there are many ways to reach God! There are many ways to heaven."

This was the pressure brought to bear upon Christians at the World Congress of Religion held in Chicago in 1993. Many religious leaders said, "If we are ever going to have unity among all peoples, Christians are going to have to drop their view that Christ is the only way to God." In other words, it is no problem for you to claim the name Christian, as long as you do not believe that He is unique and that He is the only way to God. But, of course, if you drop those beliefs, then you are no longer Christian, in the New Testament sense of the word.

Dr. Erwin Lutzer, long-time pastor of Moody Church in Chicago, attended this World Congress of Religion. He comments on this idea that there are many truths and many ways to heaven.

"Your personal opinions about religion may be true; but if so, they are also true for everyone else. If you meet a friend who says, "Christ is true for you, but not for me," tell him lovingly, "You are entitled to your own private opinion, but you are not entitled to your own private truth!"

Mathematics is transcultural; it is foolish to say that $2 + 2 = 4$ is simply a Western idea. Science and technology also rely on universal principles that apply in every country, in every era. When an astronomer finds a new star, he has not changed the nature of the universe; he has only found something that was already there. Truth exists objectively outside ourselves. We do not create it; we can only discover it.

. . . Logic requires that if there is one God then there are not two, three or ten. If what Christ said was true, then what Baha-u-llah said was false. You may live next door to a Mormon family, but Mormonism and Christianity cannot both be true. Both may be false, but both cannot be true. And if one religion of the world is objectively true, it is true for everyone. The issue is whether we have committed ourselves to a religion that reflects the way things are in the universe.

Christ presented Himself as the one and only qualified
Savior who is able to bring men and women to God the
Father . . . Logically, this excludes all other teachers/gurus
who claim that they can bring men and women to God. Nor
can Christ be the Savior for only the Western world, but not
the Eastern world. If He is the truth, He is the truth for
everyone. Whether one accepts Christ or not is a separate
question, but He is either the truth for all or the truth for
none." [13]

**2. An unbending allegiance to God rather than man.
Verses 18-20.**

Whenever we operate out of fear of man, we will likely end
up denying our God and our Savior. What is it that kills our
witness for Christ? Is it not the fear of men? What is it that
keeps you from bowing your head to give thanks for your
food when you are out to lunch with some of your co-
workers? What is it that keeps your mouth shut when
opportunities to stand up for Christ come in your everyday
world? Is it not the fear of what others might think of you?

**3. An unending dependence upon God's help. Verses 23-
31.**

It is important that the apostles immediately retreat to *"their
own companions"* or as the NIV puts it, *"to their own
people"*. Verse 23. They report and then they enter into a
prayer meeting. The prayer meeting is praise and petition.

They worship the Sovereign Lord who is in control. Verse
24. *"So when they heard that, they raised their voice to God*

---

[13]   Erwin Lutzer, Christ Among Many gods, Moody Press, Chicago, IL,
1994,page 52f

with one accord and said: "Lord, You are God, who made heaven and earth and the sea, and all that is in them . . ." They then recognize that this reaction of opposition is according to Scripture, quoting from Psalm 2 in their prayer, and they pray for boldness. They do not ask to be delivered, or that the opposition would cease, but that they would have a Holy Spirit empowered boldness. *"Now, Lord, look on their threats, and grant to Your servants that with all boldness they may speak Your word, by stretching out Your hand to heal, and that signs and wonders may be done through the name of Your holy Servant Jesus."* Verses 29-30.

The result is (verse 31) *"And when they had prayed, the place where they were assembled together was shaken; and they were all filled with the Holy Spirit, and they spoke the word of God with boldness."*

Roy Laurin writes, "Years ago, in New York City, a massive new organ was to be dedicated in a certain church. Everyone had come to hear a guest musician play the familiar songs of the sanctuary on the huge console. The service began, and as the organist pressed his fingers to the keys, he was horrified to find that not one single musical note would come forth. He pressed the start button, but still nothing happened. Then the custodian, sensing that the electricity had not been turned on, wrote a hasty note and handed it to the organist, telling him that after the invocation, the generator would be on and he could proceed with the service. The note read: "After the prayer, the power will be on."[14]

What we need today in our lives personally and in the church of Jesus Christ is not a new paradigm or format, or a new program, or a new popularity, or a new political agenda, or

---

[14] Roy Laurin, Commentary on Acts.

a new promotion. What we need today is a new Presence of the Holy Spirit to convict us of our sin and bring us to a new holiness, a new product. That new product is that our lives are utterly revolutionized by Jesus Christ, so that we have a new power, through being filled with the Holy Spirit of God. Perhaps we also need a new persecution to cause us to take our stand, but do we dare to ask for it? How about you? Do you dare ask for it?

O Jesus, I Have Promised!
(Written by John Ernest Bode in 1869)

O Jesus, I have promised
to serve thee to the end;
be thou forever near me,
my Master and my Friend;
I shall not fear the battle
if thou art by my side,
nor wander from the pathway
if thou wilt be my guide.

O Jesus, thou hast promised
to all who follow thee,
that where thou art in glory
there shall thy servant be;
and, Jesus, I have promised
to serve thee to the end;
O give me grace to follow,
my Master and my Friend.

O let me feel thee near me!
The world is ever near;
I see the sights that dazzle,
the tempting sounds I hear;
my foes are ever near me,
around me and within;

but Jesus, draw thou nearer,
and shield my soul from sin.

O let me hear thee speaking
in accents clear and still,
above the storms of passion,
the murmurs of self will.
O speak to reassure me,
to hasten or control;
O speak and make me listen,
thou guardian of my soul.

Chapter 5
The Revolution Sabotaged!
Scripture: Acts 4:32 - 5:42

A ball-point pen salesman persuaded a small business owner to order five hundred pens. He was writing the order in his sales book when suddenly the business owner exclaimed, "Hold on! I'm cancelling the order!" With that, the business owner turned to wait on a customer and ignored the salesman. The salesman left the store angry and confused. Later, the business owner's bookkeeper asked, "Why did you cancel that pen order?" "Why?" responded the man. "Because that salesman talked ball-point pens to me for a half-hour. He described the benefits. He showed me how I could use them to expand my business. He had me convinced that I could not get along without those ball-point pens. Then he turned around and wrote my order with a lead pencil. He doesn't even use his own product!"[15]

Often people are turned away from believing and trusting Christ as personal Savior because they see the inconsistencies of those who profess to know Christ but whose lives speak another message. People who say they love Christ and live most of the time for the devil are poor recommendations for Christ. People who say that Christ is Lord but who show no real level of commitment to Him turn people off.

The work of Christ and His church is often placed in jeopardy, more by those from within than by enemies from without. This is what we are confronted with as we come to Acts 5.

The Lord gave a sobering warning to His people in His treatment of Ananias and Sapphira. They were a married couple in the church at Jerusalem who were guilty of

---

[15] Dynamic Preaching Magazine, June, 1992

hypocrisy. Ananias means 'God is gracious' but he found also that God is holy. Sapphira means 'beautiful' but her heart was ugly with sin.

Doctor Luke gives us the contrast between genuine disciples and hypocritical ones.

First, let's consider **The Authentic Commitments of Genuine Disciples. Acts 4:32-37.**

1. A commitment to unity. Verse 32.

In the early days of the church, there was a spontaneous unity of heart and mind, produced by the Holy Spirit. Acts 4:32 tells us what the early church was like. *"Now the multitude of those who believed were of one heart and one soul; neither did anyone say that any of the things he possessed was his own, but they had all things in common."* Believers in Jesus Christ were of 'one heart and one soul'. They possessed a unity of bonding together in true love for each other. There was a unity of sharing their material possessions out of caring for one another. The Holy Spirit had taken away all their self-centeredness and removed their greed. This was a unity that came as a result of the transformation of their lives through Christ Jesus.

Unity is not something that comes because it is commanded but because we commit ourselves to keep the unity that the Spirit produces. Ephesians 4:1-3 tells us that we are to keep the unity of the Spirit that already has been produced by the Spirit. *"I, therefore, the prisoner of the Lord, beseech you to walk worthy of the calling with which you were called, with all lowliness and gentleness, with longsuffering, bearing with one another in love, endeavoring to keep the unity of the Spirit in the bond of peace."*

John Phillips comments: "Certainly no man-made ecumenical formulas and organizations can produce such unity. It has to be of the heart. Movements based on compromise of essential doctrine and on administrative machinery might well produce a world church, but it will be a harlot church, not the bride of Christ."[16] This is the reason all of man's efforts to produce unity of a world-wide church results in a cemetery instead of a resurrection.

Powerful preaching and effective witness comes out of this kind of Holy Spirit produced unity. Verse 33 bears witness of this. *"And with great power the apostles gave witness to the resurrection of the Lord Jesus. And great grace was upon them all."*

The preaching of your pastors and personal witness of each believer is given great power by the demonstration of harmony in the body. When we demonstrate the love of Christ to all people, regardless of background, race, economic status or any other social barriers, the unity of the love of Christ is manifested by the Holy Spirit.

2. A commitment to giving (or sharing). Verses 32-37.

One of the greatest evidences of Christ's transforming power is the change from greediness and hoarding, to generosity and sharing of our resources. This wasn't commanded by the apostles, but it was the heart-response of people whom the Lord Jesus had saved and revolutionized. Acts 4:32 declares *"neither did anyone say that any of the things he possessed was his own, but they had all things in common."* Verses 34-35 give the result of genuine sharing of their possessions. *"Nor was there anyone among them who lacked; for all who were*

---

[16] John Phillips, Exploring Acts, Commentary on Acts, Kregel Publications, Grand Rapids, MI, page 90.

possessors of lands or houses sold them, and brought the proceeds of the things that were sold, and laid them at the apostles' feet; and they distributed to each as anyone had need." A certain man by the name of Joseph, renamed by the apostles, 'Barnabas', meaning 'son of encouragement', is a specific person mentioned as an example. Verses 36-37 tells us that he brought all the proceeds from the sale of his property and laid it at the apostles' feet.

Barnabas was a man who would not fudge on his income tax forms by failing to report much of his income. How many of us have become greedy and self-protective of our income and resources, so that we fail to give to the Lord and His kingdom? When calculating our tithe, we fail to report our income to the Lord, thinking somehow He will not know. We think that the Lord will understand that we must indeed keep our money and our resources hoarded away against a rainy day. Our trust is in our stocks and bonds, our retirement funds and our Social Security checks. We live by fear, "What am I ever going to do if I get sick and can't afford to pay my hospital bills?" "What if some unexpected crisis arises? I need to keep that tithe or that money the Lord is prompting me too give to some missionary in need!"

3. A commitment to integrity.

We see in Barnabas, this 'Son of Encouragement', a person of absolute integrity. There is no pretense; what you see is what you get. He is genuine or sincere. The Greek word behind our English word 'sincere' means 'without wax'. In the New Testament times, patching a piece of cracked pottery with wax was a common practice. You could see the flaw if the piece had been patched by holding it to the sunlight. When you come under the searchlight of the Holy Spirit, are there flaws in your character that are revealed?

When it comes to the matter of giving to the Lord and the work of His kingdom, every believer is put under scrutiny by the Holy Spirit. It is then that you discover whether you have allowed the Lord to deliver you from your self-centeredness and greed. If you do not find yourself generous and joyful in your giving, then you are still patching up the old life with the wax of pretense.

Now, let's take a look at **The Awful Conspiracy of Hypocritical Disciples. Acts 5:1-11.**

The NKJV translation begins chapter 5 with "But", a more apt translation of "de" than the NIV "Now". I think Luke intended that chapter 5 is not simply a continuation of the story, but a direct contrast to the previous, namely 'Barnabas' and others who were giving all to the cause of Christ. - Phillips says, "The 'buts' in the Bible are the hinges on which great doors swing."[17]

1. An intentional pretense. Acts 5:1-2.

The Greek word "hupocrites" refers to an actor who dons a mask to pretend to be someone he is not. The actor is just playing a role.

Here we have a husband and wife, believers in Christ, part of the Christian community, conspiring with each other to pretend to give all the money they got from their property sale, when in fact they only gave a part. Ananias and Sapphira were pretending to be generous like Barnabas. They were pretending to also be giving to the common treasury for the benefit of all the community of Christians. So the selfishness of Ananias and Sapphira (Acts 5) is contrasted with the

---

[17] John Phillips, , Exploring Acts, Commentary on Acts, Kregel Publications, Grand Rapids, MI,, page 92.

selflessness of Barnabas and others (Acts 4). They wanted everyone to think that they were as spiritual and generous as Barnabas and others who gave everything they received from the sale of their properties.

How often have we been just as guilty of pretending as Ananias and Sapphira? Pretending to be generous when we know that we do not come anywhere near even tithing, let alone doing some generous act like Barnabas did?

Every once in a while, the media will publish reports on the President's and First Lady's income tax filing. Their contributions to church and charity usually fall far short of a tithe of their income for the year. Some of them have even claimed to be Baptists who professes to believe in tithing but obviously do not practice it.

But what if your giving records were posted for all to see? Would you cringe? Are you pretending to serve the Lord with gladness of heart, but griping behind the scenes to your close friends about all the work you have to do in the church? Are you pretending to be a prayer warrior when you know that you struggle to spend even five minutes a day in solitude with your heavenly Father?

Well, maybe I ought to quit meddling and let the Holy Spirit put his finger on your sin of pretense. I'm certain that there is not one of us, if we are really brutally honest before God, who is not guilty at some point.

2. A serious offense. Acts 5:3-4, 7-9.

Let's notice some of the details of the offense that Ananias and Sapphira committed, inspired by Satan filling their hearts with something other than godly thoughts and motives. Satan can influence us as Christians if we are not on guard and can lead us to do things that are despicable in God's eyes.

The offense was not in selling the land, or even in not donating all of the proceeds to the Lord. Peter's words in verse 4 makes it clear. *"While it remained, was it not your own? And after it was sold, was it not in your own control? Why have you conceived this thing in your heart? You have not lied to men but to God."* The offense, the sin, was in the pretense to be giving it all, so that they might have the applause of the church. This was an offense against the church and against their fellow Christians. More so, it was a sin of lying to the Holy Spirit, (verse 3) and lying to God (verse. 4). They were not simply lying to men, but more importantly, they were lying to God.

This is a passage that shows the Holy Spirit is God, in that 'Holy Spirit' and 'God' are used here interchangeably. Are we conscious of the fact that when we pretend to be what we are not, we are lying to the Holy Spirit? Are we consciously aware that God sees and knows every motive of our heats? Therefore we can never get away with pretending before God?

By the way, if you are not generous in your giving to the Lord, the message here is not, "It is OK not to tithe and to give generously, as long as I do not pretend that I am doing it." You still have to deal with the sin of greed and self-centeredness and let the Holy Spirit change your heart.

3. A deadly consequence. Acts 5:5-6, 9-10.

Acts 5 gives us a record of a double funeral which was a judgment upon the sin of two sinning believers. Ananias died, was carried out and buried, and three hours later, Sapphira walked into her own funeral, unaware that the ushers had just buried her husband.

Ananias and Sapphira are used as a teaching example for the early church and for us. Who of us would be alive today if God judged us as severely as He did them? We tend to brush aside our dealings with God because we feel he will not do to us what He did with Ananias and Sapphira! Stop kidding yourself, my friend! Galatians 6:7 says, *"Do not be deceived. God is not mocked; for whatever a man sows, that he will also reap."* God's judgment is often meted out upon disobedient and hypocritical believers.

We also see God's judgment upon believers in 1 Corinthians 11:27-32. *"Therefore whoever eats this bread or drinks this cup of the Lord in an unworthy manner will be guilty of the body and blood of the Lord. But let a man examine himself, and so let him eat of the bread and drink of the cup. For he who eats and drinks in an unworthy manner eats and drinks judgment to himself, not discerning the Lord's body. For this reason many are weak and sick among you, and many sleep. For if we would judge ourselves, we would not be judged. But when we are judged, we are chastened by the Lord, that we may not be condemned with the world."*

Now, don't immediately judge that if a Christian gets sick or if a Christian dies, it is because God is meting out judgment for a casual attitude toward personal sin. However, when we do get sick, we ought to search our hearts to see if God is seeking to get our attention because of some carelessness about some sin that has entered into our lives.

We brush aside such talk about a judging Savior who deals with his people by saying, "The God I believe in is a God of love." The God who loves us is the holy God who loves us so much that He died for us sinners, that we might be forgiven and empowered to live lives that please Him. The way that the love of God is often presented in the beginning of the twenty first century churches is a total distortion of the biblical revelation of God.

We hear of the "unconditional love of God" which is presented to mean that God will never make anyone feel sinful; He will never condemn or judge anyone! So somehow, people go away with a view of God as an indulging tolerant God who simply isn't too upset about our sin. SIN is really a small letter word that is not too troubling to this loving God we worship.

When you truly come to the foot of the cross, you see how big an issue your sin is with God! When you see how big an issue your sin is with God, you then begin to understand the nature of God's love that requires you to repent and identify yourself with Christ by faith.

4. A sobering influence. Verse 11.

The effect upon the church and the whole community was *"great fear came upon all who heard these things."* Verse 5b. Verse 11 repeats *"great fear came upon all the church, and upon all who heard these things."* 'Fear' is from 'phobos' from which we get 'phobia'. It is the fear that causes one to want to retreat from the cause of one's fear. It arises from a wholesome respect for the One who causes you to fear. W.E. Vine says, it is "reverential fear of God, as a controlling motive of the life, in matters spiritual and moral, not a fear of His power and righteous retribution, but a wholesome dread of displeasing Him, a fear that banishes the terror and shrinks from His presence. . ."[18]

We live in a day and age when God is trivialized by human beings generally and unfortunately by many who profess to be

---

[18]   W. E Vine, An Expository Dictionary OF New Testament Words, Fleming H. Revell Company, Old Tappan, NJ, 1940, page 84

His followers. We have developed a sub-culture of Christianity that is basically self-centered and treats God as existing for us rather than that we existing for God.

5. A Continuing Antagonistic Opposition. Acts 5:17-42.

Looking at this extended portion only briefly, we see the anger, the frustration and the continued opposition of the high priest and his cohorts from the party of the Sadducees. The disciples are thrown into prison once again, only to be miraculously brought out of prison, even with the guards being completely unaware that they were gone. They were delivered by an angel of the Lord and told by the angel to *"go, stand in the temple and speak to the people all the words of this life."* Verse 20.

The apostles are once more ordered by the high priest not to teach in the name of Jesus Christ. Peter and the other apostles once more boldly told the high priest and the other officials, *"We ought to obey God rather than men. The God of our fathers raised up Jesus whom you murdered by hanging on a tree. Him God has exalted to His right hand to be Prince and Savior, to give repentance to Israel and forgiveness of sins."* Verses 29-31.

A Pharisee named Gamaliel, a teacher of the law, finally speaks some common sense advice to the high priest and the council. *"And now I say to you, keep away from these men and let them alone; for if this plan or this work is of men, it will come to nothing; but if it is of God, you cannot overthrow it – lest you even be found to fight against God."* Verses 38-39.

After beating the apostles, they commanded them once more never to speak again in the name of Jesus. The apostles departed, rejoicing that they were counted worthy to suffer for Christ's name. Verse 42 tells us that they refused to obey men and continued their teaching and preaching of Jesus the Christ in the temple and every house.

Warren Wiersbe shares this experience from his past. "When I was pastoring my first church, the Lord led us to build a new sanctuary. We were not a wealthy congregation, so our plans had to be modest. At one point in the planning, I suggested to the architect that perhaps we could build a simple edifice with a more elaborate facade at the front to make it look more like an expensive church. "Absolutely not!" he replied. "A church stands for truth and honesty, and any church I design will not have a facade! A building should tell the truth and not pretend to be what it isn't".

Years later I ran across this poem, which is a sermon in itself:

"They build the front just like St. Mark's.
   Or like Westminster Abbey;
   And then, as if to cheat the Lord,
   They make the back parts shabby."[19]

Do you, as a professing follower of Christ, like Ananias and Sapphira, have some pretense and shabbiness to confess to your Savior, Jesus Christ? If you are a not yet saved from your sin by coming to Christ as your Savior, you need to repent and trust Him to forgive your sins and invite Him to come and dwell in you?

How bold are we as professed believers in Jesus Christ when it comes to our unabashed witness for our Lord? Do we believe like the apostles that we must obey God instead of cowering before the world system that opposes the gospel of Jesus Christ? Lord Jesus, pour out your Spirit upon us that our

---

[19]   Warren Wiersbe, The Bible Exposition Commentary, Volume 1, Victor Books, Wheaton, IL, 1989; page 421 .

mouths will not be stopped by our fear of the reactions of rebellious men!

Spirit of the living God!
(Lyrics and music by Daniel Iverson, a Presbyterian minister, 1926)

Spirit of the living God,
Fall afresh on me.
Melt me, mold me, fill me, use me.
Spirit of the living God,
Fall afresh on me.

Chapter 6
Aiding The Grace Revolution!
Scripture: Acts 6:1-15

In 1957 the First Brethren Church of Sarasota, Florida, had a ground breaking service. But instead of bringing a few shovels for a few special people to use in the ceremony, they brought an old one-horse plow. Recalling the words of Jesus, *"Take my yoke upon you,"* they borrowed an old yoke and two stalwart laymen were hitched up. But the two were unable to pull the plow. Then the members of the Building Committee were put on the rope, but even they could not move the plow. Other church officers were added, including the Sunday school officers and teachers, but still the plow did not move. Finally, every member of the congregation present took hold of the rope, and with every member pulling together, the plow moved, the ground was broken.[20]

The early church was growing rapidly and with growth came problems and stress. One cause of the problem may have been that the twelve apostles were trying to do too much by themselves. In a short time, the church had grown from 120 believers to possibly as high as 20,000 members. In a growing church like this early church of Jerusalem, it becomes necessary to get others involved. The church that is growing needs the ministry involvement of all members and the enabling leadership of many. Aiding the grace revolution is crucial work that must be done by all believers.

First of all, let's consider **The Pressing Perils of the Growing Church.**

The larger a church becomes, the more vulnerable it becomes to certain areas of attack by Satan. The church at Jerusalem

---

[20] Dynamic Preaching Magazine, May, 1994.

had experienced Satan's attacks first through persecution, then through corruption and now Satan attacks through dissension.

1. A preoccupation with a festering problem. Verse 1.

There were two groups of Jewish believers in the church as there were in the society of Jerusalem generally. There were Hebrew Jews, who were native born in Israel and spoke Aramaic. They were "the pure bred Jews". There were also Hellenistic or Grecian Jews, who were foreign born and spoke Greek primarily.

Both groups had a different perception of the problem. The complaint came against the Aramaic speaking Jews from the Grecian Jews. These foreign-born Jews felt that their widows were getting the short end in the benevolence program. We do not know whether this was actually happening or it was simply perceived that way. Whenever conflict arises, we need to listen to each other and seek to put ourselves in the other person's shoes. We need to seek to understand the other side by seeking to see through their eyes.

It would have been devastating to the early church if the twelve had allowed themselves to be preoccupied with this problem. When the church gets turned in upon itself because of some internal strife, it loses its focus upon evangelism and becomes ineffective.

2. A busyness with a secondary purpose. Verse 2.

The twelve apostles immediately recognized that their personal involvement in this important administrative work of caring properly for the widows would jeopardize the priorities that the Lord had given them to do. The twelve apostles needed to concentrate upon ministry of the word and prayer.

Chuck Swindoll wrote "A wider ministry sparks additional demands. As a result, church leaders may begin throwing aside yesterday's priorities to put out today's fires. Soon, what should be most important places second to what is most urgent."[21] I think it was Oz Guinness who wrote a little booklet years ago called "The Tyranny of the Urgent" which expresses the danger of the urgent need replacing the most important essentials.

It is very difficult for pastors to keep from getting so bogged down in the abundance of activities that seem to be required of pastoring a church these days that there is no time or energy left for preparing in study and prayer for preaching and teaching the word. John MacArthur says, "Many in the ministry today have left the emphasis on prayer and the word of God. They are so involved in the administrative details of their church that they have little time left for intercession and study."[22]

"A young man once said to the gifted expository preacher of God's word, Donald Grey Barnhouse, "I'd give the world to be able to teach the Bible like you." Looking him straight in the eye, Dr. Barnhouse replied, "Good, because that's exactly what it will cost you."[23]

3. A professional view of ministry.

It is easy to use this passage to support a view of pastoral ministry that sees it as a profession rather than a calling. It wasn't that distributing food to the needy was beneath their

---

[21] Charles Swindoll, Commentary on Acts, page 101.

[22] John MacArthur, New Testament Commentary on Acts 1-12, Volume 1, Moody Press, Chicago, IL, 1994; page 179.

[23] John MacArthur, IBID, page 180.

dignity; it was a question of priority of their assigned task under the Holy Spirit of God.

The apostle Paul did not exercise his rights to financial support of the churches, but worked manually in making tents to support himself. A pastor becomes agitated because at times he finds himself folding the bulletins or picking up a broom or mop. He ought not to be agitated because it is beneath his dignity. However folding of bulletins or doing janitor work is not the best use of his time. If he is doing these tasks all the time, he is not recruiting assistance from willing church members.

According to Scripture, there is no distinction between laity and clergy in status in the church; it is rather a matter of distinction of function. Authority is another question. Pastors and deacons are to be spiritually minded, Holy Spirit filled people who exercise authority of leadership only as a matter of function. Christ, who washed the feet of His disciples, taught them about servant leadership. There is no place for any kind of status seeking or arrogant spirit. Even Jesus, the Messiah, the Son of God said *"For even the Son of Man did not come to be served, but to serve, and to give His life a ransom for many."* Mark 10:45. The root word from which we get "deacon" means 'servant.'

4. A desire for uncommitted anonymity.

This problem is only hinted at here but I suspect that in the early church at Jerusalem there were many who wanted the benefits of the church but did not want to be involved in ministry. Many professing Christians today in our churches are not wanting to be involved. Frankly speaking, this is the attractiveness of a Willow Creek style of congregation for many who prefer to be able to attend church and keep a kind of anonymous low profile. This is a severe handicap to the work of Jesus Christ and His church.

Now let's consider and clarify **The God-Ordained Plan for the Growing Church.**

You will see in Paul's writing to Timothy that the plan is not yet implemented in its entirety. In Acts 6, you see the embryo development of a plan for the church to follow in its organization.

1. The clearly defined responsibility of leaders.

The temptation for pastors to become CEO's is not just a new trend for the modern church age. Here you see the temptation for the apostles to be sidetracked from their main responsibility in the developing church. Pastors need to know their biblically mandated responsibilities which relate to preaching and teaching the word and prayer. If they do not keep these priorities safely guarded, they will be caught up in the maze of expectations of the modern church.

After discussing many of the problems associated with the CEO approach to pastoring, T. David Gordon says, "Equally problematic, when the minister-as-CEO model of ministry is embraced, is the degrading of the office of minister of the Word. Ironically, the minister becomes more influential than he should be in areas of governance yet less influential and effective in the area of ministry of the Word. Hours in the day that ought to be devoted to prayer and the Word (Acts 6:4) become devoted to developing strategies and programs."[24]

---

[24] T. David Gordon, Article, Shepherd Or CEO?, Tabletalk Magazine, Oct. 1994, page 13.

The apostles recognized the danger and the temptation. They gathered "all the disciples together" (verse 2ff) and instructed them to choose seven men to take care of a specific need in the church community. There was nothing magical about the number seven but it seemed an appropriate number to handle this particular need in this large church community, which by this time in the short history of the church was probably over 20,000 believers.

It is the Lord's plan for the church that every believer be ministering according to the gifts given by the sovereign choice of the Holy Spirit. 1 Peter 4:10-11 teaches us that *"As each one has received a gift, minister it to one another, as good stewards of the manifold grace of God. If anyone speaks, let him speak as the oracles of God. If anyone ministers, let him do it with the ability which God supplies, that in all things God may be glorified through Jesus Christ, to whom belong the glory and the dominion forever and ever. Amen."*

2. The congregational selection of spiritual leaders.

These were not the first seven volunteers who came along. They were chosen by the congregation but there were some clear qualifications. John Phillips comments, "The criterion for public office in the church was not business acumen, financial success, or organizing ability. Nowadays those are the qualities many churches look for. The apostles had other and more significant criteria. A successful man might not be a spiritual man. On the other hand, a spiritual man might not be a sensible man." (Underscoring is my emphasis.)[25]

It doesn't mean that a successful business person does not qualify to be a church leader, but the spiritual qualifications

---

[25] John Phillips, Exploring Acts, Commentary on Acts, Kregel Publications, Grand Rapids, MI, page 117.

are as crucial as his success in business. These leaders were to be spiritually qualified leaders. Here are the biblical qualifications.

1) He must be of good reputation, a person of integrity. Verse 3. *"Therefore, brethren, seek out from among you seven men of good reputation, full of the Holy Spirit and wisdom, whom we may appoint over this business; . . ."* Stephen is a great example. In the later part of this chapter, we see that Stephen was a man who stood for Christ and the gospel, in spite of the threats of the opposing religious establishment.

2) He must be filled with the Holy Spirit. Verse 3. Such a man is one who is seeking to walk in godly purity every day, totally yielded and absolutely dependent upon the Holy Spirit.

3) He must also be filled with wisdom. Verse 3. He is a man who recognizes his dependence upon God for wisdom in all things. This is wisdom that often contradicts the supposed wisdom of the world. Stephen preaches before the Sanhedrin with power and wisdom as these Jewish leaders disputed with him. Acts 6:9-10 says, *"Then there arose some from what is called the Synagogue of the Freedmen (Cyrenians, Alexandrians, and those from Cilicia and Asia), disputing with Stephen. And they were not able to resist the wisdom and the Spirit by which he spoke."*

Even when trumped up charges (verses 13-14) are brought by false witnesses, much like Christ was accused of blasphemy, Stephen maintains his cool and reflects God's glory. Verse 15. says of Stephen, *"And all who sat in the council, looking steadfastly at him, saw his face as the face of an angel."*

A more complete list of qualifications are given in 1 Timothy 3 and Titus 1, as the church had developed more fully.

Note also the emphasis upon congregational involvement in this process. The apostles did not appoint them, but said to the congregation, *"You seek out from among you . . ." "You"* refers to the whole gathering of the believers or disciples. After the congregation decided who these seven men should be, they came to the apostles who laid their hands on them and ordained them to their position and task. Verses 3-6.

It is also interesting that the people chosen all have Greek names and were clearly going to be accepted by the complaining segment in the church, the Grecian Jews.

3. The Responsible discharge of sacred duties.

The church functions in unity and harmony when every person is doing his part in the church. Spiritual administrators are administrating and the apostles were able to devote themselves to preaching and praying. This is the biblical philosophy of ministry that we see laid out by Paul in Ephesians 4:11-16. *"And He Himself gave some to be apostles, some prophets, some evangelists, and some pastors and teachers, for the equipping of the saints for the work of ministry, for the edifying of the body of Christ, till we all come to the unity of the faith and of the knowledge of the Son of God, to a perfect man, to the measure of the stature of the fullness of Christ; that we should no longer be children, tossed to and fro and carried about with every wind of doctrine, by the trickery of men, in the cunning craftiness of deceitful plotting, but, speaking the truth in love, may grow up in all things into Him who is the head - Christ - from whom the whole body, joined and knit together by what every joint supplies, according to the effective working by which every part does its share, causes growth of the body for the edifying of itself in love."*

We do not pay pastoral staff to do all the work of ministry. They are to equip all believers to be involved in the work of ministry to the end that the body of Christ is built up and all believers move toward maturity in Christ. Pastors are not above doing the work that they are equipping others to do. They must be modeling Spirit-filled ministry. There is no distinguishing between the sacred and the secular. Everything that is done in the name of Christ is sacred and is to be done for His glory.

When the slow-moving clerk in a small store was not around one morning, a customer asked the owner's young son, "Where's Eddie? Is he sick?" "Nope, he ain't workin' here no more," was the reply. "Do you have anyone in mind for the vacancy?" inquired the customer. "Nope! Eddie didn't leave no vacancy!"[26]

We smile, but the statement which characterized Eddie applies equally to many in the church today. In serving Christ they are so weak and colorless that if they left the community their absence would scarcely be noticed. Each of us needs to consider our giftedness by the Spirit and do the work of the ministry in the power of the Holy Spirit.

If I Can Help Somebody
(By Alma Bazel Androzzo)

If I can help somebody as I pass along,
If I can cheer somebody with a word or a song,
If I can show somebody he is travelling wrong,
Then my living shall not be in vain!

Then my living shall not be in vain,
Then my living shall not be in vain!
If I can help somebody as I pass along,
Then my living shall not be in vain!

[26] From a program on my computer, Biblical Illustrator; topic: "Service".

If I can do my duty as a Christian oft,
If I can bring back beauty to a world up wrought,
If I can spread love's message that the Master taught,
Then my living shall not be in vain!

Then my living shall not be in vain,
Then my living shall not be in vain!
If I can help somebody as I pass along,
Then my living shall not be in vain!

Chapter 7
The Fuel of the Revolution
Scripture: Acts 6:8 - 8:1

Pastor Chuck Swindoll wrote these ringing words, "The buildings have weathered, the weeds have grown high, but at certain places where history was made, nothing really changes. In the British House of Commons, Winston Churchill's growl still echoes through the chambers. At Gettysburg, Abraham Lincoln's "Fourscore and seven years ago" still rings clear. In locations like these, the voices of the past seem to drift in the wind, filling the air with a nostalgic sacredness."

"One of these voices floats across time to us in Acts 7. It belongs to Stephen, the first martyr of the church. No monument marks the place where he made his final stand - only his words remain for a memorial. So as we examine these words, imagine yourself standing where he spoke them. Hear the echo. Feel the passion. For the lines were born from the courageous heart of a man prepared to die."[27]

Stephen was only the first of a long line of martyrs who have paid the ultimate price of their allegiance to their wonderful Savior and Lord, Jesus Christ. The church flourishes in the midst of persecution!

The enemies of Christ intended that the martyrs' blood should drown out Christianity but their blood fueled the revolution. One of the lessons we all need to learn is that the life that is significant and worthwhile is not measured by longevity. It is measured by our commitment to Christ and our willingness to stand faithfully with Him, no matter what the outcome.

---

[27] Charles Swindoll quote, Not certain what one of his books, this came from, but it is preserved in my accumulated Illustration files.

Stephen stands as a model of the person who had found what makes up a life that is significant in the light of eternity.

So let's pursue what it is that makes the life of a believer worthwhile and gives lasting significance.

First, there must be **The Divine Mission to Which We Are Dedicated. Acts 6:8-15.**

Stephen was a person who could not be diverted from his course. His mind and will were set upon his mission in life which was the mission of his Savior, the Lord Jesus Christ. Truly his life was totally dedicated to seeking first the kingdom of God.

1. Dedicated to a Person, not just a cause.

The focus of the opposition was upon the person of Jesus Christ. Stephen *"full of faith and power, did great wonders and signs among the people."* Acts 6:8. The Synagogue opposed Stephen because of the Person that he was proclaiming. Notice that *"these men began to argue with Stephen, but they could not stand up against his wisdom and the Spirit by which he spoke."* Acts 6:9b - 10. (NIV) Chapter 7 shows us the subject of his speech. He was showing how Jesus Christ is the promised Messiah and the fulfillment of the Old Testament prophecies.

Many radicals in our world become obsessed with a cause and are willing to dedicate themselves to that cause. Many terrorists take on revenge projects because of their perception of wrongs in society and their obsession with getting even. The worst attack on American soil until September 11, 2001 occurred on April 19, 1995 when Timothy McVeigh bombed the Murrah Federal Building in Oklahoma City. He was motivated by his dislike for the U.S. federal government and was unhappy about its handling of the Ruby Ridge incident in 1992 and the Waco siege in 1993. McVeigh timed his attack to coincide with the second anniversary of the deadly fire that ended the siege at the Branch Davidian compound in Waco, Texas.

There are others who will become martyrs for their ideology. Some radical devotees of Communism dedicate themselves to their cause even to the point of dying for the purpose of bringing about their supposed utopian solution to society's ills.

Yes, Stephen was dedicated to the cause, the mission; but it was a mission that arose out of his commitment to the person of Jesus Christ. He had met the Messiah personally through faith in Him and Christ Jesus was living in his life. Stephen was the first of a long line of martyrs who died not just for a cause, a mission, but for the Person, Jesus Christ, who had saved him from his sins and had set him on the road to heaven.

One of that long line of martyrs for Christ Jesus was a man named Polycarp who died under Roman persecution in 156 AD. Polycarp, the venerable bishop of Smyrna, a personal friend and pupil of the Apostle John, when asked to renounce Jesus Christ or be burned at the stake, replied: "Eighty and six years have I served Him and He never did me any injury. How then can I blaspheme my King and Savior?"[28]

2) Dedicated to service, not prominence.

Stephen was one of the seven chosen by the church to administer the benevolence program, the distribution of food amongst the needy widows. There is every indication that he did his job well along with the others who were appointed. The result was a growing church with many coming to believe the

---

[28] Tan - Signs of the Times, page 787.

gospel. Acts 6:7 reports *"Then the word of God spread, and the number of the disciples multiplied greatly in Jerusalem, and a great many of the priests were obedient to the faith."*

Stephen was dedicated to his mission of serving the Lord Jesus Christ. This was his motivation and it led him to faithful service to the Lord and His people, whether in food distribution or in powerful preaching of the word.

Stephen displays no trace of self-promotion or of seeking for prominence or power. Many of the prominent names in the history of Christ's mission are those who sought nothing else but to faithfully serve the Lord Jesus, even living in obscurity as far as the world is concerned. Jim Elliot, a bright and talented young graduate of Wheaton College, along with four other like-minded young missionaries, labored to reach a tribal group, the Aucas in Ecuador. They died on a remote sandbar in a river in the dense jungle of Ecuador. It is God Himself who has made the Stephens and the Jim Elliots prominent in Christian history. It is He who has used them to inspire many hundreds and thousands of others to serve Christ Jesus and His mission.

Secondly, yet of equal importance, we must proclaim **The Divine Message to Which We Are Devoted. Acts 7:1-53.**

This message given by Stephen is the longest recorded message in the book of Acts. It begins with Stephen speaking of *"the God of Glory"* (verse 2) and concludes with Stephen seeing *"the glory of God"* (verse 55). In verses 2-3, Stephen tells of *"the God of glory"* appearing to Abraham as He called him to leave Mesopotamia and to go to a country that God would show him as he, by faith, would obey. Then, in verse 55, Stephen, *"being full of the Holy Spirit, gazed into heaven the glory of God and Jesus standing at the right hand of God."*

We are devoted to the truth of the divine message. It is the unified message of the whole Bible that is woven together by the Person of Jesus of Nazareth who is the Messiah, the Christ. Remember that the New Testament is concealed in the OldTestament and that the Old Testament is revealed in the New Testament.

We will not analyze the content of Stephen's message thoroughly but just take a glimpse of it. Keep in mind that he is responding to some specific false charges that have been leveled against him. First, he was charged with speaking *"blasphemous words against Moses and God."* Acts 6:11. Secondly, he was also charged with speaking *"blasphemous words against the holy place"*, the temple. Acts 6:13. Thirdly, he was charged with saying that *"Jesus of Nazareth will destroy this place and change the customs which Moses delivered to us."* Acts 6:13-14.

1. The message rooted in biblical history.

Stephen identifies himself with the Jewish people and goes all the way back to *"our father, Abraham"* and traces God's call through Abraham, Isaac and Jacob and the patriarchs. Acts 7:2-16. He leads them through a review of God's deliverance through Moses and reminds them of the constant straying of *"our fathers"* from the commands of God. Acts 7:17-43. Then Stephen pointed out to them that Moses had told the Israelites that God would send a prophet like Moses from their own people, the Jews. (Acts 7:37 is quoting from Deuteronomy 18:15.) Then Stephen tackles the matter of the tabernacle and later the temple, the holy place. Acts7:44-50. He reminds them that even Isaiah the prophet taught them that the Most High God does not live in houses made by men. In verse 49, we find him quoting Isaiah 66:1-2. *"Heaven is My throne, and earth is My footstool. What house will you build for Me? says the LORD, or what is the place of My rest?"*

It was never God's intention that the tabernacle or temple would be permanent places of His focus. When it comes to structures like the temple, "built-in obsolescence" was part of His plan. It would pass away!

We need to keep prominently in our minds that the message that we preach is to be biblically accurate. We are not given the privilege of proclaiming a message of our own making or even our own selection, but we are devoted to biblical truth. It is not a 'new' message, but it is the old, old story that believers have loved so long. It is anchored in the promises and the covenants made to Abraham, to Moses and to David. It is the message of the Savior, the Lamb of God slain for the sin of the whole world which was so graphically predicted through the sacrifices commanded for the Jews under the Old Covenant.

2. The message interpreted by biblical precedent.

Stephen, wisely led by the Holy Spirit, seeks to help them see that the Messiah whom they had rejected, Jesus, the Christ, is just one more illustration of the fact that the stubborn nation of Israel had always done in their history. He draws attention to Joseph whom his brothers had rejected and sold into slavery in Egypt. But God had chosen Joseph and used him as their deliverer from the famine.

He then highlights Moses who was rejected as the deliverer of Israel who were in bondage in Egypt. In Acts 7:25 Stephen tells them that Moses *"supposed that his brethren would have understood that God would deliver them by his hand, but they did not understand."*

It was this rejected leader, Moses, whom God called and used to deliver them out of bondage in Egypt. Yet after all that God did through Moses in the miracles in Egypt, deliverance through the miracle at the Red Sea, and other miracles in the desert wanderings; and after Moses *"received living oracles to give to us"* (verse 38), still (verse 39) *"our fathers would not obey, but rejected. And in their hearts they turned back to Egypt. . ."* It is clear what Stephen is laying out here for these enemies of the Christ from the Jewish religious establishment, the Sanhedrin. In essence, he is forcefully telling them, "The centuries of Jewish history and the historical precedence of the actions of our fathers is a pattern which you are continuing in your rejection of the Messiah."

3. The message applied with biblical courage.

Stephen was not concerned about being politically correct or catering to their sensitivities. When you are preaching to a hostile crowd or you must speak a message from the Lord that people are not wanting to hear, there is always the temptation to pull back, to avoid it altogether, or at least to soften the message. Stephen boldly and straight forwardly says it like it is. Verses 51-53. *"You stiff-necked and uncircumcised in heart and ears! You always resist the Holy Spirit; as your fathers did, so do you. Which of the prophets did your fathers not persecute? And they killed those who foretold the coming of the Just One, of whom you now have become the betrayers and murderers, who have received the law by the direction of angels and have not kept it."*

Stephen is following in the steps of Peter and John when they faced this same hostile group of religious leaders. *"But Peter and John answered and said to them, "Whether it is right in the sight of God to listen to you more than to God, you judge. For we cannot but speak the things which we have seen and heard."* Acts 4:19-20.

Thirdly, we must serve **The Divine Master for Whom We Are Willing to Die. Acts 7:54-8:1a.**

It is my conviction that we will never begin to truly learn what it means to live a committed life of being a follower of Jesus Christ until we come to grips with whether or not we are willing to die for Him. If our faith in Him as our Savior and our commitment to Him as Lord has not reached the level where we are ready to die for Him if called upon, then we will always be compromisers with the world. Saving our skin will be more important than being faithful to our Savior.

1. Allegiance to Christ takes precedence over survival.

The natural tendency of a human being is to see survival in this life as a first priority; survival at any cost. But the martyrs who have died for Christ Jesus never saw survival as top priority. This is the way it was with Stephen. Allegiance and loyalty to Christ was of a far greater priority than safety and security.

Warren Wiersbe quotes Jim Elliot. "In 1948, Auca martyr Jim Elliot wrote in his journal, "I seek not a long life, but a full one, like you, Lord Jesus." Two years later, he wrote: "I must not think it strange if God takes in youth those whom I would have kept on earth till they were older. God is peopling Eternity, and I must not restrict Him to old men and women."[29]

2. Divine Presence enables in the face of death.

One of the evidences of the filling of the Holy Spirit is how you handle persecution or even how you face death for the name of Jesus. When you are hated and falsely accused and your face is seen by your enemies as the *"face of an angel"* (Acts 6:15) and you seek the forgiveness of your enemies (Acts 7:60), you know it is by the power of the Holy Spirit.

---

[29] Warren Wiersbe, IBID, page 433.

Stephen sees that which his enemies could not see. He saw Jesus Christ standing at the right hand of God. Verse 56. In Hebrews 10:12, we read that *"this Man, after he had offered one sacrifice for sins forever, sat down at the right hand of God."* In Ephesians 1:20 we read that the Father *"seated Him (Jesus) at His right hand in the heavenly places."* But Stephen sees Jesus standing in heaven, as if to welcome home one of his faithful servants. When we remember where we are going as believers when we die, and Who is there to welcome us home, death loses its terror.

Early church father, Augustine, said it well. "The end of life puts the longest life on a par with the shortest . . . Death becomes evil only by the retribution which follows it. They, then, who are destined to die need not inquire about what death they are to die, but into what place death will usher them."[30]

When you ponder, "Would I be able to make the ultimate sacrifice and die for Christ?" remember this. If you are completely devoted to living for Christ, He who lives in you, will enable you in that hour to be faithful, even unto death. Notice that Stephen is even enabled to be Christ-like in praying for the forgiveness of his enemies' action of taking his life. Verses 59-60.

3. Heavenly reward far surpasses earthly compromise.

If we could just get a glimpse of heaven and Christ standing at the right hand of the Father, ready to welcome us home with His "Well done, good and faithful servant", we would not give into any earthly compromise.

Luciano Pavarotti was unsure when he graduated from college whether he should be a teacher or a professional singer. His

---

[30] Augustine, Classic - "The City Of God", Daily Bread, Oct. 26, 1995.

father said, "Luciano, if you try to sit on two chairs, you will fall between them. For life, you must choose one chair." Pavarotti chose singing. It took seven more years of study and frustration before he made his first professional appearance. It took another seven years before he reached the Metropolitan Opera. But he had chosen his chair and he did not turn back.[31]

The problem with many of us as Christians is we are still trying to sit in two chairs. When you choose to allow Christ, your Savior to be your Sovereign Lord, you have chosen your chair and nothing will deter you from lovingly and faithfully serving Him, even to the point of death for His sake. Make sure you have chosen your chair!

Am I A Soldier Of The Cross?
(Written by Isaac Watts - 1674-1748)

Am I a soldier of the Cross?
A follower of the Lamb?
And shall I fear to own His cause,
Or blush to speak His name?

In the name, the precious name,
Of Him who died for me,
Through grace I'll win the promised crown,
Whate'er my cross may be.

Must I be carried to the skies
On flowery beds of ease?
While others fought to win the prize
And sailed through bloody seas?

Are there no foes for me to face?

---

[31] Adapted from a Guidepost's magazine. Saved in my illustration files, accumulated over the years of my ministry.

Must I not stem the flood?
Is this vile world a friend to grace,
To help me on to God?

Since I must fight if I would reign,
Increase my courage, Lord!
I'll bear the toil, endure the pain,
Supported by Thy Word.

Chapter 8
The Spreading Revolution!
Scripture: Acts 8:1-25

Walt Disney is recognized as a man who made his dreams come true. However he started at the bottom. Disney once recalled his early days of failure: "When I was nearly twenty-one years old, I went broke for the first time. I slept on cushions from an old sofa and ate cold beans out of a can."[32]

Hard times do not defeat some people but rather seem to spur them on to greater efforts and success. In a similar way, opposition has never stopped the church of Jesus Christ but rather it has been the soil out of which the church of Christ has grown and spread.

The work of God no one can successfully stop. God uses all opposition for His own glory. Gamaliel, the Pharisee, had it correct when he spoke to the leaders of Israel who wanted to put to death Peter and his co-worker apostles. Acts 5:38-39. *"And now I say to you, keep away from these men and let them alone; for if this plan or this work is of men, it will come to nothing; but if it is of God, you cannot overthrow it - lest you even be found to fight against God."* We see this truth fleshed out in the early history of the church of Jesus Christ. The work of God cannot be stopped by any man or satanically inspired movement.

First, we observe **The Opposition of Persecution. Acts 8:1-8.**

Stephen's death launched a torrent of violence against the Christians. Verse 1a. *"At that time a great persecution arose against the church which was at Jerusalem. . ."* A militant

---

[32] Walt Disney - Dynamic Preaching Magazine, August, 1990

Pharisee, a Jew from Tarsus, named 'Saul' was the leader of this opposition. Verses 2-3. We read that Saul *"made havoc of the church . . ."* The NIV translation says, *"Saul began to destroy the church . . ."* 'Destroy' is from a word that describes a wild animal ravaging its prey. He launched a house to house raid and dragged men and women off to prison.

Paul later describes his actions in his testimony before his accusers in Jerusalem. Acts 22:4-5, 19-20. *"I persecuted this Way to the death, binding and delivering into prisons both men and women, as also the high priest bears me witness, and all the council of the elders, from whom I also received letters to the brethren, and went to Damascus to bring in chains even those who were there to Jerusalem to be punished."* . . . *"So I said, 'Lord, they know that in every synagogue I imprisoned and beat those who believe on You. And when the blood of Your martyr Stephen was shed, I also was standing by consenting to his death, and guarding the clothes of those who were killing him."* Surely, you would think this would put a stop to this movement; but it didn't.

1. The revolutionary forces, the Christ-followers, are scattered. Verse 1b.

The persecution simply served to scatter the fire, like someone coming to a campfire and scattering the embers into all the dry leaves around. Other fires burst forth all around.

Notice that the forces that are scattered are not the apostles but the other believers. The apostles stayed in Jerusalem but other believers were scattered seeking safety from the severe oppression in Jerusalem. Do you suspect that these persecuted Christians often wondered why God would allow such persecution upon them when they had trusted the true Messiah, Jesus, the Christ?

When we go through various trials and the fires of affliction, we often do not see what God's Sovereign purpose is. But we can trust Him to work His good purpose out of what may even seem evil toward us.

2. The revolutionary message is propagated. Verses 4-8.

Acts 8:4 tells us that *". . . those who were scattered went everywhere preaching the word."* We find the believers all involved in witnessing wherever they go.

'Preached' is from a form of the Greek word 'euaggalizo' which means 'evangelize', or 'sharing the good news'. This does not speak of the formal preaching of the gospel but the 'one on one' or 'family to family' spreading of the good news.

The persecutor, Saul, could cause them to flee seeking relief from the persecution but he could not silence their tongues. Are you, as a believer in Christ, seeking to share the good news with your neighbors, your co-workers, or your own relatives?

Now we are introduced to Philip, one of the seven who had been appointed to help with the food distribution in Acts 6. Stephen, his co-worker is cut down as an evangelist, causing *"great lamentation"* over his death (verse 2) but Philip is right there to take up the work of evangelizing. Philip is a Grecian Jew and therefore not nearly so prejudiced toward the Samaritans. What wonderful evangelistic meetings he had in the city of Samaria. One wonders if the testimony of the woman of Sychar, whom Jesus reached in John 4, helped prepare the way for the favorable response to the gospel. In verses 5–6, we read that *"Phillip went down to the city of Samaria and preached Christ to them. And the multitudes with one accord heeded the things spoken by Philip. . ."* The word 'preached' here is the 'preaching to the crowd' idea. So the word spread through mass evangelism and through personal evangelism. Phillip also worked many miracles, (verse 6) and unclean (demonic) forces were being evicted from people. Paralyzed and crippled people were being healed. Verse 7. The result was *". . . there was great joy in the city."* Verse 8. Whenever people are being liberated from sin and Satan, there is great joy among believers.

3. The revolutionary boundary is expanded.

The scattering of the believers from Jerusalem was primarily into two areas, Judea and Samaria. Judea was the primary area of orthodox, pure blooded Jews. Samaria was the territory occupied by the mixed race Jews from the time of the Assyrian captivity. No self-respecting Jew would go to Samaria.

The Sovereign God used the persecution to get the Christians out of Jerusalem to begin the assigned task of being witnesses to the world. Acts 1:8 gives the commission to the Gentiles, given by Christ to His followers just before He ascended into heaven. *"But you shall receive power when the Holy Spirit has come upon you; and you shall be witnesses to Me in Jerusalem, and in all Judea and Samaria, and to the end of the earth."*

The believers had not been willing to voluntarily budge from Jerusalem to be obedient to Christ's commission. Whenever we as believers are not obedient in fulfilling the Great Commission, He may make us willing to go, as He did here in Jerusalem by bringing persecution upon the believers.

So you see the gospel crossing the prejudice boundaries, first to the despised Samaritans, then in chapter 10, to the unclean Gentiles.

There are some lessons here for every church that claims the name of Jesus. The gospel crosses all boundaries of race and geography. The church that does not reach out to all people with the gospel of Jesus Christ is disobedient to her Master. The church that is not making constant effort to extend the outreach of the gospel to the whole world is sinning against her Master, Jesus Christ. It is Christ, the head and builder of His church, who has said, *"Go into all the world and preach the gospel to every creature."* Mark 16:15.

This commission is for all believers. It is so easy to hear that this is the responsibility of the church and miss the fact that each truly born-again believer is a member of the body of Christ, the church. It is incumbent upon each of us to search our hearts and analyze our commitment to our personal witness for Christ. Are you and I involved in the Great Commission by going, praying and giving?

Secondly, we need to take a look at **The Opposition of Infiltration. Acts 8:9-25.**

Now we come into contact with a man named Simon who was a powerful individual in the city of Samaria. He was a sorcerer who performed mighty works and magical things through the power of Satan.

Don't fall for the trap of Satan that every time you see something miraculous, you assume it is of God. The magicians of Pharaoh duplicated some of the miracles that Moses performed by the power of Jehovah. When Moses threw down his shepherd's staff it became a snake. The Egyptian magicians performed the same miracle, but Moses' snake devoured their snakes. The Anti-Christ who will rule this world just before Christ returns to set up His millennial Kingdom will have miracle working power.

This Simon had managed to command the following and adoration of the whole city by his evil powers. The people even said of him that he was the "Great Power", a title for God himself. Here we find Simon seeking to infiltrate the ranks of the church.

1. A false attraction.

Simon is attracted by the spectacular power of Philip, not by the God of Philip. He saw the crowds responding to Philip and believing his message. Verse 12. According to the first part of verse 13, Simon also believed and was baptized. But notice the rest of the verse for this shows what attracted Simon. *". . . he continued with Philip, and was amazed seeing the miracles and signs which were done."* Simon was a power hungry person who saw his control slipping and seemed to be attracted to Philip's power and hoped to get in on it in order to shore up his control of the people. It seems to me that Simon's supposed conversion was a sham conversion that was motivated by all the wrong reasons. There appears to be no godly sorrow for his sin that would bring about true repentance and genuine faith in Jesus Christ.

Today in our religious world, there are many professions of salvation that are motivated by greed and the prospect of becoming rich if they follow Christ. The prosperity gospel attracts people who are struggling financially by offering them earthly riches if they simply send in their 'seed money' to the preacher's or the evangelist's ministry. The message that is preached is "Trust in Jesus and you will be rich and healthy!"

2. A false profession.

As you study this passage, I think you will clearly conclude that Simon was not truly saved. He was a hypocrite who made a profession for all the wrong reasons. He believed in the miracles, not the Master; in the signs, not the Savior.

As Peter and John come from Jerusalem, they come to officially open the doors of the kingdom of God to the Samaritans. Here in this passage we face an important side issue that is unique in the history of the church. Why did the Samaritans not receive the Holy Spirit at the time that they believed and were baptized? Verses 14-17.

In the town of Sychar, many of the people had previously believed in the Messiah, before the Holy Spirit had been given. John 4. So in this transition period, they had been baptized in the name of the Lord Jesus only. Verse 16. Other New Testament scriptures clearly teach that every believer receives the Holy Spirit when he believes. I Cor. 12:13; Rom. 8:9, etc. I like Warren Wiersbe's comment. "It was necessary for two of the Apostles, Peter and John to come from Jerusalem, put their hands on the converts, and impart to them the gift of the Spirit. Why? Because God wanted to unite the Samaritan believers with the original Jewish church in Jerusalem. He did not want two churches that would perpetuate the division and conflict that had existed for centuries. Jesus had given Peter the "keys of the kingdom of heaven" (Matthew 16:13-20), which meant that Peter had the privilege of "opening the door of faith" to others. He opened the door to the Samaritans. Later, he would open the door to the Gentiles (Acts 10)."[33]

Peter's condemnatory words to Simon makes it clear what Peter thought of his profession of faith and his baptism. Acts 8:21-23 says, *"You have neither part nor portion in this matter, for your heart is not right in the sight of God. Repent therefore of this your wickedness and pray God if perhaps the thought of your heart may be forgiven you. For I see that you are poisoned by bitterness and bound by iniquity."*

---

[33] Warren Wiersbe, IBID, pages 435-436.

Just as the newly forming church in the city of Samaria was about to welcome in Simon, a phony, to their fellowship, so churches are constantly in danger of welcoming in people flying falsely under the flag of Christianity. Like Simon, you may make a profession of faith and even be baptized, but if you are not truly repentant and truly saved, you are just as lost as before. All your baptism means is that you got wet and your heart is still not right with God.

3. A false motive.

Simon's evil heart before God is revealed. He desired power for his own selfish interests. Simon did not seek holiness; he sought personal honor. He did not desire purity; he desired power. He did not seek God; he sought to be a god.

What is your motive when you come to profess faith in Christ? Do you really recognize your sinfulness and your total unworthiness in the presence of the Savior? Or are you coming to Christ for some ulterior motive? Over the years of pastoring, I have seen those who want to join the church for personal reasons. It gives them a whole new clientele to contact for their business purposes! Or it will give them some influence in the community if they can claim to be a good "church-going" Christian. Or the rich man thinks that he can buy acceptance and prestige by giving large donations to the church. True motives are often revealed by wanting public credit and recognition.

4. A false method.

Simon sought to buy what he wanted by offering money to the apostles. The apostle Peter has some very strong words for Simon in verses 20-21. *"Peter said to him, "Your money perish with you, because you thought that the gift of God could*

*be purchased with money! You have neither part nor portion
in this matter, for your heart is not right in the sight of God."*

Tragically today, even in evangelical churches, we have
deteriorated to the point where we depend upon methods
instead of the Master; upon money instead of the majesty of
our Lord; upon the spectacular rather than the Holy Spirit.

Jesus's words to the crowds who came again after the miracle
of the feeding of the 5000, are significant. John 6:26-27.
*"Jesus answered them and said, "Most assuredly I say to you,
you seek Me, not because you saw the signs, but because you
ate of the loaves and were filled. Do not labor for food that
perishes, but for the food which endures to everlasting life,
which the Son of Man will give you, because God, the Father
has set His seal on Him."*

John Phillips comments, "The faith that rests on miracles is not
worth much. If we win people with sensationalism we will
need sensationalism to keep them. People who come for loaves
and fishes will have to be kept by loaves and fishes."[34]

We feel that the secret of the power is in the method. We think
that if we just have the "right formula" for starting churches,
that it will insure success. And we may attract hosts of people
who like the formula but are we building true churches of truly
repentant, converted, transformed believers? We seek to
attract the unsaved with the bread of entertainment or the husks
of the spectacular, and unless you seek to retain them with
another show more impressive than the last, they will go off to
some other show.

---

[34] John Phillips, Exploring Acts, Commentary on Acts, Kregel Publications,
Grand Rapids, MI, page 152.

God's word is powerful, sharper than a two-edged sword. Hebrews 4:12. It is the gospel that is the power of God unto salvation. Romans 1:16. So whatever method you use, you better not be depending upon the method, but upon the power of God to save people from their sin and from eternal hell.

Let's seek to be genuine believers who seek nothing else but the glory of God and His Sovereign power. We are planning some 'Spiritual Power' meetings in January and have invited an evangelist to preach the word. Some say that won't work; this kind of method is outdated. That is also exactly what many say about preaching the word on Sunday mornings. As songwriter, Daniel Whittle, has written, "I know not how the Spirit moves, Convincing men of sin. Revealing Jesus thru the Word, Creating faith in Him."

The signs are all around us that opposition to Christ and His people is growing even in our western world. Believe me, persecution has the effect of sorting out the true from the false, the genuine from the hypocrite. It may also scatter the true believers but it will not silence their witness!

Cleanse Me!
(Written by J. Edwin Orr – 1936)

Search me, O God, and know my heart today,
Try me, O Savior, know my thoughts, I pray;
See if there be some wicked way in me;
Cleanse me from every sin, and set me free.

I praise Thee, Lord, for cleansing me from sin;
Fulfill Thy word and make me pure within;
Fill me with fire, where once I burned with shame;
Grant my desire to magnify Thy name.

Lord, take my life, and make it wholly Thine;
Fill my poor heart with Thy great love divine;
Take all my will, my passion, self and pride;
I now surrender, Lord, in me abide.

O Holy Ghost, revival comes from Thee;
Send a revival, start the work in me;
Thy Word declares Thou wilt supply our need;
For blessings now, O Lord, I humbly plead.

Chapter 9
Witnesses for the Revolutionary!
Scripture: Acts 8:26-40

George Barna reported in 1995, "This year, 2.2 million people will die in America. Their passing will lead to months of grieving by tens of thousands of family members and friends. To them, the death of 2.2 million people will be a big tragedy.

"Only God knows how many of those people who die will wind up in a state of eternal separation from Him, which we commonly refer to as hell. Research suggests, however, that more than 1 million of those people who die will go to hell. Perhaps the number will be more, perhaps less. Nothing in our social science arsenal enables us to measure the true contours of the heart and soul with absolute accuracy; that is in God's purview and His alone. But our best research techniques suggest that every day, thousands of people leave this planet for a known and permanently agonizing eternity."[35]

The death of a dear loved one has the effect of giving us a 'wake-up call' spiritually. Our family experience this past week-end, as Bev's brother passed away, was that many of the relatives were very open to consider the gospel and their own relationship with God. But even then, there are very few of us that will even venture to get into a conversation with an unsaved relative to seek to bring them to personal faith in Christ as their Savior.

It is so very clear in Scripture that it is God's will that every believer should be a witness for Christ Jesus. But many of us feel awkward or afraid to share the gospel with anyone. Many of us have just given up the thought of even trying to witness for Christ. We'll leave that to the professionals.

---

[35] George Barna, Evangelism That Works, Regal Books, 1995, page 11.

Being an effective witness is possible only through the power of the Holy Spirit alone. From this account of Philip's witness to the Ethiopian eunuch, we gain some important insights about effective witnessing for Christ.

First we see that **He Is Available for The Holy Spirit's Use.**

One of the huge problems in fulfilling the Great Commission of our Lord is that most Christians never share the gospel with other people as a way of life. They are glad that they have heard the gospel and have responded to accept Christ as their Savior, but they have not committed themselves to seek to be a witness for Christ.

Philip is an example of one who is available to be used by the Holy Spirit in evangelizing the world with the gospel. Verse 4 of this chapter has made it clear that Christians who were scattered by the persecution went everywhere 'preaching', that is 'evangelizing' the word. Philip is specifically mentioned as one of them.

Philip was available to preach to the masses in a city of Samaria. He had been experiencing the great blessing of God in his evangelistic campaign in the city and many were responding in repentance and faith. Acts 8:25 tells us that they returned to Jerusalem, *"preaching the gospel in many villages of the Samaritans"* along the way. But as you read this next passage, Acts 8:26 – 40, you find that Philip is available to be directed by the Holy Spirit in evangelizing for Christ elsewhere. He is directed by the Spirit to leave Jerusalem again and to make his way toward the south along the road that leads from Jerusalem toward Gaza. Verse 26.

The question is not so much our ability, but our availability. That does not mean that we do not need to improve in our ability. If we do not study the word and develop our ability to clearly share the gospel with someone, it is not likely that we will be used by the Holy Spirit. 2 Timothy 2:15 commands us, *"Be diligent to present yourself approved to God, a worker who does not need to be ashamed, rightly dividing the word of truth."*

Do you have a heart that desires to be obedient in witnessing? Are you making yourself available to the Holy Spirit for His use? Do you pray about this aspect of your Christian life? Are you doing anything to be equipped to witness more effectively? Do you bother to attend seminars that we provide that teach us how to be more fruitful in our daily witness for Christ?

Secondly**, He Is Sensitive to The Holy Spirit's Prodding. Verse 26.**

Verse 26 tells us that, in Philip's case, the Holy Spirit uses an angel, a messenger of some kind to communicate to Philip. God doesn't usually send an angel to tell us where we are to go to meet someone with whom we can share the gospel. In Philip's case, the angel was needed to relocate Philip to reach an Ethiopian who would then spread the gospel to another continent. However, usually we are to witness as the Spirit of God opens doors of opportunity with relatives, with neighbors, with co-workers, or even with some stranger that you chance to meet. If you are available to be a witness for Christ and you are being obedient in praying about being a witness, the Holy Spirit will direct you. Believers who are available to the Holy Spirit will find opportunities to be a witness. Just be sensitive to the burden that the Lord puts on your heart.

Thirdly**, He Is Obedient to The Holy Spirit's Commands. Verse 27.**

When God clearly gives you a command, set out to be obedient. Philip does just exactly what the angel had commanded him, although from a logical viewpoint, it probably didn't make a lot of sense. Why not return to a very successful work there in Samaria where there were crowds of people listening and responding to the gospel? Why go to a desert place, a desolate area like the road going to Gaza?

Philip obeyed without any idea of why he was to go there! He exercised faith like Abraham did when God told him to leave Haran and go a land that He would show him. He left Haran, not knowing where God was leading him.

Perhaps you are saying, "I would be obedient if God sent an angel to me and made it so abundantly clear what I was to do." However, the commands of Scripture are clear; so why do we need an angel? Mark 12:30-31 tell us, *". . . you shall love the Lord your God with all your heart, with all your soul, with all your mind, and with all your strength.' This is the first commandment. And the second, like it, is this: 'You shall love your neighbor as yourself.' There is no other commandment greater than these."* Then Mark 16:15 commands us *"Go into all the world and preach the gospel to every creature."* Just before His ascension into heaven, Jesus could not have been more clear, as recorded in Acts 1:8, *"But you shall receive power when the Holy Spirit has come upon you; and you shall be witnesses to Me in Jerusalem, and in all Judea and Samaria, and to the end of the earth."*

How often have you sensed a strong burden to go to some neighbor or some relative to seek to lovingly minister to their need and to seek to share the good news, but you have ignored it?

Fourthly, **He Is Ready for The Holy Spirit's Opportunity. Verses 27 - 28.**

When a Christian is obedient to God's command to be a witness and is available, you will be looking for the opportunities that the Holy Spirit opens to you. This is exactly what Philip does. I think he was looking all along the way, seeking to understand the reason that the Holy Spirit had him on this journey to Gaza.

He met a procession traveling the road. It turns out that it is an important Ethiopian man, on his way back from Jerusalem. These facts about the man's identity and that he had been to Jerusalem to worship were not then known to Philip. This is the record of the historian, writing after the fact. Luke tells us that the man was the treasurer of Queen Candace of Ethiopia.

Philip observed a black man, obviously very important as he traveled with his whole retinue of servants. It is incredible timing, guided by the Holy Spirit. The Lord placed Philip right there in the right place when this man was passing that way. This is not simply coincidence. It is a 'God-thing'.

Keep your eyes open to the opportunities that God gives for you to share a word of witness, to sow the seed or do a little watering of seed already sown. As you are controlled by the Holy Spirit as a Christian, the contacts that you have are not just coincidental and circumstantial. Why has God placed you in your neighborhood where you live? You may be the only one on your street who is born again and alive in Christ! Why are you, as a Christian, working at a job? Are you just there to earn a pay check? You are a student at school and all around you are other students, most of whom are not on their way to heaven. Do you see yourself as a servant of God for whom the Holy Spirit is creating opportunities for witness? As you are flying on a particular plane or eating in a particular restaurant, or shopping in a particular store, is there some opportunity that the Lord is creating for you to be a witness?

Fifthly, He Is Alert to The Holy Spirit's Working. Verse 29-30.

The Spirit of God tells Philip to *"go near and overtake this chariot."* Verse 29. Did Philip hear an audible voice? Probably not; more than likely the Holy Spirit spoke through a strong impulse to go near the chariot. Verse 30 tells us that Philip ran to intercept the chariot. John Phillips comments, "Run, Philip, run. It was not just that he might miss the traveler, he might miss the text."[36]

He also observed that the man was reading a scroll which he discovered was a scroll of Isaiah. Here was a God fearing Gentile, probably a Jewish proselyte, who had been to Jerusalem on a pilgrimage of worship of the God of the Jews. As a Gentile and a eunuch, he would be allowed only in the outer courts of the temple. He apparently still was searching for something that he had not found in Jerusalem. Perhaps he had purchased some Old Testament scrolls in Jerusalem and he was reading, probably in the Greek Septuagint translation.

Philip is alert to the fact that the Holy Spirt is working in this man's heart and he is searching in the right place, the Scripture. The same Holy Spirit that had brought Philip from Jerusalem is the one who had this man reading in the book of Isaiah.

The Holy Spirit is working today in the hearts and lives of many unsaved people, seeking to draw them to Christ. John 16:7-11 makes the working of the Holy Spirit clear. *"Nevertheless I tell you the truth. It is to your advantage that I go away; for if I do not go away, the Helper will not come to you; but if I depart, I will send Him to you. And when He has*

---

36 John Phillips, Exploring Acts, Commentary on Acts, Kregel Publications, Grand Rapids, MI, page 161.

come, He will convict the world of sin, and of righteousness, and of judgment: of sin, because they do not believe in Me; of righteousness, because I go to My Father and you see Me no more; of judgment, because the ruler of this world is judged."

Trust the Holy Spirit to be at work, preparing the hearts of unsaved people. Attach yourself to someone's chariot. Attach yourself to people. Get in conversation with people and explore to see whether the Holy Spirit has prepared a person for a witness of Christ.

Sixthly, He Is Knowledgeable of The Holy Spirit's Methods. Verses 30-35.

As Philip heard the man reading the prophet Isaiah out loud, he asks a good exploratory question, *"Do you understand what you are reading?"* Verse 30. We need to learn a lot of good exploratory questions that you can use in various situations.

I carry a little blue booklet in my shirt pocket that has been written by Larry Moyer and is printed by his organization, Evantell. On the front is a large question mark and simply asks, "May I ask you a question?" Then the question is posed inside the booklet, "Has anyone ever taken a Bible and shown you how you can know for sure that you're going to heaven?" Then it goes on to share the gospel message.

Here are several other exploratory questions:
> • Do you ever read the Bible? Do you understand it?
> • Have you ever thought about God and whether or not God exists?
> • Have you ever wondered who you really are and if you are any different than the animals? What makes you different?

- As a father or mother, have you ever considered your responsibility to teach your children some spiritual truths and values?
- Are spiritual things important to you?
- Have you ever wondered if there is anything after this life? If so, where will you be?
- Would you mind if I shared with you how I came to believe in Jesus Christ?
- Did you have any church background as you were growing up as a child?

The Ethiopian gives an interesting response to Philip's question, *"Do you understand what you are reading?"* He responds, *"How can I unless someone explains it to me?"* Verse 31. It is the Holy Spirit's desire to use you, a believer, to explain the truth of the Scriptures to others who are not yet seeing the truth. Notice verse 35. *"Then Philip opened his mouth, and beginning at this Scripture, preached Jesus to him."* We need to get from whatever passage of Scripture or whatever topic to the important topic, Jesus Christ. John Phillips enlightens us, "It is only a step from the Scripture portion to the Savior's person."[37]

The Holy Spirit creates hunger and brings conviction when one begins to explore the Scriptures. Use the Bible rather than your own plausible human arguments. Anchor your witness in the Scriptures and always share Jesus Christ. Then depend upon the power of the gospel. Believe and trust Romans 1:16. *"For I am not ashamed of the gospel of Christ, for it is the power of God to salvation for everyone who believes, for the Jew first and also for the Greek."*

Seventh, **He Is Trusting in The Holy Spirit's Power. Verses 36-39.**

---

[37]   John Phillips, IBID, page 163.

The Ethiopian responded to Philip's witness but it was the Holy Spirit who brought about faith and a true new birth in his life.

The Ethiopian immediately asked to be baptized. Most think that Philip explained baptism to him in his witnessing to him. Regardless, we see that the immediate response of this Ethiopian was to obey the command to be baptized. Baptism is not a condition of salvation, but a confession of salvation.[38]

We are to be witnesses, instruments to bear the message of the word of God to people. It is the Holy Spirit's responsibility to bring people to the point of salvation through faith. Campus Crusade's founder, Dr. Bill Bright, used to say "Successful witnessing is simply sharing the gospel in the power of the Holy Spirit and leaving the results to Him." Even when people do not respond in faith to receive Christ, our witness is successful, because they are then without excuse. As someone has said, "the preaching of the gospel to someone will either make him sad, or mad or glad."

There is nothing more thrilling for the follower of Christ Jesus than to be an instrument used by God to bring someone to faith in Christ. Here Philip is "snatched away" (verse 39) which is from the same Greek word as we find in I Thess. 4:17, speaking of the rapture of believers.[39] The Ethiopian went on his way rejoicing.

It would be a tragedy to know the solution to curing AIDS or cancer and to keep it a secret. To know Jesus Christ and that

---

[38] Verse 37 is omitted in the NU and the M-Text manuscripts. Verse 37 is found in the Western texts, including the Latin traditional texts. It was probably added to Luke's writing by some later scribe. Nevertheless, it is consistent with the teaching of the New Testament.

[39] The root Greek word is "arpago".

Jesus Christ alone is the only way to heaven. When we aren't actively involved in spreading the "good news", it is the greatest tragedy of all.

I Love To Tell The Story
(Written by Arabella K. Hankey, 1866)

I love to tell the story of unseen things above,
Of Jesus and His glory, of Jesus and His love;
I love to tell the story, because I know 'tis true,
It satisfies my longings as nothing else would do.

Refrain:
I love to tell the story,
'Twill be my theme in glory,
To tell the old, old story
Of Jesus and His love.

I love to tell the story, more wonderful it seems
Than all the golden fancies of all our golden dreams;
I love to tell the story, it did so much for me,
And that is just the reason I tell it now to thee.

I love to tell the story, 'tis pleasant to repeat,
What seems each time I tell it more wonderfully sweet;
I love to tell the story, for some have never heard
The message of salvation from God's own holy Word.

I love to tell the story, for those who know it best
Seem hungering and thirsting to hear it like the rest;
And when in scenes of glory I sing the new, new song,
'Twill be the old, old story that I have loved so long.

Chapter 10
A Trophy of the Grace Revolution!
Scripture: Acts 9:1-31

Ronald Rusty Woomer, 35, died in an electric chair on April 27, 1990 in South Carolina. He was guilty of one of South Carolina's most notorious murder sprees as he killed four innocent people.

Bob McAlister tells of his first contact with Rusty. "Late in the evening, as I walked up to the last cell, I saw a sight I will never forget: Rusty, his face the color of chalk, sitting on the floor - motionless. Crawling aimlessly like so many drunks, dozens of roaches covered the walls and floor. But what froze my soul were roaches crawling on the man - his lap, his shoulders - and such was his despair that he did not flick them off.

I sat down on the floor and tried to talk to him. He could not talk back. He just stared. It was a perfect picture of sin: filthy, degrading, and hopeless. In vain I tried to rouse a response. Frustrated and scared, I prayed aloud that God would cut through the evil in that cell and pierce the heart of its inhabitant.

"Rusty, just say the word Jesus," I pleaded. With much effort, he pursed his lips together and whispered, "Jesus." "Just look at you," I gently chided. "Your cell's filthy and so are you. The roaches have taken over and you're spiritually a dead man, son. Jesus can give you something better."

I asked Rusty if he wanted to accept Jesus as Lord and Savior. Through tears he nodded, then prayed. "Jesus, I've hurt a lot of people. Ain't no way that I deserve You to hear me. But I'm tired and I'm sick and I'm lonely. My mama's died and she's in heaven with You, and I never got to tell her good bye. Please forgive me, Jesus, for everything I've done. I don't know much about You, but I'm willing to learn, and I thank You for listening to me."

I went back to see him the following Monday. I walked up to his cell; it was spotless. Gone were the dirt and roaches and porno magazines. The walls were scrubbed, the bed was made, and the scent of disinfectant hung in the air.

"Bob, how do you like it?" exclaimed a smiling, energized Rusty. "I spent all weekend cleaning out my cell 'cause I figured that's what Jesus wanted me to do." "Rusty," I blurted, "it took all weekend to clean out your cell, but it took Jesus an instant to clean out your life."

In the four and half years of his appeals, Rusty grew mightily as a Christian. He was able to forgive an abusive father who had neglected him during his childhood and made it very difficult for Rusty's mama. He found even forgiveness from Lee Hewitt, a younger brother of Della Louise Sellers, for whose murder Rusty was executed. Lee also had become a Christian and knew that he must forgive Rusty. Lee later said, "Rusty and I are now brothers in Christ, and I had no choice but to forgive him. I love him."[40]

The transforming power of Christ is still evident as lives are changed by His grace.

You might be saying, "It isn't fair! Rusty shouldn't be forgiven, after all he is a murderer." But that is God's immeasurable grace!

---

[40] From Jubilee, Prison Fellowship, July, 1990, written by Bob McAlister, volunteer.

We come to the account of the salvation of Saul of Tarsus who also was a murderer. He participated in the murder of Stephen and was responsible for the persecution and death of many Christians. In fact, when Saul is arrested by Christ Jesus, he was on his way to wreak more havoc upon Christians in Damascus. If Saul of Tarsus and Rusty Woomer could be saved, anyone can! The power of God's grace to transform a lost sinner is seen in Saul of Tarsus, this trophy of the grace revolution.

First we see **Saul's Confrontation. Acts 9:1-9.**

Not everyone is going to be confronted personally by Jesus Christ in a visible frightening encounter like Saul was. However, every person who is saved by grace, will have a confrontation with Christ. You have to come to grips with who Christ is and what He has done for you, or you cannot be saved.

The Lord brought many of the common people and a number of the Jewish leaders to faith in Him as Savior and Lord through more normal means. Some were reached through preaching and others through personal witness. However, Saul was a hard-nut to crack, a rebel with a cause, who thought he was serving Jehovah God by seeking to stamp out this movement, this following of Jesus. Acts 9:1-2. *"Then Saul, still breathing threats and murder against the disciples of the Lord, went to the high priest and asked letters from him to the synagogues of Damascus, so that if he found any who were of the Way, whether men or women, he might bring them bound to Jerusalem."*

In the actual confrontation with Jesus, Saul was knocked from his horse and lay prostrate on the ground, blinded by a sudden flashing light from heaven. Verse 3 – 4a. Christ Jesus speaks to him personally. Verse 4b. *"Saul, Saul, why are you persecuting Me?"* Jesus takes persecution against His people as personal persecution of Himself.

Saul immediately recognized this confrontation to be by Someone whom he addresses as *"Lord"*. Saul said, *"Who are you, Lord?"* Verse 5. Then Jesus gives His personal identification: *"I am Jesus whom you are persecuting."*

His fellow travelers, his enforcers, did not see anyone, although they heard the sound, and saw the results of Saul's confrontation. Total blindness came upon Saul. Saul was blind and saw everything clearly, while the others accompanying him gazed all around and saw nothing.

A person comes under deep conviction as Jesus Christ is preached and many walk out unmoved. Are you running from God's pursuit? Are you seeking to escape the conviction of your sin? Are you trying to avoid Jesus Christ when the Holy Spirit is speaking to your heart? Are you seeking to deny your need or to bury the confrontation with Jesus by some diversionary activity? Look out! God may bring you to your senses real quickly by some confrontational tactic.

What a humbling of Saul takes place! He is no longer this arrogant, blustery, enforcer of suffering but he is blind, being led into Damascus by the hand. Such a humbling must come to anyone of us if we are to truly be saved from our sins. We must recognize our awful sins and our need of a Savior. We must come to Jesus as an unworthy sinner.

Next we see **Ananias's Consternation. Acts 9:10-16.**

Ananias, some obscure Christian disciple in Damascus, becomes God's targeted servant to deal further with Saul. He is only mentioned here and in Paul's later testimonies. The Lord gives him specific instructions as we read verses 11-12.

"So the Lord said to him, "Arise and go to the street called Straight, and inquire at the house of Judas for one called Saul of Tarsus, for behold, he is praying. And in a vision he has seen a man named Ananias coming in and putting his hand on him, so that he might receive his sight." There is no fogginess in the Lord's instructions. A specific street with a particular house, it is all spelled out for him.

There is a great deal of consternation and apprehension in Ananias's heart as he hears his assignment from the Lord. Lord, are you sure? Is this a trap? *"Then Ananias answered, "Lord, I have heard from many about this man, how much harm he has done to Your saints in Jerusalem. And here he has authority from the chief priests to bind all who call on Your name."* Ananias saw Saul as a murderer and an enemy of Christians, for his reputation was widely known. But the Lord saw Saul as *"a chosen vessel of Mine to bear My name before Gentiles, kings and the children of Israel. For I will show him how many things he must suffer for My name's sake."* Verses 15-16. Warren Wiersbe comments, "The fact that Saul was praying instead of preying should have encouraged Ananias."[41]

Can you imagine being in Ananias's shoes? Would your heart be in your throat? Would you be filled with fear? It is hard to accept some people into the family of God when you know their reputation! A prostitute, a homosexual or lesbian, or a murderer who repents and trusts Jesus Christ to save them! Can God's mercy and grace be extended to such a despicable enemy of the cross as Saul?

Corrie Ten Boom tells about her struggle to reach out a hand of forgiveness and accepting love to the man who was the mean guard when she and Betsy were confined at

[41]   Warren Wiersbe, IBID, page 440.

Ravensbruck Concentration Camp. He had showed up at a meeting where she was speaking about her experiences. He had identified himself and told her of his repentance and faith in Jesus. Can you imagine the struggle to reach out your hand of acceptance to one who had treated you so badly?

Now we see **Saul's Conversion. Acts 9:17-19.**

Here is the real time of Saul's new birth. Ananias places his hands upon him and he receives his sight physically and spiritually, and the Holy Spirit comes into his life. Verses 17-18. *"And Ananias went his way and entered the house; and laying his hands on him he said, "Brother Saul, the Lord Jesus, who appeared to you on the road as you came, has sent me that you may receive your sight and be filled with the Holy Spirit." Immediately there fell from his eyes something like scales, and he received his sight at once; and he arose and was baptized."* A new believer is born-again by the Holy Spirit entering his life and transforming him. Romans 8:9 tells us that *"if anyone does not have the Spirit of Christ he is not his."*

Ananias calls him *"Brother Saul,"* What a powerful greeting! *"Brother Saul."* This murderer, this enemy of Christ Jesus and His people is now *"brother Saul."* Oh, the powerful work of God's grace who takes hopeless sinners, total rebels, and turns them around to be trophies of His grace.

He got up and was baptized! Verse 18b. Again we see baptism, immersion in water as an identification with the death, burial and resurrection of Christ. It is a confession of salvation, not a condition of salvation, nor a means of salvation.

Have you been confronted by Jesus Christ? Have you repented and trusted Him? Have you publicly confessed your faith by obeying the Lord's command to be immersed in water?

Baptize (a transliteration rather than a translation from the Greek word 'Baptizo') means 'to dip or immerse'. It is the only mode of baptism that was practiced in New Testament times. Sprinkling was added much later in church history. Immersion is the only mode that pictures death, burial and resurrection. When one is lowered into the water and submerged, it is the picture of death and burial. When one is raised out of the water, it is the picture of resurrection and new life.

Verse 19b says, *"Saul spent several days with the disciples in Damascus."* Wow! The very ones that Saul came to persecute and imprison are now his brothers and sisters in Christ, and he is now accepted in their midst and spends time with them.

Now we witness **Saul's Confession. Acts 9:20-22.**

"Immediately he preached the Christ in the synagogues, that He is the Son of God. Then all who heard were amazed, and said, "Is this not he who destroyed those who called on this name in Jerusalem, and has come here for that purpose, so that he might bring them bound to the chief priests?" But Saul increased all the more in strength, and confounded the Jews who dwelt in Damascus, proving that this Jesus is the Christ."

When you really meet Jesus Christ and respond to Him in faith, there is a significant change. And Saul's life does a great 360 degree turn-about. The persecutor is now the preacher. The accuser of Jesus is now the defender. During these days, Saul quickly became a powerful apologist, proving to the Jews that Jesus is indeed the Christ, (the Messiah). Verse 22.

Often to our shame, we manipulate prominent people who become Christians. We parade them out to share their testimony because they are sports personalities or some noted celebrity. It is not wrong to let them share their testimony, but make sure they understand that they need to be discipled. They need to be protected from Satan's tactics to use their pride to defeat them. They need to go through the school of character development before they become leaders in Christ's church.

This leads to **Saul's Conflict. Acts 9:23-25, 29.**

Verse 23 begins with *"Now after many days had past. . ."* It is generally agreed that this 'many days' was about three years, during which time Paul withdrew to the Arabian Desert, where he received his instruction in the gospel from the Lord himself. Galatians 1:11-17.

John Phillips says, "His gospel was not of man and not received of man. He needed time to effect fully and systematically the change in his thinking initiated on the Damascus road, so he retired into Arabia with his copy of the Old Testament in his bag. He returned some time later with the great truths of Romans, Ephesians and Thessalonians in his heart. By the time he returned from the solitude of Sinai, his essential theology was formed."[42]

When he returned to Damascus, he became the focus of a plan to kill him. With the aid of his Christian brothers, he escaped by being let down in a basket or sling at night time, through an opening in the wall.

Verse 29 shows that in Jerusalem, he runs into the same kind of opposition and they are trying to kill him there also. So he is ushered away to Caesarea and he departs to Tarsus, his homeland. The apostle Paul was now the recipient of persecution instead of the perpetrator of persecution of Christians.

---

[42] John Phillips, IBID, page 183.

If you really stand up for the Lord and witness for him verbally, backed up as well as by your transformed life, you will inevitably run into conflict. This old world is not a friend to grace and you will run into the opposition of those who are rebellious toward God.

Next we meet **Saul's Confidante (or Companion). Acts 9:26-28.**

Now a tough test comes to Saul, after probably about three years of time has elapsed since his conversion. The disciples at Jerusalem are not about to take Saul into their family, their inner circle. They didn't trust him. Verse 26. *"And when Saul had come to Jerusalem, he tried to join the disciples; but they were all afraid of him, and did not believe that he was a disciple."*

Sometimes, it is hard for new believers to break into our circles of Christian friends, not necessarily because we do not trust them, but because we do not care enough to reach out to include new believers.

Barnabas surfaces again, as the encourager. He takes Saul under his wing and vouches for him. Through Barnabas, Saul is accepted by the church in Jerusalem.

Saul goes through a growth process in order to become the kind of servant that God can use. Somehow we have visions of Saul becoming the great apostle, Paul, overnight. But years are involved of very difficult experiences. He spends three years of virtual isolation in the Arabian Desert. He is rejected by Jews in Damascus and by the church in Jerusalem. Then he is rejected by the Grecian Jews in Jerusalem and he is shipped off to anonymity in his birthplace in Tarsus. Then Paul resurfaces in Acts 11:25 as Barnabas sends for him to come to assist in the teaching ministry in Antioch. There are probably

Rick Warren

several years between Acts 9 and Acts 11. According to
Wiersbe, about 7 years after the end of Acts 9, and about 10
years after his conversion.

There is no easy road to becoming "God's chosen instrument"
for ministry. There is no immediate way to become mature in
Christ! Chuck Swindoll says, "God does everything possible
to stop the energy of the flesh."[43]

Some prominent sinners are pursued by the Lord in personal
confrontations and dramatic conversions, like Saul. Others of
us less prominent, even unknown sinners are confronted by
Christ in less dramatic fashion, through preaching or personal
witness. Nevertheless, if you are to be saved from your sin,
born again into God's kingdom and placed on your way to
heaven, confrontation by Christ must happen. Every sinner, in
order to be saved, must arrive at the point of desperation,
realizing the immensity of his sinful lostness. He must be made
conscious by the Holy Spirit's conviction in his heart that he
personally is a rebel against God and that he is totally
unworthy of God's love and salvation. He must become
conscious of the fact that he is destined for hell without Christ.
Then he will understand the immensity of the grace of God,
the Father, in making His Son Jesus, the Messiah, the sacrifice
for his sin.

The Billy Graham Evangelistic Association produced a film
about Chuck Colson, called 'Reluctant Prophet'. His story is
of a confrontation through the witness of Tom Phillips,
president of Raytheon Corporation. The confrontation with
Jesus Christ came as Chuck Colson sat in his car on a rain
drenched night, unable to drive for a half hour because of the
tears in his eyes. He, like Saul, was convinced of two things:
His sinfulness and his unworthiness, and Who Jesus Christ is

---

[43] Charles Swindoll, Commentary on Acts, Volume 1, page 155.

and what He had done for Chuck Colson on the cross. It was the night of his conversion, his new birth by the Spirit.

You also can become a trophy of God's grace revolution. Do you see who Jesus really is? He is the Creator God! You would not be if He hadn't created you and given you physical life. He is the Redeemer God, the Lamb of God, slain for your sin upon a rugged Roman cross! He is the resurrected Christ, Who conquered sin and death for you! It is hard for you to keep kicking against the goads. Surrender to Him and accept Him as your Lord and Savior. Accept Him and receive His free gift of eternal life. Then be baptized as you surrender your life to Him. You also will become a trophy of His grace!

Pass Me Not, O Gentle Savior!
(Written by Fanny Crosby in 1868)

Pass me not, O gentle Savior,
Hear my humble cry;
While on others thou art calling,
Do not pass me by.

(Refrain)
Savior, Savior,
Hear my humble cry;
While on others thou art calling,
Do not pass me by.

Let me at thy throne of mercy
Find a sweet relief;
Kneeling there in deep contrition,
Help my unbelief. [Refrain]

Trusting only in thy merit,
Would I seek thy face;
Heal my wounded, broken spirit,

Save me by thy grace. *[Refrain]*

Thou the spring of all my comfort,
More than life to me,
Whom have I on earth beside thee?
Whom in heaven but thee? *[Refrain]*

Chapter 11
The Grace Revolution Breaks Down Barriers!
Acts 10:1 - 11:18

Prejudice is a cancer in our lives and our society. In the spring of 1992, an incident with the Los Angeles Police Department and a motorist by the name of Rodney King led to a violent outburst in Los Angeles that seemed unbelievable as we watched the pictures on TV. When the smoke had finally cleared, an estimated 5200 buildings had been destroyed or damaged and losses were estimated at close to a billion dollars. Almost 17,000 people had been arrested, 2,383 were injured and 54 people killed.

Here in Acts 10, we see the breaking down of the walls of prejudice that was absolutely essential for the world-wide expansion of the cause of Christ. God is an impartial God who offers His grace and mercy to all people. Christ died for all the world, not just for the Jews. This is Paul's teaching in Ephesians 2:11-22, where he teaches us that the wall between Jews and Gentiles has been broken down by Jesus Christ. Those Gentiles, who once were aliens and foreigners, are now brought near. Now Jews and Gentiles, those who were near and those who were *'far-off'* have access by one Spirit to the Father.

The mindset of the Jewish people toward Gentiles was an immense barrier. This was a very difficult hurdle to cross in order for God to accomplish His will. Barriers needed to be broken down that had been long standing barriers of prejudice.

This is a lengthy passage before us. We will simply refer to certain parts of it. We will only touch upon some of the truth herein contained as we seek to see the wonderful transformation that occurs on this historically significant occasion.

If it was not for the breaking down of these barriers in Acts 10 and 11, the gospel would have continued to be a gospel for the Jews only. But the gospel is for *"the Jew first, and also for the Gentile"*, as the New Testament so often declares, for example in Romans 1:16. *"For I am not ashamed of the gospel of Christ, for it is the power of God to salvation for everyone who believes, for the Jew first and also for the Greek."*

First, we witness **The Transforming God at Work.**

When you seriously study the Bible, you see that God is not a God who created the world and withdrew into some celestial corner to ignore the world and His creation. Even though sometimes God is seemingly silent in His Sovereign ways, He is very much involved in His transforming ways. God's loudest statement of His involvement came when He sent His Son, Jesus Christ to our world, and He hung on a rugged cross in our place, and was raised again from the dead. That is the message that we find Peter proclaiming as he comes to the home of this Gentile Roman centurion, Cornelius. While we probably do not have all the words that Peter preached, it is the basic gospel message that he shares with this Gentile crowd. Acts 10:34-43.

"Then Peter opened his mouth and said: "In truth I perceive that God shows no partiality. But in every nation whoever fears Him and works righteousness is accepted by Him. The word which God sent to the children of Israel, preaching peace through Jesus Christ - He is Lord of all - that word you know, which was proclaimed throughout all Judea, and began from Galilee after the baptism which John preached: how God anointed Jesus of Nazareth with the Holy Spirit and with power, who went about doing good and healing all who were oppressed by the devil, for God was with Him. And we are witnesses of all things which He did both in the land of the Jews and in Jerusalem, whom they killed by hanging on a tree.

Him God raised up on the third day, and showed Him openly, not to all the people, but to witnesses chosen before by God, even to us who ate and drank with Him after He arose from the dead. And He commanded us to preach to the people, and to testify that it is He who was ordained by God to be Judge of the living and the dead. To Him all the prophets witness that, through His name, whoever believes in Him will receive remission of sins."

The first nine chapters of Acts focus upon the gospel being preached to the Jews. The church that is established in those first four or five years is basically a Jewish church. You see the wonderful transforming, saving work of God through His Son Jesus Christ, as lives of many Jewish people are saved through faith in Jesus Christ. But the time had come for the gospel of Jesus Christ to be offered to the whole world. That is what we see happening here in Acts 10.

It was always God's eternal will that the whole world, all nations, might be blessed through the seed of Abraham Who was the promised Messiah. Genesis 22:18. *"In your seed all the nations of the earth shall be blessed, because you have obeyed My voice."* In this wonderful account we see God working in His transforming power to save us from our sins. That is God's eternal purpose, to bring us alienated and desperately lost sinners back into a personal relationship with Him.

Think about the timing of His work with Cornelius and with Peter They are located in two places about 30 miles apart. The appearance of the angel to Cornelius giving commands to send for Peter had to take place early enough to allow messengers to get to Joppa, at precisely the right time to coincide with what God was doing in Peter's life through his vision. We also see that God knows precisely where we are. He tells Cornelius through His angel just exactly where Peter is. Verses 5-6.

Now we need to take a look at Peter. **The Transformed Jewish Christian.**

Let's first take a look at what the Lord is doing in Peter's life, then we will come back to Cornelius. Peter was not yet ready to respond to God's will because of his prejudice against Gentiles. He had been raised in a Jewish culture where Gentiles were despised as unclean.

Prejudice, according to Webster, is "preconceived judgment". To the Jewish mind, any Gentile was an idolater and Gentiles were to be avoided, so as not to be contaminated by their presence. Lest we be too hard on Peter's prejudice, let's allow Chuck Swindoll ask us some pertinent questions about our own prejudices.

"Take a moment for a quick personal prejudice test. What images come to mind when you think of blacks or whites or Hispanics or Asians? How about those who are poor? Or those who are wealthy? Do you categorize people by the length of their hair or the cosmetics they wear or don't wear? Politically, what about liberals? Conservatives? How do you feel about people who have failed? Who are divorced? Who've been in psychiatric hospitals?

"What about religious prejudices? How do you view those who attend a different church? Who worship differently than you do? Or who have a different list of do's and don'ts? A tattooed motorcycle gang member roars into the church parking lot one Sunday. The Lord tells you to welcome him into the service.

"It's painful to face our own prejudices. And like being trapped in a smoke filled building, it's hard to see through the negative misconceptions we've had all our lives."[44]

This Jewish Christian, Peter, needed a transformation of his thinking in order to be open to do what God was calling him to do. We find Peter, waiting for lunch to be ready, goes to the roof-top to meditate and pray; He is hungry, and falls into a trance. Verses 9-10. The word 'trance' comes from the Greek word, "ekstasis", from which we get the word 'ecstasy'.

Leviticus 11 gives a whole list of dietary laws. Some things were to be eaten and many other things were on the forbidden list. Peter sees a sheet from heaven with all kinds of clean and unclean creatures in it. Three times this vision comes! 'Three' was significant in Peter's life! He had denied Jesus three times. And the Lord had asked him three times, "Do you love me, Peter?" It became obvious that God was seeking to tell him something more than just a lesson about Jewish dietary laws.

Peter's response to the command to *"rise Peter, kill and eat"* is a contradiction in terms; he says, *"Not so, Lord! For I have never eaten anything common or unclean."* Verse 14. When dealing with God's commands to us, we must drop one or the other; either drop the 'no' or drop the term 'Lord'.

Verse 15 is the message for Peter from God, although he did not immediately perceive its application. *"What God has cleansed you must not call common!"* As he is pondering the meaning of this vision, visitors arrive from Cornelius. Peter is learning rapidly and he responds in obedience to God's commands, goes to the home of Cornelius and ends up preaching the gospel to the Gentiles for the first time.

---

[44] Charles Swindoll, Commentary on Acts, Volume 2, page 1-2, 15.)

Do we, like Peter, need a transformation of our hearts so that we will reach out to all people for whom Christ died? Alexander Whyte is quoted by Charles Swindoll, "If you would take a four cornered napkin . . . and write the names of the nations, and the churches, and the denominations, and the congregations, and the ministers, and the public men, and the private citizens, and the neighbors, and the fellow-worshippers, all the people you dislike, and despise, and do not, and cannot, and will not, love. Heap all their names into your unclean napkin, and then look up and say, 'Not so, Lord'. I neither can speak well, nor think well, nor hope well, of these people. I cannot do it, and I will not try." If you acted out and spoke out all the evil things that are in your heart in some such way as that, you would thus get such a sight of yourselves that you would never forget it."[45]

There are many other things we could say about Peter, but we must move on.

Now let's consider **The Transformed Gentile.**

Our introduction to Cornelius (verses 1-8) tells us considerable about a Gentile seeker of the true God. He was a good man but not saved. While Cornelius did not yet know the Holy Spirit, the Holy Spirit knew him and knew all about him. He was sincere, devout, seeking to live up to the truth that he had. God took notice of him and revealed to him through this vision of an angel, what he should do further, in order to truly know God. Cornelius's experience confirms to us that those who sincerely seek God with their whole heart shall find Him. Jeremiah 29:13 teaches this truth: *"And you will seek Me and find Me when you search for Me with all your heart."*

---

[45]   Charles Swindoll, Commentary on Acts, Volume 2, page 7.

It is interesting that God does not reveal the message of the gospel through the angel, but commands him to send for Peter, a man who would give him God's message. God's spreads His word through us, not by angels.

Cornelius was obedient, and as Peter arrived, he already had gathered a crowd of family and friends together to hear what Peter had to say. Verses 23b - 27. *"On the next day Peter went away with them, and some brethren from Joppa accompanied him. And the following day they entered Caesarea. Now Cornelius was waiting for them, and had called together his relatives and close friends. As Peter was coming in, Cornelius met him and fell down at his feet and worshiped him. But Peter lifted him up, saying, "Stand up; I myself am also a man." And as he talked with him, he went in and found many who had come together. Then he said to them, "You know how unlawful it is for a Jewish man to keep company with or go to one of another nation. But God has shown me that I should not call any man common or unclean."*

Cornelius bowed down to worship Peter but Peter immediately refused that adoration. Peter humbly recognized that he too is a man, and was not any more important in God's sight than this Gentile. Prejudice always spawns feelings of superiority over others and prevents sharing the good news. Peter realized that God was doing something special in spreading the gospel to the Gentiles. Therefore he could not continue to court what the Jews regarded as unlawful – *"for a Jewish man to keep company with or go to one of another nation."* From now on, he could not *"call any man common or unclean."* Verse 28.

Verse 33 tells us that they were receptive people, eagerly waiting to know how to be saved. What a treat it would be for a pastor to have such an audience when one preaches the gospel of Jesus Christ! People sitting on the edge of their chairs, eager to hear Peter's message to them.

Cornelius and the others gathered in his house are responsive, believing in Christ Jesus who died for them and rose again. Verses 44-48. *"While Peter was still speaking these words, the Holy Spirit fell upon all those who heard the word. And those of the circumcision who believed were astonished, as many as came with Peter, because the gift of the Holy Spirit had been poured out on the Gentiles also. For they heard them speak with tongues and magnify God. Then Peter answered, "Can anyone forbid water, that these should not be baptized who have received the Holy Spirit just as we have?" And he commanded them to be baptized in the name of the Lord. Then they asked him to stay a few days."*

The converting work of the Holy Spirit occurred before the ordinance of baptism occurred. They are baptized after they are born again! In fact, Peter doesn't make baptism optional, but he *"commanded them to be baptized."* Every truly born-again believer must be baptized or he is being disobedient to Christ's command. The Great Commission, given by Jesus to His disciples, commands them to baptize those who become followers (disciples) of Jesus Christ. Matthew 28:16-20. He who is not willing to confess Christ publicly through immersion in water may seriously question whether or not he has anything inwardly to confess.

The 'speaking in tongues' is a sign to Peter and the Jewish Christians, who accompanied him, that this offer of salvation to the Gentiles is God's will and plan. This was the same occurrence at this critical historical juncture as had happened in Jerusalem on the day of Pentecost. When Peter is back in Jerusalem, Peter says this, *"And as I began to speak, the Holy Spirit fell upon them, as upon us at the beginning. Then I remembered the word of the Lord, how He said, 'John indeed baptized with water, but you shall be baptized with the Holy Spirit.' If therefore God gave them the same gift as He gave us* *when we believed on the Lord Jesus Christ, who was I that I could withstand God?" When they heard these things they became silent; and they glorified God, saying, "Then God has also granted to the Gentiles repentance to life." A*cts 11:15-18.

If you are still unsaved take a lesson from Cornelius. You too can be saved today by repenting of your sins and trusting Christ alone and His death alone as your means of being declared righteous before God.

Next we need to understand **The Transformed Church.**

Acts 11:1-18 tells us about the struggle that occurred in the established Jewish church. Peter, as he made his journey back to Jerusalem is criticized by his Jewish Christian brothers for going to the house of a Gentile. It reminds me of Christ Himself, who was criticized for His association with tax collectors and sinners.

Observe how Peter handles this! He doesn't pull a power play and reprimand them for questioning his authority as an apostle. People have a right to raise legitimate questions. Peter rehearses in painstaking detail what happened and leads them to his conclusion that this is God's doing. He reminds them that he was not alone. Six other Jewish Christians were with him. Verse 12. Then, in verse 17, Peter poses the logical question, *"If therefore God gave them the same gift as He gave us when we believed on the Lord Jesus Christ, who was I that I could withstand God?"*

The conclusion of the church is given in Acts 11:18. *"When they heard these things they became silent; and they glorified God, saying, "Then God has also granted to the Gentiles repentance to life."* The church of Jesus Christ was forever changed as the gospel of salvation was now given to the whole world.

Let's not allow our prejudices to prevent us from reaching out to all people with the good news of Jesus Christ, who died for all and is not willing that any should perish but that all should come to repentance.

Maybe you are very much like Cornelius, religious and devout, seeking to be God's servant, but not yet saved. You've been baptized as an infant, gone through catechism and you go to the mass or the Lord's Supper once in a while! You've been told that is how you are made right with God. You need to come to God in his prescribed way through his Son, Jesus Christ.

Believe in Jesus Christ! Trust Him and His provision for you on the cross of Calvary! Make up your mind to repent of your sin right now, trust Him as your Savior and determine to follow Him in your life. How about sincerely from your heart, having this talk with God?

"Lord, I confess before You that I am a sinner, deserving of your punishment. Lord Jesus, I thank You that You took my place on the cross and what I deserve You suffered for me. I thank You that You shed your blood and died in my place. Right now, I repent, and I place my trust in You alone as my Savior and Lord. Forgive me for my sins and receive me as Your redeemed child into Your family. Amen."

My Faith Has Found A Resting Place!
(Written by Eliza E. Hewitt, 1891)

My faith has found a resting place,
Not in device or creed;
I trust the ever-living One,

His wounds for me shall plead.

(Refrain)
I need no other argument,
I need no other plea,
It is enough that Jesus died,
And that He died for me.

Enough for me that Jesus saves,
This ends my fear and doubt;
A sinful soul I came to Him,
He'll never cast me out.

My heart is leaning on the Word,
The living Word of God,
Salvation by my Savior's name,
Salvation through His blood.

My great physician heals the sick,
The lost He came to save;
For me His precious blood He shed,
For me His life He gave.

Chapter 12
Key Factors In The Spreading Revolution!
Acts 11:1-30

Perhaps you have heard the revealing story about the young wife who always cut both ends off of a ham before she cooked it. It bothered her new groom whenever she did it. One day he could take it no longer. "Please tell me, honey," he said, "why do you always cut a piece off of both ends of a ham before you cook it?" "I don't know," she answered, "that's just the way my mother always did it."

One day he bravely asked his new mother-in-law why she cut both ends off of a ham before she cooked it. "I don't know," she answered, "but that's the way my mother always did it." Finally he asked his wife's grandmother why she always cut both ends off of a ham before she cooked it. "Oh," she said, "it's because I only had one pan to bake with, and it was too small for the whole ham."

Often we are so locked into our traditional ways that we find it hard to break out of their restrictions. We are so accustomed to doing things as we have always done them that we fail to ask "Why do we do this program?" or "Why do we do ministry this way?"

The early church, even after the first few years of her existence, was no exception. This eleventh chapter of Acts is a pivotal, critical juncture in the life of the growing church and the Lord's plan to reach the whole world. You quickly become aware of some key factors that led to the spread of the gospel to the Gentiles. As we look at these key factors, let's allow the Lord to apply these truths to our own lives and to our own church.

A Key Shift in Church Thinking. Acts 11:1-21.

In the last chapter, we looked at the breaking down of the barriers of prejudice in Peter's heart and his response to the request of Cornelius to come to his home. Peter obeyed and through the preaching of the gospel, the first Gentiles were reached with the gospel and were saved.

The Jewish church had a hard time accepting this step forward. The "circumcised believers" criticized Peter for going into a uncircumcised Gentile's house and eating with them. Acts 11:1-3.

Peter's way of handling the criticism gives us a pattern for dealing with conflict situations. Verses 4-17. Peter made it clear that to not go to Cornelius and to not share the gospel would have meant opposing God. However, Peter was patient with his critical brothers as he explained all the details of his visit from God in Joppa. Peter did not chastise them for asking questions about his violation of Jewish tradition and law.

The Jewish believers reached the right conclusion and they praised God that the Gentiles are included. Verse 18. *"When they heard these things they became silent; and they glorified God, saying, "Then God has also granted to the Gentiles repentance to life."*

It seems that it is still very difficult for the Jewish believers to allow their practice to catch up with their new understanding of the Gentiles being included. Verse 19. *"Now those who were scattered after the persecution that arose over Stephen traveled as far as Phoenicia, Cyprus, and Antioch, preaching the word to no one but the Jews only."*

Wouldn't you expect, after the lesson Peter was taught in Chapter 10, that Peter would launch a Gentile missions program? But he didn't! Those Jewish believers who had been scattered from Jerusalem by the persecution (Acts 8:1-4) continued to share the gospel just with the Jews.

Finally some of the Jewish believers, men from Cyprus and Cyrene (present day, Libya) went to the city of Antioch and began to speak to Hellenists, telling them the good news about the Lord Jesus. Verse 20. The Hellenists were Jews who lived or had lived in the Greek world and had adopted Greek cultural elements and spoke Greek. We see that the focus of the mission of spreading the gospel was the Jews, even for some time following the conversion of Cornelius and his household.

Even after Paul and Barnabas are commissioned by the church in Antioch and are sent off to preach the gospel, they were preaching to Jews in the synagogues. After their preaching to the Jews in several cities, they finally come to Antioch of Pisidia, where they preach the gospel to the Jews in the synagogue. In Acts 13:45-48, we find them finally turning to the Gentiles to share the gospel. *"But when the Jews saw the multitudes, they were filled with envy; and contradicting and blaspheming, they opposed the things spoken by Paul. Then Paul and Barnabas grew bold and said, "It was necessary that the word of God should be spoken to you first; but since you reject it, and judge yourselves unworthy of everlasting life, behold, we turn to the Gentiles. For so the Lord has commanded us: 'I have set you as a light to the Gentiles that you should be for salvation to the ends of the earth.'" Now when the Gentiles heard this, they were glad and glorified the word of the Lord. And as many as had been appointed to eternal life believed."* If Paul and Barnabas hadn't taken this step, the church of Jesus Christ was in danger of becoming provincial and inward looking.

In our church, we need also to be open to some shifting of our thinking if we are to keep moving forward in what the Lord is doing in our midst and in our community. We are in a building program that is necessary to provide for facilities that allow us to reach more people with the gospel. It would be easy to be content with a full worship center and crowded Christian Education facilities. Perhaps the Lord is wanting us to go to two services so that more people have the opportunity to hear the gospel. That will require an openness to new ways and new schedules.

It would be more comfortable to just praise the Lord for what He has done in the past and be content with a full and thriving church. If we do so, that will mean that our church will become inward-looking and we will abandon our commitment to help fulfill the Great Commission.

Now let's consider the importance of **Some Key Servant Leaders. Acts 11:19-26.**

Leadership is crucial to the work of the Lord being accomplished. The church needs leaders with servant hearts who are mature in Christ and filled with the Holy Spirit.

There are three leaders mentioned here in chapter 12 that are key to the spreading revolution.

1) Pioneering leaders, those like these Jewish leaders from Cyprus and Cyrene who risk the criticisms of their fellow church members in going against the prejudicial traditions. While they did not yet take the gospel to the Gentiles, at least they began to preach to the Hellenists, the Jews who were regarded by the Hebraic orthodox Jews as contaminated by the Gentile culture. Verses 19-21.

The church needs pioneering leaders who are willing to risk criticism with their new vision and new dreams.

2) Barnabas, the mature, encourager who comes to these new Christians in Antioch and is used of the Lord in the initial work of establishing them in the faith. Verses 22-24. We've seen him twice before in Acts. Barnabas was committed to Christ all the way, as he sold his property and gave all the proceeds to the church to meet the necessities of the needy believers. Acts 4:36-37. By the way, others did the same, although Barnabas is named. It was also Barnabas who reached out to Saul as a new believer who was being rejected by other fearful believers. Acts 9:26-28.

Barnabas soon saw that this was a much bigger work than he could handle, so he needed to recruit other leadership help. Note that he doesn't go back to Jerusalem to seek help from Peter or John. The Lord leads him to seek out a person he had not seen for some time, Saul.

3) So Saul enters the picture. Saul, who later is renamed Paul, is God's choice servant to reach the Gentiles. Verses 25-26. The word "seek" (verse 25) indicates that Barnabas had to do a hard search for him. The time frame is not easy to pin-point, but Saul had probably been a believer for from 6 to 9 years at this point.

For some years now, Paul had probably felt like he had been put on the shelf, after being ushered out of Jerusalem because of opposition from fellow Jews. Charles Swindoll says, "Whomever God chooses, He uses . . . but not always right away. God chose Saul at his conversion. ". .. . *he is a chosen instrument of Mine,"* God told Ananias, *"to bear My name before Gentiles and kings and the children of Israel."* Acts 9:15. But the Lord didn't fully use Saul until years later, when Barnabas came looking for him in Tarsus.

Do you feel that God has chosen you for a special purpose but has left you waiting in Tarsus? Are you struggling with this - anxious for Him to quit stalling?"[46]

God uses many different kinds of leaders but he only can use those who are humble and dependent upon Him. He doesn't just use those who are gifted as leaders, which leads us to the next point.

We need to understand the role of **Many Key Growing Believers. Verses 26-30.**

This new church at Antioch becomes a strong local body that becomes a sending church, as we see later in Acts 13. Here we see the church becoming strongly established as new believers are grounded in their faith. They are 'Christ-like' in character. Verse 26 tells us *"the disciples were first called Christians in Antioch."* They were called "Christians" or "Christ-ones"! Perhaps this name for believers was first used derogatorily, but not necessarily. It is a privilege to be named after our Lord and Savior, the Christ.

Barnabas had challenged them correctly and they had responded in obedience. Verse 23. The NIV says, Barnabas *"encouraged them to remain true to the Lord with all their hearts."* 'Remain true' is from the Greek word, 'prothesis', meaning 'to set forth' or 'to purpose'. The KJV translates this *"exhorted them all, that with purpose of heart they would cleave unto the Lord."*

If you want to be a growing Christian who serves the Lord, you must decide to be committed to Him and to His work. It is a whole hearted commitment to Christ that makes the difference. When you are saved by trusting Christ alone for

---

[46] Charles Swindoll, Commentary on Acts, Volume 2, page 32.

your salvation, it is just the beginning of your relationship with God. You are to grow in grace and knowledge of Christ, and you are to be committed to Christ and His Kingdom. We must learn what it is to seek first His kingdom and His righteousness.

These new Christians at Antioch quickly become giving, caring Christians. Verses 29-30. Agabus, a prophet from the church in Jerusalem predicts a severe famine over the whole Roman world. These Gentile believers at Antioch are moved to send a relief offering to the Jewish Christians living in Judea. What a demonstration of the love of Christ as these Gentiles give to help those who had formerly despised them!

One of the truest signs of the new birth is the conversion of our wallets and bank accounts. Paul tells us that we are all to do a weekly stewardship check! 1 Corinthians 16:1-2. *"Now concerning the collection for the saints, as I have given orders to the churches of Galatia, so you must do also: On the first day of the week let each one of you lay something aside, storing up as he may prosper, that there be no collections when I come."*

First, you are not to neglect your regular worship on the first day of every week. As you are going to worship, you are to do an accounting. "What income have you had this past week?" Give according to your ability, in other words, as God has blessed you. If every believer just tithed his income to the Lord's work, there would be no lack to do the work of the Lord.

Let's consider **Some Key Ministry Principles.**

1) The "Key Center" principle.

Although there is no indication that the disciples or even those missionaries who went to Antioch thought this way, it seems clear that the Holy Spirit led in starting this church at Antioch because it was a strategic center for the expansion of the mission to the Gentiles. As you follow Paul in his missionary journeys, the Holy Spirit led him to evangelize in key cities. Then as a church was established in a key city, he moved on to another city. Believers in the cities then reached their metro and country-side areas.

Antioch would not be our first choice of a place to start a church from the human standpoint. Lloyd Ogilvie comments, "Syrian Antioch was a formidable place to begin a ministry. It was third only to Rome and Alexandria in prominence at the time. Known as one of the "eyes" of Asia, it was the residence of the Roman prefect and the seat of political power for that area of the Roman Empire. The culture of this metropolitan city at the mouth of the Orontes River was Greek. Strategically located fifteen miles from the Mediterranean Sea, Antioch had become very cosmopolitan. But something else had made the very name of the city synonymous with rampant immorality. In this "sin city", chariot racing, gambling, and debauchery took priority in the persistent pursuit of pleasure."[47] To start a church plant in Antioch would be like deciding to start a church in Las Vegas or San Francisco.

However, the Holy Spirit targeted people in Antioch and they were saved and the church became strong, a key center in the mission to the Gentiles.

2) A second principle: Keep the gospel message clear!

There is only one way to the Father, the Lord Jesus Christ and His saving work on the cross. That was Peter's message to Cornelius and his household. As Peter was reporting to the

---

[47] Lloyd Ogilvie, Drumbeat Of Love, The unlimited power of the Spirit as revealed in the Book of Acts, Word Books, 1976 pages 152f

church in Jerusalem, he made it clear to them that the angel that had stood in Cornelius's house had communicated to him. *"Send men to Joppa, and call for Simon whose surname is Peter, who will tell you the words by which you and your household will be saved."* Acts 11:13-14. The NIV says it this way, *"He will bring you a message through which you and all your household will be saved."* That was the message to the people at Antioch. It was the same message, the 'good news' that men from Cyprus and Cyrene preached to the Hellenist Jews as they came to Antioch. Acts 11:20. *". . .some of them were men from Cyprus and Cyrene, who, when they had come to Antioch, spoke to the Hellenists, preaching the Lord Jesus."*

However, after people accepted Christ by faith and were saved, they were exhorted or encouraged to grow in their commitment. Barnabas *". . . encouraged them all that with purpose of heart they should continue with the Lord."* Verse 23.

Today, in our efforts to start churches in our modern ways, we hear pastors saying things like, "We can't talk to our people about tithing or about supporting missionaries or even about obedience to being baptized as a believer by immersion; they are not ready for that yet. It might drive them away!" The front-line apostles were not even thinking that the truth might drive people away. They preached and taught the truth and trusted the Spirit of God to use the truth to transform those who believed.

3) Another principle is that the church of Jesus Christ must be a Bible teaching church. Acts 11:26.

Barnabas searched to find Paul and brought him back to Antioch to assist in grounding these new believers in the faith. *". . . so for a whole year they assembled with the church and taught a great many people. And the disciples were first called Christians at Antioch."*

New Christians will never become strong Christians unless you get them into studying the word of God, learning to obey the word. How are you doing as a Christian? Are you still in the word of God? Are you committed to the Lord and His work? Or have you just settled back into a leisure life-style as a Christian, content to know you're saved?

4) Another principle is to depend totally upon the Holy Spirit.

Strategies are not nearly as significant as being led and anointed by the Spirit of God. Wherever and however you gather people together, (programs or individual contacts), preach and teach the gospel and preach and teach God's word. We are not here to entertain! We are here to evangelize people and disciple believers who are serious about following Christ Jesus!

As you read through Acts, you get the impression that these pioneers of the faith are not so much developing their plans and strategies, as they were being led along by the Holy Spirit. Verse 21 says, *"The hand of the Lord was with them, and a great number believed and turned to the Lord."* Fruitfulness comes when *"the hand of the Lord is with us."*

The work of the Lord in the grace revolution is a divine enterprise. So I challenge all of us to rededicate ourselves to the Lord and trust Him to pour out His Holy Spirit upon us. Be fervent in our prayer lives and obedient to the Lord. Wait upon the Lord and see what He will do to glorify His great name. *"Now to Him who is able to do exceedingly abundantly above all that we ask or think, according to the power that works in us, to Him be glory in the church by Christ Jesus to all generations, forever and ever. Amen."* Ephesians 3:20-21.

Take My Life And Let It Be Consecrated!
(Written by Frances R. Havergal, 1874)

Take my life and let it be
Consecrated, Lord, to Thee.
Take my moments and my days,
Let them flow in endless praise.

Take my hands and let them move
At the impulse of Thy love.
Take my feet and let them be
Swift and beautiful for Thee.

Take my voice and let me sing,
Always, only for my King.
Take my lips and let them be
Filled with messages from Thee.

Take my silver and my gold,
Not a mite would I withhold.
Take my intellect and use
Every pow'r as Thou shalt choose.

Take my will and make it Thine,
It shall be no longer mine.
Take my heart, it is Thine own,
It shall be Thy royal throne.

Take my love, my Lord, I pour
At Thy feet its treasure store.
Take myself and I will be
Ever, only, all for Thee.

Chapter 13
Pray For A Faith Lift!
Acts 12:1-19

This Passover mentioned in Acts 12 is the eleventh anniversary of the crucifixion and resurrection of Jesus Christ. We have already read of several attacks upon Christians in these eleven brief years of the history of the church. Another wave of persecution strikes the church of Jesus Christ.

Peter is arrested by Herod and placed in prison, to be held until after the feast of unleavened bread, the seven day feast following the Passover. Jewish laws did not allow for trial or sentencing to death during these seven days.

This Herod is Herod Agrippa I, the grandson of the Herod who murdered the children when Jesus was born. He was a politician in the bad sense of that word. A.T. Robertson comments, "Herod Agrippa I . . . was anxious to placate his Jewish subjects while retaining the favor of the Romans. So he built theatres and held games for the Romans and Greeks and slew Christians to please the Jews."[48]

We read in Verse 2-3: *"Then he* (Herod) *killed James the brother of John with the sword. And because he saw that it pleased the Jews, he proceeded further to seize Peter also. Now it was during the Days of Unleavened Bread."* This James was the brother of John, the two sons of Zebedee. Herod was more concerned about his popularity than he was about his integrity. Therefore, when he was on a roll with the Jews, he decided that another good target would be the big fisherman, Peter, himself.

---

[48] A.T. Robertson, Word Pictures in The New Testament, Broadman Press (1930, 1932, 1933), pages 163f.

So we find Peter locked in prison, *"bound with two chains between two soldiers; and the guards before the door were keeping the prison."* Verse 6. He was guarded by double the usual force, *'four squads of soldiers'* Verse 4. It is the last night before his trial and probable execution. Whether a Peter physically locked away in prison or a believer who seems imprisoned by his or her difficult problems, the situation seems impossible. You may find yourself in such a circumstance where it seems to you an absolutely impossible situation.

When God's people are under attack, the genuineness of their faith is revealed. In this chapter, we have a portrayal about real faith and how it operates.

True Faith Commits To The Lord Unreservedly.

When you trust Christ as your Savior and you are born again through faith in Him, it will not take you long to discover that not everyone is happy that you have become a follower of Jesus Christ. Some will consider you foolish, a religious fanatic. Others will suggest that you are a weak person who needs a crutch. Others will display hostility and, if it were possible legally, they would vote for your demise from this world.

In America today, Christians are about the only group of people that can be attacked, ridiculed and scoffed at on the media, and they can get away with it. On the ABC network, the Dana Carvey show is an example. He repeatedly attacks Christians and thinks it is humorous.

Remember that this old world is not 'Christian' and it is not under the lordship of Jesus Christ. 1 John 5:19 says, *"We know that we are of God, and the whole world lies under the sway of the wicked one."* In John 15:18-19, Jesus spoke clearly of what his followers would face. *"If the world hates you, you know that it hated Me before it hated you. If you were of the world, the world would love its own. Yet because you are not of the world, but I chose you out of the world, therefore the world hates you."* Also, John 16:33 expressly says, *"These things I have spoken to you, that in Me you may have peace. In the world you will have tribulation; but be of good cheer, I have overcome the world."*

Therefore everyone who will be a follower of Jesus Christ must decide to commit his or her life unreservedly to Him. Whether it means life or death in this world, Jesus Christ is my Lord and my Savior.

One of the clear evidences of true faith, being truly born again by the Holy Spirit, is that you decide for Jesus Christ when the pressure is on. All around this world, there are countries where Christians have been hauled off to prison, sent away to the Gulag, and even annihilated for no other crime other than being a dedicated follower of Jesus, the Christ. There is a great discrepancy in statistics reported about how many martyrs for Christ there are in the world every day. According to 'Open Doors', eleven Christians per day die for their faith.[49]

If you are not committed to Jesus Christ to stand up for Him, when at your work place some co-worker scoffs at Christ or

---

[49] https://www.opendoorsusa.org/christian-persecution/stories/11-christians-killed-every-day-for-their-decision-to-follow-jesus/ "The Christian persecution we read about in Scripture and history books is not a thing of the past. It still exists. Today, in the 21st century, we are living in a time when persecution against Christian believers is the highest in modern history. According to Open Doors' 2019 World Watch List—an in-depth investigative report focusing on global Christian persecution—persecution is increasing at an alarming rate. Research for the List indicates that each day, a staggering 11 Christians are killed for their faith in the top 50 countries ranked on the World Watch List."

Christians, then you have not dealt with the issue of your unreserved commitment to Him. He died for you! Have you died with him? Galatians 2:20 is my chosen life's verse. *"I have been crucified with Christ; it is no longer I who live, but Christ lives in me; and the life which I now live in the flesh I live by faith in the Son of God, who loved me and gave Himself for me."*

True Faith Submits to God's Sovereign Will.

Peter's faith is seen in his submission to the will of God. James had been put to death, and as far as Peter knew, that would be his fate also. Yet you find Peter very much at peace about it all. Verse 6 tells us that *"Peter was sleeping . . ."* If I was expecting to be put to death tomorrow morning, I don't think I would be sleeping tonight.

The only way to be at peace in your difficult situation is to believe in God as the Sovereign LORD over everything that exists. You must believe in the God of the Bible who really does work everything according to His Sovereign plan. Ephesians 1:11-12 reminds us, *"In Him also we have obtained an inheritance, being predestined according to the purpose of Him who works all things according to the counsel of His will, that we who first trusted in Christ should be to the praise of His glory."*

His plan is not to make us permanent citizens of this world but to take us home to be part of His eternal kingdom. This old world is someday going to burn and it will be replaced by the new heaven and the new earth, wherein righteousness reigns, because Jesus Christ is King. So our difficult circumstances must be viewed in that light. That is what real faith is!

God's plan for His redeemed people is to transform them into the image of Christ, and trials are a part of that process. Ponder

Paul's words to the Roman church in Romans 5:3-5. *"And not only that, but we also glory in tribulations, knowing that tribulation produces perseverance; and perseverance, character; and character, hope. Now hope does not disappoint, because the love of God has been poured out in our hearts by the Holy Spirit who was given to us."*

When things are going on in our lives that we can't understand or make sense of, faith holds on to the fact that the Sovereign LORD knows all about it and He will work it out according to His eternal plan. Romans 8:28-29 is still in the Bible and it is still as true today as it was in Paul's day. *"And we know that all things work together for good to those who love God, to those who are the called according to His purpose. For whom He foreknew, He also predestined to be conformed to the image of His Son, that He might be the firstborn among many brethren."*

James was killed by Herod's sword and Peter was delivered from prison miraculously; both were according to God's Sovereign will. The attitude of faith is that expressed by Paul in Phil. 1:18-21. *"What then? Only that in every way, whether in pretense or in truth, Christ is preached; and in this I rejoice, yes, and will rejoice. For I know that this will turn out for my deliverance through your prayer and the supply of the Spirit of Jesus Christ, according to my earnest expectation and hope that in nothing I shall be ashamed, but with all boldness, as always, so now also Christ will be magnified in my body, whether by life or by death. For to me, to live is Christ, and to die is gain."*

True Faith Rests in God's Constant Care.

It is an amazing statement in verse 6. *"And when Herod was about to bring him out,"* (to trial and death) *"that night Peter was sleeping . . ."* You would expect him, humanly speaking to be anxious, agitated, fuming and fretting, but he is sleeping. How different Peter is now in his personal storm than he was out there on Galilee when Jesus was sleeping in the boat while the disciples thought they were about to perish. The Lord had rebuked them, *"O you of little faith!"* But with the prospect of being soon put to death, just as James had been, he is at peace and able to sleep soundly.

You are never prepared to live until you are prepared to die, and you are never prepared to die until you are living your life totally committed to Jesus Christ. For these last eleven years since the events of the crucifixion and resurrection of Christ, Peter had been living all out for His Master. So, with the impending execution, he was able to rest peacefully in the care of the Lord. He was confident that no one, not even Herod could take his life, unless the Lord Jesus allowed it. Most importantly, Herod could not end his eternal life.

Remember, eternal life is a gift you have the minute you trust Christ as your Savior. You are now living your eternal life! You do not wait until you die to get eternal life. Because you live in Christ Jesus, you will never die spiritually. Physical death is just a transition to a new phase of your eternal existence with God. Remember the words of Jesus to Martha when Lazarus had died. John 11:25-26. *"Jesus said to her, "I am the resurrection and the life. He who believes in Me, though he may die, he shall live. And whoever lives and believes in Me shall never die. Do you believe this?"*

So you are going through some terrible experience right now; you're been laid off from work; or your marriage mate has been unfaithful and ditched you for some other person; or one of your children has rebelled against the Lord and given you all kinds of grief; or whatever deep valley you are going through. Your prison walls seem just as formidable as they were for Peter, and your situation seems to be impossible!

Listen to Chuck Swindoll's words. "Whenever we view a problem as impossible, we are actually falling into a subtle trap - the trap of focusing on the externals. Paul told the Corinthian believers, "You are looking at things as they are outwardly" (2 Cor. 10:7a), and we do the same thing by seeing only the wall and not the God of the wall. God is not limited like we are. He never faces dead ends. He doesn't even know what one looks like."[50]

Does God know all about it? Do you believe Jesus Christ cares? Do you believe that He is able to do anything about it? When we commit our situation to the Lord and trust Him to work out His Sovereign will, then we can rest in Him. Here is Peter's advice, probably learned in prison, chained between two soldiers, sleeping soundly and suddenly awakened by an angel visitor. 1 Peter 5:7 (NIV). *"Cast all your anxiety on him because he cares for you."* Remember the invitation of Jesus in Matthew 11:28: *"Come to Me, all you who labor and are heavy laden, and I will give you rest."*

True Faith Prays To God Earnestly.

Acts 12:5 informs us *"Peter was therefore kept in prison, but constant prayer was offered to God for him by the church."* The whole church in Jerusalem was praying for Peter, but a special all night prayer meeting was going on this particular night in Mary's house. In verse 12, when Peter shows up early in the morning, probably while it is still dark outside, we find *"many were gathered praying."* This was the home of Mary, the mother of John Mark, a place where Peter had often enjoyed the fellowship of other believers.

---

[50] Charles Swindoll, Commentary on Acts, Volume 2, page 34.

How does the church pray? The word 'constant' in verse 5 is probably better translated 'fervent' or 'earnest' prayer. 'Constant' (NKJV) is from "ektenees", meaning "to be stretched out, an intentness of mind, or earnest"[51] They were stretched out before God in interceding for God's work in Peter's situation. What were they praying for? I don't think they were necessarily praying for God to deliver him out of prison. Otherwise, why would they have been so skeptical about Rhoda's report that Peter was knocking at the door? Perhaps, they were more intent upon praying that Peter would be strengthened to go through this experience of being executed like James had been, and that he would not weaken in his commitment to Christ.

God does perform a wonderful miracle for Peter and the church at Jerusalem, but neither Peter nor the Jerusalem church seem to be expecting the miracle. An angel comes, pokes Peter in the ribs to awaken him, and tells him to be quick, get up, put on his clothes and sandals and follow him. The angel escorts him out of the prison, all of this happening without awaking two sets of guards. Note that God doesn't do everything for Peter, only that which he can't do for himself. God loosed the chains silently, without awaking the guards, and he led Peter past the sentries, and opened the locked prison gates miraculously.

When we pray, we must be prepared to take action to do what God enables us to do. If you are out of work, don't pray and then sit around, doing nothing. Get out and look for places that are hiring and fill out applications. Verse 10b says, after exiting the prison gate, *"they went out and went down one street, and immediately the angel departed from him."* He was

---

[51] Thayer's Greek - English Dictionary, Zondervan, Grand Rapids, Michigan, 1962.

on his own now! Not really, the living Christ is always with us.

Verse 11 says, *"And when Peter had come to himself, he said, "Now I know for certain that the Lord has sent His angel, and has delivered me from the hand of Herod and from all the expectation of the Jewish people."* To that point, Peter thought it was still a dream or a vision. Verse 9. But now it dawned on him that this was really happening. He was free! *"Had come to himself"* is from the same word used of the prodigal son in Luke 15, as he came to his senses out there in the pig pen, in his desperate situation. When you come to your senses and see what God is doing, you take action. Peter decides to get out of there before Herod sends his henchmen searching for him.

True Faith Rejoices in God's Deliverance.

Whatever God does for you, make certain that you give God the glory and rejoice in His wonderful ways. When the prayer meeting broke up and they realized that Peter was actually released, they at first were *"astonished."* Verse 16.

As we pray faithfully and earnestly, we also will often be astonished, surprised at what God chooses to do in our midst and in our behalf. He doesn't always choose to do a miracle but sometimes He will. Often what God does for you cannot be technically called a miracle, but it is so wonderful to you that you will regard it as God's miraculous working. The praying church of Jerusalem rejoiced at what God had done and gave God the glory.

Herod is a different story in the end of this chapter. When the jail guards couldn't find Peter and didn't know what had happened to him, Herod was incensed and commanded that all the guards should all be put to death. Verse 19. Then Herod takes refuge in his palace at Caesarea, his Mediterranean Sea coast mansion. Sitting on his throne and giving an oration to the people. Herod is praised as the people shouted, *"The voice of a god and not of a man!"* Verse 22. Herod accepted the praise and worship of people, and *"an angel of the Lord struck him, because he did not give glory to God. And he was eaten by worms and he died."* God Almighty has no competitors and does not tolerate any who touch His glory!

Chuck Swindoll has some fitting remarks that can help us keep our eyes on the Lord when the church body or we, as individuals, are faced with imposing prison walls. "This story reminds us of two principles that will keep our heads up when circumstances appear bleak. First, we are all faced with a series of great opportunities brilliantly disguised as impossible situations. An impossible situation can turn into an opportunity for God to show His power. Second, if there is to be a solution, it will take divine intervention.[52] A dear friend of mine from Canada, Harold Phillips, used to say, "Problems are simply opportunities to see God at work!"

Therefore commit your heart to our great and mighty God, and surrender your desperate situation to the Lord! Pray much and wait upon the Lord to see His hand at work!

It Took a Miracle
(Written by John Peterson)

My Father is omnipotent,
and that you can't deny;
A God of might and miracles,
'tis written in the sky.

(Chorus)
It took a miracle to put the stars in place;

---

52 Charles Swindoll, Commentary on Acts, Volume 2, page 39.

It took a miracle to hang the world in space.
But when He saved my soul,
Cleansed and made me whole,
It took a miracle of love and grace.

Though here His glory has been shown,
we still can't fully see
The wonders of His might, His throne,
twill take eternity.

The Bible tells us of His power
and wisdom all way through;
And every little bird and flower
are testimonies too.

The greatness of the Lord
is seen in everything He made,
But greater far the work He did
when on Him my sin was laid.

Chapter 14
Front Line Troops for the Grace Revolution!
Acts 13:1-4

World War II posed one of the greatest threats to the free world that has ever been encountered. Some of us are old enough to remember those battles as you participated as "front line troops".

One of our members, Art Jones, shared his testimony of those days when he was ministered to by what, he believes, was an angel. I would agree, as I heard his testimony. He shared about being badly injured on the front lines and a soldier appeared with a completely clean uniform. This was unusual as they were fighting in rain and mud. This soldier carried him back to the medics' tent where he received immediate help for survival. Then this soldier just disappeared. Was this soldier a ministering angel from the Lord? There is no doubt in my mind, or in Art's mind.

In order for the front line troops to be successful, there was a mobilization of America and Canada. It was necessary for all to sacrifice in order for the front line troops to be supplied with what they needed to fight the war. Some remember the gas rationing; the fact that you could not buy rubber tires; and women were hired to work in the armament plants. My sister-in-law worked in one such plant in New Brighton, Minnesota.

In Acts 13, we find that the church in Antioch became the key sending church for the spreading of the gospel to the Gentile world. All three of Paul's missionary journeys began here in Antioch and he reported back to this key local church.

If the world is going to be reached with the gospel, local churches must pattern their missionary vision and zeal after this church in Antioch. Front line troops are needed and we in the local church play a key role. Let's learn from the believers at Antioch.

First we observe **A Maturing Local Church.**

If the missionary task is going to be accomplished, local churches must be strong. If local churches are to be strong, individual believers must be strong in the Lord. Not only must individual believers be strong in the Lord but they must be fervently committed to the local church. There are far too many who call themselves followers of Christ who are "lone rangers". There are far too many of us church members who are not taking seriously our responsibility to be committed to the local body of Christ. This is totally contrary to God's will and plan.

1. They responded to a biblical teaching ministry. Acts 11:25-26.

When Saul comes to Antioch with Barnabas, they begin the process of discipling these new believers. *"For a whole year, they assembled with the church and taught a great many people."* Verse 26.

There is no way for a believer to become a strong Christian or for a church to become a strong church without solid Bible teaching. Get into the word personally in verse by verse Bible study. Be faithful in your commitment to worship services and soak up every morsel of the word of God that you can. KNOW the word and DO the word, and you will grow strong in Christ Jesus. In the church at Jerusalem, you see the same pattern. Acts 2:42. *"And they continued steadfastly in the apostles' doctrine and fellowship, in the breaking of bread, and in prayers."*

As a pastor, I am concerned about some of you who are so irregular in your commitment to the worship services. I am burdened for many of you who never stay to study the word of God in Sunday Bible classes. I remind many of you as parents who are not staying with your children so that your children can be taught the word of God in their age-graded Sunday school classes. Let me meddle a little further. How is your personal and family life when it comes to time in the word and in prayer? Parents, you will be held accountable for your children! King Solomon, looking back with some regret upon his own failures, remarks in Ecclesiastes 12:1, (NIV) *"Remember your Creator in the days of your youth, before the days of trouble come and the years approach when you will say, "I find no pleasure in them"*

2) They were respectful of spiritual leaders. Acts 13:1.

The church at Antioch was well blessed with good solid spiritual leaders. They were "prophets and teachers," Prophets were preachers, forth-tellers, not just foretellers. Teachers were those skilled in giving clear understanding of the Scriptures. A.T. Robertson, comments, "All prophets were teachers, but not all teachers were prophets . . .(The construction "The double use of 'te' here) makes three prophets (Barnabas, Simeon, Lucius) and two teachers (Manaen and Saul)"[53]. G. Campbell Morgan writes, "Prophets are men of insight and foresight, who seeing into the heart of truth, and far on into the economy of God, as the result of personal fellowship with Him, speak forth the words of God. Teachers are men of understanding, who having that understanding, are able to impart their knowledge to others."[54]

---

[53]   A. T. Robertson, IBID, page 177.

[54]   G. Campbell Morgan, The Acts of Apostles, Fleming H. Revell Company, 1924, page 308.

These are not self-appointed leaders; though in this case, being a newly established church, they do not seem to have been appointed by congregational vote, as the seven deacons were appointed in the church at Jerusalem. Acts 6. This team of leaders seem to have been appointed by God in the process of forming this church. Barnabas is first named and was sent to Antioch by the established church in Jerusalem. Simeon, called Niger, meaning 'black', was probably from North Africa. Some think this was the same Simon of Cyrene who carried the cross of Jesus. Lucius of Cyrene, was probably one of the original evangelists mentioned in Acts 11:20, who brought the gospel to Antioch in the first place. Manean was, literally 'foster-brother' of Herod, the tetrarch. Finally, Saul, was the former persecutor of Christians.

Barnabas, named first, was probably the leader of the team, serving in a kind of 'senior pastor' role. Note the order in which "Barnabas and Saul" are first mentioned. Then later in Acts 13:13, the order shifts to *"Paul and his party"*. From verse 42 and following the order is *"Paul and Barnabas."*

The people at Antioch respected these leaders and responded to their preaching and teaching ministry. The church was rapidly maturing and becoming strong.

3) They faithfully worshiped the Lord. Verse 2.

We read that the church is involved in their regular routine of worshiping the Lord. The KJV says, *"While they ministered to the Lord . . ."* The word 'ministered' is from 'leitourgeo' from which we get our word 'liturgy.' This word is common in LXX (the Septuagint – the Greek translation of the Old Testament) of the priests who served in the tabernacle. Here it is referring to the gathered church, meeting to worship, to minister to the Lord in praise and worship. G. Campbell Morgan comments, "The Church is an institution for worship, its members minister to the Lord, and then they are sent forth to be of service. Worship and work are always intimately associated. If we try to work without worship, we shall disastrously fail. If we worship and never work, we shall become ritualists. (my comment —"just going through the motions, the forms") The attitude to which the Spirit can reveal Himself is that of worship."[55]

Note also that they were fasting. There was no pot-luck dinner to attract people to come to worship. Fasting is an act of intense desire to know the Lord's will. God is not more responsive to us when we do not eat, but is more responsive to the heart desire that leads one to forgo a meal because of intense longing to commune with Him. It was *"As they ministered and fasted, the Holy Spirit said . . ."* When we gather with a right heart and a fervent desire, the Holy Spirit speaks. Verse 2.

4) They listened to the voice of the Holy Spirit.

How did the Holy Spirit speak? In an audible voice? Probably not, but probably through one of the leaders. The insight of G. Campbell Morgan is helpful. "One cannot say definitely how the Spirit spoke to the Church at Antioch. I do not for a moment imagine that the assembly heard a voice. That is the mistake we too often make. We try to force ourselves into ecstasies in order to hear the voice, and then we imagine we hear it! That is not the suggestion here. He made known His will to the assembly, probably through one spokesman, whose word produced agreement. We are not told through which of them (the leaders) the Spirit spoke. The method of the Spirit is ever that of obscuring the instrument. In those days of worship and fasting, one of their number probably rose and spoke, and immediately in the whole assembly there was unanimity,

---

[55] G. Campbell Morgan, IBID, page 310.

absolute conviction that this is the mind of the Spirit."[56] I believe it was much the way in which the Holy Spirit has been leading in our decisions regarding our building addition. As we have met and worked through this process, there has come unanimous agreement that this is the will of the Lord.

There must be a right heart attitude on the part of God's people in order to hear the Holy Spirit speak. The Psalmist expresses this proper desire of the heart of the believer. *"As the deer pants for the water brooks, so pants my soul for You, O God. My soul thirsts for God, for the living God."* Psalm 42:1. We want to know you, Lord, and we want more than anything else to know and do your will.

Next we witness **An Obedient Local Church.**

1. They recognized God's specific call to a specific task.

Remember that this is not the original call of Barnabas and Saul to the ministry of the word as pastors or preachers. They had already been called to that role. Saul was called at his conversion on the Damascus Road to preach the gospel to the Gentiles.

Being a pastor or a missionary is not just a human choice of vocations or a choice of careers. Unfortunately the church of Jesus Christ is plagued with many who are trying to pastor who have never been called by the Spirit of God. Again I refer you to G. Campbell Morgan. "No man can go (Author's comment – "'should go' as obviously some endeavor to go into pastoral ministry on their own initiative) unless the Spirit calls him. Men cannot make a minister, not even the Church, nor her theological halls. He must be called of the Spirit. Unless he hear that call sounding in his soul, ringing like a trumpet night

---

56   G. Campbell Morgan, IBID, page 311.

and day, giving him no rest until he is compelled to say, 'Woe is me if I preach not; then in God's name let him stay where he is, in his present calling."[57]

In Acts 13:2, the Holy Spirit is calling two of their pastors to be front line troops in the missionary work of spreading the gospel to the Gentiles. The Holy Spirit says to the church at Antioch, *"Now, separate to Me Barnabas and Saul, for the work to which I have called them."*

Most of us are called to stay in our Antioch, and to faithfully serve the Lord in the church so that our community is touched by the gospel. However, it is God's doing to send some of them out as laborers into other parts of His world-wide harvest field. Remember the command of Jesus in Matthew 9:37-38. *"The harvest truly is plentiful, but the laborers are few. Therefore pray the Lord of the harvest to send out laborers into His harvest."*

2) They remembered Christ's world vision.

They continued to fast and pray (verse 3a), seemingly a reaffirming that indeed it is the Holy Spirit who has spoken. As they did so, I am certain that they probably checked it out according to the Lord's word. This guidance from the Holy Spirit is consistent with the Lord's instructions to them as recorded in Acts 1:8. *"But you shall receive power when the Holy Spirit has come upon you, and you shall be witnesses to Me in Jerusalem, and in all Judea and Samaria, and to the end of the earth."* It was also consistent with what Saul had been shown by the Lord on the Damascus Road.

We need to remember that the Holy Spirit always speaks consistently with the revealed word. The Spirit of God never

---

[57] G. Campbell Morgan, IBID, page 312.

guides us as individuals or as a church body to do anything that contradicts the teaching of the word of God.

If we as a local church are going to be doing the will of the Lord, we must keep the vision of the whole world before us. If Antioch had been a self-centered and self-serving body, they would have tried to keep Barnabas and Saul right there in Antioch. They would have tried to keep their most capable and gifted leaders ministering to them in Antioch. These missionaries had already demonstrated their call as pastors and had been shown to be effective in doing the work of evangelism and pastoring.

One doesn't become a missionary by crossing the ocean or crossing a cultural barrier. Anyone that the Holy Spirit separates to be part of the front-line missionary troops will demonstrate his call by his effective use of Holy Spirit given gifts in his local church. We also learn from the church at Antioch, that the church that does not have a world vision will never be a strong biblical, Christ-honoring church.

3) They released the 'called ones' to obey the Holy Spirit.

It is not technically accurate to say that Antioch was a "sending church". Verse 4 makes it abundantly clear that the sending agent is the Holy Spirit. The church at Antioch placed their approval upon what God was doing. The "laying on of hands" was a confirming act that indeed the Holy Spirit was sending Barnabas and Saul to embark on this missionary venture.

The Antioch church did not support them financially but this is probably a failure of the church, certainly not to be construed as the way it should be. Paul mentions in Philippians 4:15 that the church at Philippi was the only church that shared with them in giving. Barnabas and Saul primarily supported themselves financially by being tentmakers. It is important that we support those called by the Holy Spirit to serve on the front lines in the missionary cause of Christ. We need to support them in prayer and in our financial giving.

God has raised up some from our congregation who are called of the Lord to be out on the front-lines of the world-wide mission of our God. They have demonstrated their commitment to Christ, have grown in grace, and have authenticated their call from the Holy Spirit. Let's be vigilant and hear the Holy Spirit as He continues to send forth others from our local church.

The grace revolution is a world-wide revolution. Even the Psalmist frequently speaks of all the nations praising Jehovah. Psalm 67:1-3 tells us, *"God be merciful and bless us, and cause His face to shine upon us, that your way may be known on earth, Your salvation among all nations. Let the peoples praise You, O God; Let all the peoples praise You."*

Send The Light!
(Written by Charles H. Gabriel, 1888)

There's a call comes ringing o'er the restless wave,
"Send the light! Send the light!"
There are souls to rescue, there are souls to save,
Send the light! Send the light!

(Refrain:)
Send the light, the blessed Gospel light;
Let it shine from shore to shore!
Send the light, and let its radiant beams
Light the world forevermore!

We have heard the Macedonian call today,
"Send the light! Send the light!"

And a golden offering at the cross we lay,
Send the light! Send the light!

Let us pray that grace may everywhere abound,
"Send the light! Send the light!"
And a Christ-like spirit everywhere be found,
Send the light! Send the light!

Let us not grow weary in the work of love,
"Send the light! Send the light!"
Let us gather jewels for a crown above,
Send the light! Send the light!

Chapter 15
A Bicycle Built for You!
Acts 13:4 - 14:28

I have found this writing, called 'The Road of Life', inspiring and encouraging. Unfortunately the author unknown.

At first, I saw God as my observer, my judge,
keeping track of the things I did wrong,
so as to know whether I merited heaven
or hell when I die.
He was out there sort of like a president.
I recognized his picture when I saw it,
but I really didn't know Him.

But later on when I met Christ,
it seemed as though life were rather like
a bike ride, but it was a tandem bike,
and I noticed that Christ
was in the back helping me pedal.

I don't know just when it was
that He suggested we change places,
but life has not been the same since.
When I had control, I knew the way.
It was rather boring, but predictable.
It was the shortest distance between
two points.

But when He took the lead, He knew
delightful long cuts, up mountains,
and through rocky places at breakneck
speeds. It was all I could do to hang on!
Even though it looked like madness,
He said, "Pedal!"

I was worried and was anxious and asked,
"Where are you taking me?"
He laughed and didn't answer, and I
started to learn to trust.
I forgot my boring life and entered into
the adventure. And when I'd say, "I'm
scared," He'd lean back and touch my hand.

He took me to people with gifts that I
needed. Gifts of healing, acceptance
and joy. They gave me gifts to take
on my journey, my Lord's and mine.
And we were off again. He said, "Give
the gifts away; they're extra baggage,
too much weight." So I did, to the people
we met, and I found that in giving I
received, and still our burden was light.

I did not trust Him, at first, in control
of my life. I thought He'd wreck it;
but He knows bike secrets,
knows how to make it bend to take sharp corners,
knows how to jump to clear high rocks,
knows how to fly to shorten scary passages.

And I'm learning to shut up and pedal
in the strangest places, and I'm beginning
to enjoy the view and the cool breeze
on my face with my delightful constant
companion, Jesus Christ.
And when I'm sure I just can't do anymore,
He just smiles and says, "Pedal".

As you look at chapters 13 and 14 of Acts, you see that Paul
and Barnabas experience all kinds of ups and downs as they
serve the Lord on their first missionary journey. That is the

way life is! Whether or not you are a frontier missionary, you as a believer in Christ will also experience your mountain tops and your valleys as you walk with the Lord. And if you do not trust the Lord to be on the front of your bike that is built just for you and Him, you'll get discouraged by the obstacles that He alone can overcome.

Living consistently for Christ requires enduring in faith, believing that God is working all things for good to those who love Him and are called according to His purpose.

First we observe **The Obstacles the Gospel Encounters.**

If you are a believer in Christ, you have probably already come to the realization that knowing Christ as Savior does not relieve you of problems. In fact, when you see all of the trouble that Paul and Barnabas ran into as they were being obedient to Christ, you will understand that experiencing difficulty and trouble does not necessarily indicate that you have missed the will of God.

1) They encounter direct opposition from Satan's forces. Acts 13:4-12.

Coming to the town of Paphos on the western end of the island of Cyprus, Paul and Barnabas met two men. The first is Bar-Jesus (son of salvation) who was also called Elymas (skillful one), who was a Jewish magician or sorcerer, a false prophet who was operating by demonic powers. The second one mentioned is Sergius Paulus, the Roman proconsul, who had Elymas as his attendant.

Note Paul's statements about this Elymas in Acts 13:9-11. *"Then Saul, who also is called Paul, filled with the Holy Spirit, looked intently at him and said, "O full of all deceit and all fraud, you son of the devil, you enemy of all righteousness, will you not cease perverting the straight ways of the Lord? And now, indeed, the hand of the Lord is upon you, and you shall be blind, not seeing the sun for a time." And immediately a dark mist fell on him, and he went around seeking someone to lead him by the hand."*

Remember that when you are one of God's redeemed children who is seeking to faithfully serve the Lord, and you are actively sharing the gospel with others, you will at times be opposed by those who are controlled directly by Satan. Even in our day, there are those who have sold out their souls to Satan and oppose the work and word of the Lord as emissaries of Satan. Stand in the authority of Christ Jesus, our Lord, and do not be afraid. 1 John 4:4 promises us, *"You are of God, little children, and have overcome them, because He who is in you is greater than he who is in the world."*

So God blinded the eyes of Elymas, the one who refused to see the truth. The one who longed to see the truth, God opened his eyes. Sergius Paulus witnessing what had happened, believed in Christ, *"being astonished at the teaching of the Lord."* Verse 12.

2. They are disappointed through the failure of others. Acts 13:13.

Luke makes only a brief statement about John Mark, this young cousin of Barnabas (Col. 4:10), who forsakes the missionary team and returns to Jerusalem. We do not know why he leaves but it upset Paul so much that it led to a division between Paul and Barnabas regarding their plans for their second journey. Acts 15:36-41. Perhaps the rigorous demands and opposition that they experienced were too much for him. Perhaps he was upset because he thought that Paul was taking over from Barnabas and his cousin was getting "second fiddle" treatment.

As a Christian, you need to keep your eye on the Master, because if you do not, you will often get disillusioned by the failures of your fellow Christians. The Lord does not call us to be accountable for others who may not be carrying their weight in ministry or may not do what they say they will do.

3. They faced the jealousy of arrogant religious leaders. Acts 13:13-52.

In this section Luke describes their efforts to expand their mission up into Asia Minor, centering primarily upon their experience in seeking to reach the Jews and God-fearing Gentiles who had attached themselves to the synagogue of Antioch of Pisidia. As they attend the synagogue, after the traditional reading of the Law and the Prophets, the synagogue rulers invite them to speak *"any word of exhortation for the people. . ."* Verse 15.

Paul preaches the gospel based upon Old Testament history and prophecies. He briefly reminds them of the ways in which God has led the Jewish people. He refers to John, the Baptist as the forerunner of the Messiah. He quotes from the Psalms and Isaiah regarding the death and resurrection of Jesus, the Messiah. In verses 38-39, Paul gives the gospel invitation to his hearers. *"Therefore let it be known to you, brethren, that through this Man is preached to you the forgiveness of sins; and by Him everyone who believes is justified from all things from which you could not be justified by the law of Moses."*

The following week, on the Sabbath, large crowds gathered to hear them again. This popularity of Paul and Barnabas brought to the surface, a jealous reaction of the religious leaders. Acts 13:45. *"But when the Jews saw the multitudes, they were filled with envy; and contradicting and blaspheming, they opposed the things spoken by Paul."* Then Paul and Barnabas announced that they were turning to the Gentiles with their message of salvation in Christ. Acts 13:46-48. *"Then Paul and Barnabas grew bold and said, "It was necessary that the word of God should be spoken to you first; but since you reject it, and judge yourselves unworthy of everlasting life, behold, we turn to the Gentiles. For so the Lord has commanded us: 'I have set you as a light to the Gentiles, that you should be for salvation to the ends of the earth.'" Now when the Gentiles heard this, they were glad and glorified the word of the Lord. And as many as had been appointed to eternal life believed."*

Whenever God is at work, people are being truly saved by faith alone, in Christ alone, by grace alone, there will be jealous reactions from religious establishment leaders. You will sometimes find that nasty things are being said behind your back by other religious leaders. Pay no attention and go on with the work of Christ! In spite of the opposition, we find the disciples are living victoriously. They are *"filled with joy and with the Holy Spirit"*. Verse 52.

4. They suffer physical abuse and attempted murder. Acts 14:1-20.

In Chapter 14, we find Paul and Barnabas are pursued by jealous Jews and Gentiles whom the Jews had incited in an attempt to do away with their lives. Many Jews and Gentiles at Iconium believed (Acts 14:1) and Paul and Barnabas moved on to Lystra, keeping a step ahead of their murderous pursuers.

As you read this passage, you find the people of Lystra hailing them as "gods" because of their wonderful miracle works, and then shortly they are stoning them to kill them. Doesn't this remind you of Palm Sunday as the crowds hailed Jesus as their king? Within a few days, the same crowd was crying out "Crucify Him! Crucify Him!"

Verse 19 tells us that these jealous Jewish leaders, who made their way from Antioch and Iconium, stirred up the crowd, and they finally work their murderous efforts. *"Then Jews from Antioch and Iconium came there, and having persuaded the multitudes, they stoned Paul and dragged him out of the city, supposing him to be dead."*

Paul makes a marvelous recovery (verse 20) and Paul and Barnabas leave for Derbe the very next day. Just think of Paul's injuries. He was pelted with stones and rocks, bruised and battered until they thought he was dead. Yet he recovers to the point of leaving for Derbe on the very next morning. Now, let me ask you, if you are discouraged as a Christian because of the trouble you are going through, how would you and I respond if we were in their shoes? Hebrews 12:3-4 exhorts us, *"For consider Him who endured such hostility from sinners against Himself, lest you become weary and discouraged in your souls. You have not yet resisted to bloodshed, striving against sin."*

Now let us consider **The Ways the Witnesses Endure. Acts 14:21-23.**

"And when they had preached the gospel to that city and made many disciples, they returned to Lystra, Iconium, and Antioch, strengthening the souls of the disciples, exhorting them to continue in the faith, and saying, "We must through many tribulations enter the kingdom of God." So when they had appointed elders in every church, and prayed with fasting, they commended them to the Lord in whom they had believed." Acts 14:21-23.

1. Accept opposition to Christ as normal and inevitable. Acts14:21-22.

It is much easier to endure opposition when you are expecting it! Jesus Himself warned His disciples of this kind of treatment. John 16:33. *"These things I have spoken to you, that in Me you may have peace. In the world you will have tribulation; but be of good cheer, I have overcome the world."* Paul, the apostle, wrote to his young protégé pastor in 2 Timothy 3:10-13, *"But you have carefully followed my doctrine, manner of life, purpose, faith, longsuffering, love, perseverance, persecutions, afflictions, which happened to me at Antioch, at Iconium, at Lystra - what persecutions I endured. And out of them all the Lord delivered me. Yes, and all who desire to live godly in Christ Jesus will suffer persecution. But evil men and impostors will grow worse and worse, deceiving and being deceived."* So don't be shocked and taken off guard when opposition comes!

2. Select strong spiritual leaders. Acts 14:23a.

They appointed elders or pastors for these new churches. These were not just casually selected but those appointed to such responsible leadership positons had to meet some important criteria. These pastors whom they appointed were solid mature spiritual men who were not self-serving or arrogant. These were men who responded to the discipling that was provided by Paul and Barnabas. They had not been believers for a long time, but they had responded to follow the Lord and to be obedient to the apostles' doctrine.

Make certain that you choose to follow the right spiritual leaders. Follow pastors who have proven themselves to be godly, humble, and dependent upon the Holy Spirit. Follow faithful and capable preachers and teachers of the word of God.

3. Persist in prayer and fasting. Acts 14:23b.

The early church was a praying church, totally dependent upon the Lord. I doubt that they were just praying and asking for things, but I suspect their prayers centered on knowing the Lord better and seeking the power of the Spirit to be the kind of persons He wanted them to be.

One of the major reasons that our prayers are not answered is that we are selfish in our praying. Our lives must be centered on the Lord and we must be "seeking the kingdom of God first". As Tony Evans once said, "The Holy Spirit isn't interested in blessing you with his presence and power if you are not about kingdom work."

4. Remain true to the faith. Acts 14:22a.

They were *"strengthening the souls of the disciples, exhorting them to continue in the faith . . ."* When troubles come, Satan wants you to give up your faith in Christ and the truth of Scripture. He seeks to discourage you so that you will throw it all over board. 1 Peter 5:8-9, in the context of suffering for godly living, tells us, *"Be sober, be vigilant; because your adversary the devil walks about like a roaring lion, seeking whom he may devour. Resist him, steadfast in the faith, knowing that the same sufferings are experienced by your brotherhood in the world."*

5. Trust in the continuous care of the Sovereign Lord. Acts 14:23c.

They *". . . prayed with fasting, they commended them to the Lord in whom they had believed."*

We have trusted Christ to save us from our sins and give us eternal life. That is settled from the time we were born again in response to faith in His shed blood and His resurrection from the dead. Now the issue is to trust Him each day for every situation, every trial, and every need.

Is He really the Sovereign God who is working all things together for good to us who love Him and are called according to His purpose? What is your trouble right now? Is it your health, your job, your financial crunch, or you are being persecuted at work because of your witness for Christ? Will you endure in trusting Christ through every trial?

Paul and Barnabas then returning to Antioch, *"gathered the church together"*, and joyfully reported what God had done. Charles Swindoll aptly concludes, "In Paul's report, he must have marveled at what God had done through his sickness, John Mark's departure, the opposition, the stoning. The same is true for us when our storm passes and we can see clearly again. For after the suffering we realize that God has been perfecting, confirming, strengthening and establishing us all along."[58]

"And I'm learning to shut up and pedal in the strangest places, and I'm beginning to enjoy the view and the cool breeze on my face with my delightful constant companion, Jesus Christ. And when I'm sure I just can't do anymore, He just smiles and says, "Keep on pedaling!"

I Have Decided To Follow Jesus!

(A Christian hymn that originated in Assam, India. According to Dr P. Job, the lyrics are based on the last words of Nokseng, a Garo man, a tribe from Meghalaya which then was in Assam, who along with his family decided to follow Jesus Christ in the middle of the 19th century through the efforts of an American Baptist missionary. Called to renounce his faith by the village chief, the convert declared,

---

[58] Charles Swindoll, Commentary on Acts, page 101.

"I have decided to follow Jesus." His two children were killed and in response to threats to his wife, he continued, "Though no one join me, still I will follow." His wife was killed, and he was executed while singing, "The world behind me, The cross before me." This display of faith is reported to have led to the conversion of the chief and others in the village.)

I have decided to follow Jesus;
I have decided to follow Jesus;
I have decided to follow Jesus;
No turning back, no turning back.

The world behind me, the cross before me;
The world behind me, the cross before me;
The world behind me, the cross before me;
No turning back, no turning back.

Tho' none go with me, I still will follow,
Tho' none go with me I still will follow,
Tho' none go with me, I still will follow;
No turning back, no turning back.

My cross I'll carry, till I see Jesus;
My cross I'll carry till I see Jesus,
My cross I'll carry till I see Jesus;
No turning back, No turning back.

Will you decide now to follow Jesus?
Will you decide now to follow Jesus?
Will you decide now to follow Jesus?
No turning back, no turning back.

Chapter 16
Grace Under Attack!
Acts 15:1-35

It was July of 1961 and the Green Bay Packers football team, made up of mostly grizzled veterans, were starting the first day of training camp. They had ended the last season with a heartbreaking defeat when the Packers blew a lead late in the 4th quarter and lost the NFL Championship to the Philadelphia Eagles. This stunning defeat had been nagging them for the entire off-season. They were anxious to get started on a new season and wanted to redeem themselves.

Vince Lombardi stood before his team and began the training camp with these famous words, as he held a pigskin in his hands. "Gentlemen, this is a football!" With this, he took his team back to the basics, the fundamentals, reviewing how to block and tackle, and how to hold onto the football to avoid fumbling. He took nothing for granted. Max McGee, the Packers' Pro Bowl wide receiver, joked, "Uh, Coach, could you slow down a little? You're going too fast for us." With a smile, Lombardi continued a training camp that was all about the basic foundations of the game. Six months later, the Green Bay Packers beat the New York Giants 37-0 to win the NFL Championship.[59]

You can't get much more basic than that! That is what the church should be doing on a regular basis - getting back to the basics, making certain that we stay on track with God and his word.

---

[59] Information gleaned from::David Maraniss, When Pride Still Mattered: A Life of Vince Lombardi. New York, NY: Simon & Schuster.1999.

This issue of salvation by grace was a crucial issue that needed to be defended without compromise. Acts 15:1 begins by laying out an issue that was basic to the survival of the church of Jesus Christ and the survival of salvation by grace alone. *"And certain men came down from Judea and taught the brethren, "Unless you are circumcised according to the custom of Moses, you cannot be saved."*

Working out this basic issue of salvation by grace alone involved some conflict. Conflict is inevitable even in the church, just as we see in the early church. Differences of opinion can lead to growth or they can lead to disunity and division.

Chapter 15 of Acts deals with the attack upon the grace principle of salvation. As we study this chapter, we can also learn how these important issues get resolved in a way in which the unity of the church is preserved!

First, we must have **The Right Attitude. Acts 15:1-7a.**

Whenever conflict comes, it is important to do an attitude check-up. Obviously, this issue facing the Council called in Jerusalem was a doctrinal issue that was crucial with which the leaders of the church had to deal. However, most conflicts in churches do not come because of doctrinal issues; most come because of personality conflicts or hurt feelings. The church where I grew up as a teenager went through a church split during a building program because of two strong personalities who argued over where the money would be borrowed to complete the building. Paul writes to the church at Philippi about two women who were at odds with each other. Philippians 4:2-3.

1. Be Certain the Issue is Central Truth.

For many people today, even those who claim to be Christian leaders, standing for truth takes second place to keeping the peace. This often leads to compromise of basic important truths for the sake of "Let's just get along!" You will notice that Paul and Barnabas did not fall into this trap. Acts 15:1-2. *"And certain men came down from Judea and taught the brethren, "Unless you are circumcised according to the custom of Moses, you cannot be saved." Therefore, when Paul and Barnabas had no small dissension and dispute with them, they determined that Paul and Barnabas and certain others of them should go up to Jerusalem, to the apostles and elders, about this question."*

Paul and Barnabas knew that this was a crucial issue that could destroy the gospel of grace. So the dissension and dispute was no small issue. Jude 1:3-4 is instructive at this point. *"Beloved, while I was very diligent to write to you concerning our common salvation, I found it necessary to write to you exhorting you to contend earnestly for the faith which was once for all delivered to the saints. For certain men have crept in unnoticed, who long ago were marked out for this condemnation, ungodly men, who turn the grace of our God into lewdness and deny the only Lord God and our Lord Jesus Christ."*

The secret is to learn how to contend for the faith without being contentious in attitude. Now obviously we need to make sure that we are contending for the central issues of truth and not for some obscure point, where we end up debating about semantics or issues that are not crucial to our faith. Here the issue of salvation by grace alone was at stake which was absolutely crucial to the gospel.

In Galatians 1, Paul contends that those who were adding their legalistic conditions to the gospel were preaching *"another gospel"* which really is not the gospel. So strongly did he feel about this that he said, *"If any one preaches any other gospel to you than what you have received, let him be accursed."* Verse 9.

2. Seek the Wise Help of Other Church Leaders. Acts 15:2b.

Often when doctrinal issues come up, they cannot be resolved by those who are initially involved. The church at Antioch decided to send Paul and Barnabas to Jerusalem to seek the wisdom of the apostles and elders on this question. Verse 2b. Over the years of the history of the Christian Church, various important Councils have been called to resolve important doctrinal issues that have arisen, usually sparked by some heresy that was being taught by some church leader.

Doctrinal issues are not just some private matter which each individual decides for himself. Seek the wise counsel of respected Bible teachers who are solidly anchored in their faith in the infallible word of God. This does not mean that we simply look to someone who has a degree in theology or who claims to be speaking for God. Many such people do not believe in the basic orthodox faith once committed to the church by the apostles.

Having established that one must have a strong commitment to the inerrancy and authority of God's word, we are not to be isolationists who act as our own authority for truth. Authority rests in God and His word, properly interpreted and firmly believed. Authority for truth does not rest in the church, or in some papal pronouncement, either by the Roman Catholic pope or some self-appointed "pope".

3. Give an Honest Hearing to All Viewpoints. Acts 15:4-7.

The Council meeting in Jerusalem begins with Paul and Barnabas being warmly welcomed by the church and the apostles and elders (pastors). Verse 4. Paul and Barnabas gave a report of what God was doing through them. Then in verse 5 the believers who were still giving allegiance to the Pharisees stood up and spoke: *"It is necessary to circumcise them, and to command them to keep the law of Moses."* They were not speaking about simply obeying the Ten Commandments and the moral law, which all Christians should seek to obey, but the ceremonial laws. They were saying in essence that you can't be a Christian just by grace through faith alone. There are other requirements that you must keep. In other words, "You must also be circumcised, or become a proselyte Jew."

Verses 6-7 informs us that there was a great deal of dispute and some lively discussion! Each viewpoint was adequately heard and sufficiently discussed. Sometimes when we meet for conferences as church delegates, we avoid discussion of doctrinal issues. In my opinion, we want to keep peace at any cost to the detriment of sharpening ourselves in understanding and standing upon the truth. There are issues that need to be discussed, even if we do not always reach a consensus. Such issues as the issue of salvation by grace alone through faith alone through Christ alone; the meaning of the new birth; the issue of baptism and church membership; the issue of a woman's role in the church and ministry; charismatic issues and other applications of the gospel to our secular culture.

Secondly, we must take **The Right Approach. Acts 15:6-21.**

1. Define the Real Issue.

It is important to define what the issue is, and the Council at Jerusalem did that. Verse 6 says that *"the apostles and elders came together to consider this matter."* They clearly defined the issue. Specifically, is it essential for Gentiles to be circumcised and to obey the law of Moses in order to be saved? Verse 5. The church and the leadership of the church did not ignore the issue. They dealt with it up front, knowing that this was critical to the future of the church of Jesus Christ and her stand for the true gospel.

2. Review the Workings of God.

After much discussion, then Peter gets up to address them all. Verses 7-11. Peter speaks because he was the person directly involved by God in taking the gospel to the Gentiles. Peter's makes several salient points in his arguments.

1) He shares what the Lord did in his experience with Cornelius and his household. He points out that this was obviously the work of the Holy Spirit.

2) He reminds them all that they (the Jews) weren't able to obey the law either, so why now insist on putting this yoke on the necks of the Gentile believers.

3) He then gives a clear authoritative statement about how they themselves were saved. Acts 15:11 *"But we believe that through the grace of the Lord Jesus Christ we shall be saved in the same manner as they."*

Verse 12 then tells us about Paul's and Barnabas's accounts of the miraculous works that the Lord was doing among the Gentiles. The whole assembly is spellbound and *"they became silent."* When you are tempted to get disturbed by some issue that you think is crucial, take a look at what God is doing and how God is working.

As our local church has been deciding on our building program, we have differences about the details. But it is important to have harmony over these issues for the sake of the larger purpose, namely the salvation of souls that God is enabling us to reach. We need to recognize what God is doing here as a week from tonight, we will be baptizing six adults who will be professing their faith in Christ.

3. Listen to the Wisdom of God's Appointed Leader.

In Verse 13, we find James speaks up and says *"Men and brethren, listen to me!"* It is generally conceded that James was the pastor of the church there at Jerusalem. James observes that the events that Peter has shared about the Gentiles coming to Christ is consistent with Scripture. He is quoting from Amos 9:11-12, probably from the Septuagint (Greek) translation. *"After this I will return and will rebuild the tabernacle of David, which has fallen down; I will rebuild its ruins, and I will set it up; So that the rest of mankind may seek the Lord, even all the Gentiles who are called by My name, says the Lord who does all these things."* Acts 15:16-17.

The principle is to evaluate everything that is happening according to the clear message of Scripture. Don't interpret Scripture by your experience; but evaluate your experience according to Scripture.

James's authority is not based merely upon his position as pastor, but the fact that he is judging the matter according to the authority of the clear message of God's word. James gives his biblical judgment to which the assembly in unity agrees. Verses 19-21.

4. Seek the Witness of the Peace of Christ. Verse 28.

There is a very interesting comment in the written message that is sent to the church at Antioch in verse 28. *"It seemed good to the Holy Spirit and to us . . ."* A consensus of peace seems to come upon the assembly that indeed this is the right decision.

That is how the Holy Spirit leads us, through giving to us the settled peace of Christ in our hearts. Colossians 3:15 says, *"And let the peace of God rule in your hearts, to which also you were called in one body; and be thankful."*

Thirdly, we must reach **The Right Appraisal. Acts 15:19-35.**

1. The Principle of Salvation by Grace Alone. Verse 11.

Peter got it right, and we better not lose track of this principle of grace alone for salvation. Verse 11. *". . .we believe that through the grace of the Lord Jesus Christ we shall be saved in the same manner as they."*

Salvation can never be in any degree by our merit, our works or our efforts. To add any other requirement for us to be saved, other than faith in our Lord Jesus Christ and his atoning death is to destroy the grace of God. If we are saved by our works, or by trying to keep the law, then it is no longer salvation by grace. Romans 4:1-6. *"What then shall we say that Abraham our father has found according to the flesh? For if Abraham was justified by works, he has something to boast about, but not before God. For what does the Scripture say? "Abraham believed God, and it was accounted to him for righteousness." Now to him who works, the wages are not counted as grace but as debt. But to him who does not work but believes on Him who justifies the ungodly, his faith is accounted for righteousness, just as David also describes the blessedness of the man to whom God imputes righteousness apart from works: "Blessed are those whose lawless deeds are forgiven, and whose sins are covered; Blessed is the man to whom the Lord shall not impute sin."*

Paul continues on in Romans 4, clarifying the very issue that arose in the Council at Jerusalem in Acts 15. He points out that Abraham was justified by his faith before he was circumcised.

Note James' words in Acts 15:19 (NIV). *"It is my judgment, therefore, that we should not make it difficult for the Gentiles who are turning to God."*

Many people respond in a similar way when they hear the gospel. Some will say, "Oh, it just can't be that easy!" Too often, we want to make it more difficult by adding some other requirements. In essence, we are saying, "Clean up your life, then come and trust Christ!" Jesus would probably say, "It's like fishing for fish. Fish for men. You catch them and let Me clean them."

2. The Principle of a Godly Lifestyle. Acts 15:20.

James addresses those Gentile believers, not about further things that they need to do in order to be saved, but now that you are saved by grace through faith, how are you to live? Acts 15:19-20. *"Therefore I judge that we should not trouble those from among the Gentiles who are turning to God, but that we write to them to abstain from things polluted by idols, from sexual immorality, from things strangled, and from blood. For Moses has had throughout many generations those who preach him in every city, being read in the synagogues every Sabbath."*

There were some things that they were to avoid as believers. Verses 28-29 state this in the actual letter written to the church in Antioch. *"For it seemed good to the Holy Spirit, and to us, to lay upon you no greater burden than these necessary things: that you abstain from things offered to idols, from blood, from things strangled, and from sexual immorality. If you keep yourselves from these, you will do well."*

Immorality is a moral issue and is always wrong, an abomination in God's sight. This is clearly forbidden in both the Old and New Testaments. As a true believer, you are to do your best by the Holy Spirit's power to live a pure and godly life. The principle of grace alone for salvation never puts its stamp of approval upon immoral and careless living. We are to live in a way that honors our Holy God whom we believe in and serve. We live godly lives, not to add to our salvation in any way but to *"escape the corruption of this present world"* by the power of Jesus Christ, our Savior.

In this world of corruption in which we live, we must live godly lives if we are to have any impact in our witness. Linda Bowles wrote, "No-fault living has become the order of the day in America. "Sin" is an archaic idea. Right and wrong as moral concepts have been abolished. Moral discernment has been deemed judgmental and discriminatory. God is scorned - but tolerated if He stays in His place."[60]

Our liberty in Christ is not to be used as a license to sin against God. Galatians 5:13. *"For you, brethren, have been called to liberty; only do not use liberty as an opportunity for the flesh, but through love serve one another."*

The church at Antioch is also requested to *"abstain from things offered to idols, from blood, and from things strangled."* Acts 15:21 gives their reasoning for asking the Gentiles to avoid these questionable and debatable issues. It is not adding to requirements for their salvation which is by grace alone. Rather it is for the consideration of the Jewish believers who still gathered in the synagogues and their consciences were still not at liberty to violate the laws of Moses which they heard read every Sabbath.

---

[60] Linda Bowles, writer for Creators Syndicate, in Article, "Moral Decay is Bigger Worry than the Economy". (AFA Journal, June, 1996, page 16.)

3. This leads us to the next principle, **The Principle of Love for Others.**

There are two other issues that James addresses, one for the Gentiles and one for the Jews. These are "stumbling-block" issues, clearly addressed in Romans 14:13-15. *"Therefore let us not judge one another anymore, but rather resolve this, not to put a stumbling block or a cause to fall in our brother's way. I know and am convinced by the Lord Jesus that there is nothing unclean of itself; but to him who considers anything to be unclean, to him it is unclean. Yet if your brother is grieved because of your food, you are no longer walking in love. Do not destroy with your food the one for whom Christ died."*

For the Gentiles who had been saved out of idolatry, the stumbling-block for many of these new Christians was that Christians would eat meat offered to idols which was then sold in the marketplace. Those who regarded this meat to be alright for consumption, because they knew that idols were not valid deities, were exhorted to love their Gentile Christian brothers and sisters and not cause them to stumble by their freedom in Christ. They were encouraged to abstain from eating meat offered to idols in consideration of their brothers in Christ who would be offended by their liberty.

For the Jews who had been saved, the issue was eating meat that had been improperly killed (it wasn't kosher) or eating the blood of an animal because that was forbidden in Jewish law. They were exhorted to love their Jewish Christian brothers and sisters and not do anything that would easily offend them.

The issue that brought such conflict, and thankfully was resolved correctly in the Jerusalem Council, was that "we are saved by grace alone through faith alone in Christ alone." It was not once for all settled by the apostles and elders in Jerusalem however, for this same truth was the one that was recovered through the great conflict brought on by the struggle of Martin Luther. Peace came to his heart when he came to believe that *"the just shall live by faith."*

Some of you may have never experienced salvation through grace alone; you have never been born again by the Spirit of God. What is grace? Charles Swindoll writes, "You received an end of the month pay check - that's not grace. You give your son an allowance for doing his chores - that's not grace. You return a favor by baby-sitting your neighbor's kids - no grace here. Where can we find grace?

"Grace is the prodigal son returning home to a party in his honor or Jesus spying a wicked little man in a sycamore tree and saying, "Zacchaeus, today I must stay at your house" (Luke 19:5b). Grace is Jesus saying to the thief who languishes on the cross next to His: "Today, you shall be with me in Paradise" (Luke 23:34)."[61]

Open up your heart to Jesus. Confess to Him that you are an unworthy lost and condemned sinner. Invite Christ Jesus into your life and trust Him to save you and make you one of His redeemed children! Receive Him as your personal Savior and He will give you eternal life as a free gift. John 1:11-13. *"He came to His own, and His own did not receive Him. But as many as received Him, to them He gave the right to become children of God, to those who believe in His name: who were born, not of blood, nor of the will of the flesh, nor of the will of man, but of God."*

Grace Greater Than Our Sin!
(Written by Julia H. Johnston, 1910)

Marvelous grace of our loving Lord,

---

[61] Charles Swindoll, Commentary on Acts, Volume 2, page 120.

Grace that exceeds our sin and our guilt!
Yonder on Calvary's mount outpoured,
There where the blood of the Lamb was spilled.

(Refrain)
Grace, grace, God's grace,
Grace that will pardon and cleanse within;
Grace, grace, God's grace,
Grace that is greater than all our sin!

Sin and despair, like the sea waves cold,
Threaten the soul with infinite loss;
Grace that is greater, yes, grace untold,
Points to the refuge, the mighty cross.

Dark is the stain that we cannot hide;
What can we do to wash it away?
Look! There is flowing a crimson tide,
Brighter than snow you may be today.

Marvelous, infinite, matchless grace,
Freely bestowed on all who believe!
You that are longing to see His face,
Will you this moment His grace receive?

Chapter 17
Can't We Just All Get Along?
Acts 15:36-41

"What we really need today in the church is to get back to being the New Testament church!" Every once in a while you will hear someone make that statement, as if that is going to make us spiritual or almost perfect.

Which New Testament church would you choose to be like? Maybe, the church at Corinth? Really? With all of its problems - with schisms, immorality, carnality, and doctrinal error, you want to have that church as our model?

Even in the early churches founded by the apostles, there were problems and imperfections. Now as we continue on in Acts 15:36-41, we find conflict continues! And the conflict is between the leaders of the missionary movement.

There is this little humorous poem, the author of which is unknown.

"To live above with saints we love,
Oh, that will be glory.
But to live below with saints we know,
Well now, that's another story."

This time the conflict is not a doctrinal issue as we looked at in the previous chapter, but it is a personal clash between two co-workers. How do Paul and Barnabas handle it? Do you think they resolved their conflict in the right way?

How should we as Christians handle personal conflict when it arises? These are questions that may be answered as we seek to learn some lessons from this conflict between Paul and Barnabas.

Why Does Conflict Occur?

Paul and Barnabas have been at Antioch for some lengthy time now, involved in settling the doctrinal issue at the Council meeting in Jerusalem, and strengthening the Christians there at Antioch. They begin to discuss the need to go and visit the churches that had been started when they were on their first missionary journey. Barnabas brings up the subject, "Oh, by the way, John Mark would like to go along again!" "Oh, no! No way!" says Paul.

The conflict comes over the question, "Should a defector be given a second chance?" We discover that conflict in our lives and in our churches comes often,

1. Because of Deeply Held Convictions.

Convictions involve principles which are sometimes firmly based in Scripture, but not always. Sometimes we hold to 'convictions' which are nothing more than preferences that we stubbornly hold. You know how it is; "My wife is stubborn, but I have convictions."

For Paul and Barnabas, the conflict comes because they each had some strongly held personal convictions which probably each could support with Scripture. The imperfect tenses of the verbs in Verses 37-38, tell us that they felt strongly about their positions on this matter. The word "*determined*" (verse 37) is the idea of "*continually insisting.*" Barnabas probably was arguing that the Lord taught us to forgive, to be patient, to be kind, to give people another chance. The NIV translators used the words "*did not think it wise to take him*" in an attempt to convey the idea of Paul "*keeping on insisting*" that they not take Mark along. I can imagine Paul might have used Scripture also, reminding Barnabas that *"he who puts his hand to the plow and turns back is not fit for the kingdom of God."*

2. Because of Differing Opinions (or Viewpoints).

Our opinions or our view-points are the way we see an issue. We need to remember that the glasses through which we are viewing the issue are colored by our personality and our experiences. Each of us has a background and how we were raised and the experiences we have had provide us a filter system through which we hear and perceive others' views. Our opinions may be right or they may be wrong; or they may need to be modified by seeing things from another's perspective.

There is an ancient Hindu story about six blind men who were brought to "see an elephant". "It is very much like a wall," said the first man as he touched the side of the elephant. "It is much like a spear", said the second man as he stroked the elephant's tusk. And the third man, taking the elephant's squirming trunk in his hands, said, "It is very much like a snake!" "Nonsense", the fourth man shouted. Stretching his arms around one of its legs, he concluded, "This wondrous beast is very much like a tree!" The fifth man, touching the elephant's ear, cried, "Even the blindest can tell this animal is very much like a fan." And the sixth, grabbing the tail, assured his friends that "the elephant is really like a rope."

By listening to the view of others, we may come to see the picture more completely.

This leads us to consider **Who Is Right in His Viewpoint?**

Could it be that both of them were right in some aspects and both of them were wrong in some aspects? In fact, in a lot of conflicts in which we find ourselves involved, whether in our marriages, our families, our work, or our church family, it is really a matter of perspective rather than who is right and who is wrong.

1. Paul's View Favored The Task.

Paul probably had in mind the enormous task that had been laid upon him to take the gospel to the Gentile world. It was crucial that they be able to accomplish their task and be unhindered by the desertion of any member of the team. It happened once and it could happen again.

If you are a soldier going into battle, you want to make certain that your buddy is not going to chicken out and flee when the battle gets intense. That's what John Mark did on their last journey, and Paul kept on insisting that they should not take such an unproven soldier into battle again. Perhaps he had in mind Proverbs 25:19 (NIV). *"Like a bad tooth or a lame foot is reliance on the unfaithful in times of trouble."*

2. Barnabas's View Favored The Person.

Barnabas was known as a person of consolation and encouragement. You can just imagine how his reasoning went as he kept on insisting that they take Mark along once more. "Paul, sure Mark deserted us, but he was just a kid. Now he has matured and he has learned his lessons. It is only right to give him a second chance! Everyone deserves a second chance." "Besides, Paul, don't you remember how I took your side when the believers were so afraid of you! You had been our enemy and I gave you a chance to prove yourself!"

Charles Swindoll and Ken Gire wrote, "Barnabas was people oriented; Paul was more task oriented. Barnabas was a man of compassion; Paul was a man of conviction. Barnabas was a builder of men; Paul was a planter of churches.

Paul looked at the issue from the viewpoint of the overall good of the ministry. Barnabas looked at the issue from the viewpoint of the overall good of the man."[62]

How Should Conflict Be Resolved?

Now we need to take a look at the options in solving conflicts. In this passage, we find only one solution, which seems the least desirable one.

1. It Is A Negative Solution.

Verse 39 tells us that *"the contention became so sharp that they parted from one another. . ."* The word for "sharp disagreement" is "paroxysm". Roy Laurin says this is a medical term meaning "a fit" or an "exacerbation." This was a very unpleasant scene, causing lots of sharp and convulsive problems for these two co-workers.

As Barnabas took Mark and they got on the ship to sail to Cyprus, it is not likely that Paul was there to see them off. Sometimes it may be necessary to part ways as far as ministering together, because of strong convictions or for other reasons, but should it not be done with a right spirit, with agreeing to disagree?

2. Some Possible Compromises.

We need to observe again that the Scriptures do not paint the pictures of all of God's notable servants as perfect saints. Here we see some of the choice servants of Christ with feet of clay.

Could they not have found some other solution than separating from each other? Leslie Flynn suggests some options. "Could

---

62   Charles Swindoll and Ken Gire, Grace Awakening, Thomas Nelson Publishing, 2006, page 81.

Paul have said, "We'll tell him he's on probation? If he doesn't work out the first month, we'll ship him home again." .Or perhaps Barnabas could have conceded, "We do need dedicated workers on our team. Let's give Mark a minor assignment to see how he does. Meanwhile we'll start on our journey and, if we hear he's measuring up, we'll send for him to join us along the way." Or could they have agreed on a contingent plan? "Let's take Mark, but others also. If Mark deserts us again, we'll have others to fall back on." Either the inventiveness of love should have discovered some middle ground, or the submission of love should have yielded the point entirely."[63]

When conflict arises with another, care enough for the other person to work it through. Charles Swindoll advises, "Don't run from conflict. Don't quit your job, your church, or your marriage because of disagreements. Slamming down the phone or slamming shut the door doesn't help matters, and neither does resorting to the silent treatment. Truly caring about a relationship means you're willing to face the issue and, with God's help, work it out in love."[64]

What Are The Results Of Conflict?

First, we see a very negative effect of this conflict between Barnabas and Paul.

1. Separation From A Christian Brother.

You never see Barnabas surface again in the New Testament, or in Paul's life. It seems that they just go their separate ways. We have no knowledge of this rift in the relationship between

---

[63] Leslie Flynn, When Saints Come Storming In, Victor Books, Wheaton, IL, page 67.
[64] Charles Swindoll, Commentary on Acts, Volume 2, page 129.

Paul and Barnabas ever being resolved. However, we do have some clues of some positive results!

2. Growth in maturity.

Certainly we know that John Mark matured, because he became a reliable worker for the Lord, serving much with the apostle Peter. John Mark is the writer of the Gospel of Mark. Paul in several references mentions Mark as a profitable servant of the Lord. Colossians 4:10 *"Aristarchus my fellow prisoner greets you, with Mark the cousin of Barnabas (about whom you received instructions: if he comes to you, welcome him) . . ."* In 2 Timothy 4:11, Paul writes, *"Only Luke is with me. Get Mark and bring him with you, for he is useful to me for ministry."* These expressions from Paul indicate some growth in Paul also as he accepts Mark as a fellow worker in the gospel.

3. Expansion Of God's Kingdom.

God has His way of bringing good about even in times of our failures. Two missionary teams are formed instead of one. Barnabas and Mark take care of Cyprus. Paul takes Silas and returns to the churches in Galatia and continues to venture out further into the unevangelized territories of Asia and Europe.

Isn't it encouraging to see how God uses people with various personalities with all kinds of different backgrounds? Does it lift your spirit to know that even when you blow it in life that God will still forgive and give you another chance, as long as you turn back to Him? Doesn't it inspire you to serve the Lord when you see that he uses less than perfect people to perform his work?

The late Dr. Robert Cook used to say, "God reserves the right to use people who disagree with me!" When conflict arises, humble yourself and make the effort to work it out.

Remember, as a church of Jesus Christ, we are a family; we are Christ's body, and He commands us to love one another. For this is how they shall know that we are His disciples!

Blest Be The Tie That Binds

(John Fawcett served for seven years, despite a small income and a growing family. It seemed only practical that he move to a church that paid a larger salary. When he received a call in 1772 to the large and influential Carter's Lane Baptist Church in London, he planned to accept the call. But at the last minute he changed his mind, and remained at Wainsgate where his salary was £25 a year. To commemorate this event, in 1782 he wrote the words to his "Blest Be the Tie that Binds" hymn, his most famous hymn by far.)

Blest be the tie that binds
Our hearts in Christian love.
The fellowship of kindred minds
Is like to that above.

Before our Father's throne
We pour our ardent prayers.
Our fears, our hopes, our aims are one
Our comforts and our cares.

We share each other's woes,
Our mutual burdens bear.
And often for each other flows
The sympathizing tear.

When we asunder part
It gives us inward pain,
But we shall still be joined in heart,
And hope to meet again.

Chapter 18
When God Shuts The Door!
Acts 15:40 - 16:15

The word "failure" has a terrible ring to it! But failure s should be viewed as a matter of perspective. Often our failures may be a matter of God shutting a door to give us a new direction.

That was true of that noble patriot and orator Patrick Henry. For years of his life he was a miserable failure. He and his brother opened a store, but it failed. Next Patrick's father-in-law set him up in farming. Patrick was given 300 acres, a house, and six slaves. Even with that start, though, Patrick couldn't make it as a farmer. Finally, on the advice of friends, Patrick turned to law. He was a natural persuader and a captivating orator. As a lawyer, Patrick was an instant success. Further, his voice was exactly the voice that was needed to launch the colonies toward a break with England. Patrick Henry was not a failure. He was simply in the wrong field for much of his life.[65]

Every Christian believer will find that God sometimes closes doors in order to open other doors for us. Paul and Silas experienced this early in their second missionary journey.

Let's learn some practical lessons that will enhance our faith when we seem to be up against God's brick walls. We are to walk by faith, not by sight. We take one step at a time, relying on our Lord to lead us in His way. When we are able to commit our way unto Him, we find that His way is always best. Then we can thank Him for closed doors and open doors. We must learn to trust His good purpose in every door He closes and see His love in every door He opens.

---

[65] Dynamic Preaching Magazine - July 1, 1991.

First we need to understand **The Process of God's Guidance.**

Acts 15:40-41 informs us that Paul and Silas began their missions work on this second trip by going through Syria and Cilicia which is basically the area we know of as Turkey today. The churches they visited were started on their first journey, Derbe, Lystra and Iconium. They spent their time *"strengthening the churches"* (verse 41) and they achieved their purpose. Acts 16:5. *"So the churches were strengthened in the faith and increased in number daily."*

Next we find them venturing into new territory where they had not been on their first journey, pushing further north and west into Asia Minor. It seems that Paul and Silas just assumed that this was the will of the Lord that they should now reach into Phrygia and Galatia, and then just continue their outreach efforts into Asia. Acts 16: 6-12 give us the details of their efforts. *"Now when they had gone through Phrygia and the region of Galatia, they were forbidden by the Holy Spirit to preach the word in Asia. After they had come to Mysia, they tried to go into Bithynia, but the Spirit did not permit them. So passing by Mysia, they came down to Troas. And a vision appeared to Paul in the night. A man of Macedonia stood and pleaded with him, saying, "Come over to Macedonia and help us." Now after he had seen the vision, immediately we sought to go to Macedonia, concluding that the Lord had called us to preach the gospel to them. Therefore, sailing from Troas, we ran a straight course to Samothrace, and the next day came to Neapolis, and from there to Philippi, which is the foremost city of that part of Macedonia, a colony. And we were staying in that city for some days."*

1) The Holy Spirit Guides Us Personally.

The text in verses 6-7 tells us that the Holy Spirit shut some doors but it doesn't tell us how He shut the doors.

We need to be careful that we do not interpret difficulty or hardship as God shutting a door. The Apostle Paul's life and ministry was filled with hardship, suffering and trouble. 2 Corinthians 4:8-11 is one of several passages in his writings where he expresses some of this hardship that he endured for Christ and the gospel. *"We are hard-pressed on every side, yet not crushed; we are perplexed, but not in despair; persecuted, but not forsaken; struck down, but not destroyed - always carrying about in the body the dying of the Lord Jesus, that the life of Jesus also may be manifested in our body. For we who live are always delivered to death for Jesus' sake, that the life of Jesus also may be manifested in our mortal flesh."* So experiencing hardship doesn't necessarily mean that we are out of the will of the Lord. These afflictions and trials that Paul describes as his constant experiences as he was doing God's will were obviously the attempts of Satan and his followers to close the door on the Lord's work.

The Lord definitely opens doors that lead to the advancement of His kingdom. But Satan, the Adversary, will actively oppose the Lord's work using all of his henchmen who will operate with him. In 1 Corinthians 16:8-9, Paul writes about an open door in Ephesus. *"I will tarry in Ephesus until Pentecost. For a great and effective door has opened to me, and there are many adversaries."* Paul was delaying his visit to Corinth because God had opened a door there in Ephesus which led him to stay in Ephesus a while longer, even though he was encountering much opposition. So, Lord, give us discernment to know when You are closing a door, or are we simply facing our adversaries and therefore we must press on through the opposition to Your will.

The Holy Spirit is seen here as the companion of the believer, the one called alongside to guide us. Acts 16:6 tells us that *"they were forbidden by the Holy Spirit to preach the word in*

Asia. "'Forbidden' is a strong word, indicating that the Holy Spirit was slamming the door shut and God was making it clear to them.

But how does He guide Paul and Silas? How did the Holy Spirit forbid them to go into Asia? G. Campbell Morgan thinks that Paul might have gotten sick and couldn't go to those places, but needed to get to Troas for treatment, and there met Dr. Luke. In other words, the Holy Spirit shut the door through circumstances. However, there is no indication of this in the text. It may simply be that God shut the door by giving Paul and Silas a sense of uneasiness, a lack of peace about this move. Colossians 3:15 plainly teaches us that we are to *"let the peace of God rule in your hearts, to which also you were called in one body; and be thankful."* In my life, I have experienced the leading of the Spirit by this rule. If the Holy Spirit is not giving me absolute confidence and peace about moving forward in a necessary decision, I take that lack of His peace as a "No!"

When you experience something in your life where it seems that a door is slammed in your face, how do you react as a Christian? The company that you work for is down-sizing and you get laid off. It's an uncontrollable event in your life. Is God in charge of that event or is the corporation in charge of your life? In Psalm 37:23 (NIV) David writes *"If the LORD delights in a man's way, he makes his steps firm; . . ."* The NKJV says, *"The steps of a good man are ordered by the Lord, and He delights in his way."* Someone has commented, "The stops, as well as the steps of a good man are ordered by the Lord."

2) The Holy Spirit Guides An Active Servant.

Paul and Silas are out there doing something for the Lord. They were dedicated to the Lord, committed to serving Him, seeking first his kingdom. Some Christians sit around doing nothing, seeking to find out what the Lord wants them to do. Someone has observed that you can't steer a car that isn't moving. However, sometimes God has to stop us before He can turn us in another direction.

3) The Holy Spirit Shuts Some Doors And Opens Other Doors.

Paul and Silas experienced God shutting some doors and they end up at Troas with the sea in front of them, having traveled through miles and miles of the mountain passes, with apparently no productive work accomplished.

Some doors God slams shut through circumstances over which you have no control. Accept the closed door in faith and do not grumble. Other times, the Holy Spirit will resist your attempt to open a door by giving you a disturbed sense inside - a lack of peace. If you persist, the Holy Spirit may allow you to push the door open, but my advice is "Don't push it open!" If you push it open, it will be to your detriment. Revelation 3:7-8 speak clearly of Christ Jesus as the One who opens and closes doors with a finality in His actions. *"And to the angel of the church in Philadelphia write, 'These things says He who is holy, He who is true, "He who has the key of David, He who opens and no one shuts, and shuts and no one opens." "I know your works. See, I have set before you an open door, and no one can shut it; for you have a little strength, have kept My word, and have not denied My name."*

Next we need to consider **The Results of God's Closed Doors.**

Don't get discouraged when God shuts a door, because this is the Holy Spirit's way of guiding you. Remember that God never makes a mistake. He will open other doors before you as you wait on Him in faith. Sometimes, it takes time, perhaps even a few years to see the 'big picture' and to understand why the Holy Spirit closed a door and opened another door. We see at least three positive results for Paul and Silas.

1) New Relationships.

Paul found a new co-worker, Timothy, at Lystra, the place where he had been stoned and left for dead on the first visit there. Timothy was a growing disciple, well-spoken of by the other believers. Verse 2. Probably Timothy had been won to Christ's cause through Paul's ministry on his first missionary journey as he shared the gospel in Lystra. The context in Acts 14 tells us that Timothy likely observed all that happened to Paul, being stoned and left for dead, and yet Paul was still committed to Jesus Christ, and rose up to go on preaching the good news.

Timothy, therefore, became a follower of Christ Jesus, saved through faith in Christ alone. He was committed to Christ and committed to the cross. He was saved by the cross and he served by the cross. Timothy was a disciple of Christ who had learned to practice the words of Christ in Luke 9:23. *"Then He said to them all, "If anyone desires to come after Me, let him deny himself, and take up his cross daily, and follow Me."* Timothy was Paul's son in the faith, and became a strong pastor in the early church. This relationship became a precious one to both of them as Paul was like a father to this young man, Timothy.

Paul and Silas pick up another companion, Dr. Luke, at Troas and Luke travels with them from then on. Note the change in pronouns used by Luke in his writing of his account. Luke uses "they" previous to verse 10, and "we" from verse 10 forward.

2. New Opportunities.

Through the vision of the man from Macedonia, Paul is guided to press on into Greece and the gospel is preached in Europe for the first time. Places like Philippi, Thessalonica, Corinth and Athens are reached with the gospel. Whenever God closes a door, as a Christian dedicated to serving Him, you can expect that God will open other doors before you which will give you fresh fruitful and fulfilling opportunities.

Personally, when I first heard the call of the Lord to serve Him in fulltime ministry, my mind was set on becoming a missionary pilot but God closed the doors to that training. He redirected me to being a pastor. To me, it was very disappointing at the time, but I leave it to your judgment whether or not it was for the best in God's overall plan.

3) New Fruitfulness.

Acts16:13-15 tell of their first fruits in Europe. There was no synagogue in Philippi as there was not a large Jewish population there. However, there was a place of prayer down by the river, where some women gathered on the Sabbath day. One specifically mentioned is Lydia, a business woman from Thyatira, who responded to accept Christ. She may have been in Philippi just for a time on a business trip. However, she did have a home there as she invites Paul and Silas to stay at her house. Verse 15. She and her household are baptized. They are the first recorded believers in Europe. It is interesting that the vision Paul had at Troas was a man pleading to *"come over to Macedonia and help us."* Acts 16:9. However, the first convert there was a woman. This is the launching of the gospel to Europe and it set the whole course of history.

The story of history might have been much different if Paul and Silas had been allowed by God to turn east toward Asia. Perhaps Europe and the rest of the western world would not have been reached with the gospel. If you are yielded to Him and earnestly wanting to do His will, obstacles or closed doors must be viewed with the faith that God has some better plan for you.

Charles Swindoll writes, ". . . in our lives, God will sometimes shut down an exciting ministry or allow obstacles in our paths like sickness, financial difficulties, job failure, or a relationship breakup. At times like these, it's easy to become frustrated and disheartened. We can't imagine why God would shut some doors that He does. So we try to explain it, saying, "Maybe we just made a mistake . . . or maybe we need to try harder." But when Christ closes a door, He has His sights on something better - something around the bend we can't see yet. For Paul, that something was Europe.[66]

Has a relationship that you cherished ended and you were certain that you had found your life's dream mate? Has your business failed in spite of all your efforts? When disappointment in the form of a closed door faces you, take the time to get on your knees and pray about it. Seek to understand what is God trying to tell you by closing the door on your plan, and your vision for your life? Is He trying to protect you? Is He redirecting you? Recognize that a closed door may be a blessing, but you may not recognize it as a blessing right now. Ask God to reveal that blessing to you and to show you where and why He is leading you in another way.

John Nelson Darby shared this story of God's sovereignty in opening and closing doors. "Newscaster Paul Harvey told a remarkable story of God's providential care over thousands of allied prisoners during World War II, many of whom were Christians. One of America's mighty bombers took off from the island of Guam headed for Kokura, Japan, with a deadly cargo. Because clouds covered the target area, the sleek B-29

---

[66] Charles Swindoll, Commentary on Acts, Volume 2, page 136.

circled for nearly an hour until its fuel supply reached the danger point. The captain and his crew, frustrated because they were right over the primary target yet not able to fulfill their mission, finally decided they had better go for the secondary target. Changing course, they found that the sky was clear. The command was given, "Bombs away!" and the B-29 headed for its home base. Sometime later an officer received some startling information from military intelligence. Just one week before that bombing mission, the Japanese had transferred one of their largest concentrations of captured Americans to the city of Kokura. Upon reading this, the officer exclaimed, "Thank God for that protecting cloud! If the city hadn't been hidden from the bomber, it would have been destroyed and thousands of American boys would have died." God's ways are behind the scenes; but He moves all the scenes which He is behind. We have to learn this, and let Him work." Clearly that protecting cloud was a closed door, slammed shut by God!

Our wonderful Lord Jesus Christ died for our sins, has saved everyone who has repented and simply trusted His provision through the shedding of His atoning blood on the cross. He has opened the door to heaven for all who will enter! On our pathway through this life, sometimes He closes doors so that He can open other doors to new opportunities that He has mapped out for us. His way is always best!

He Leadeth Me!
(Written by Joseph H. Gilmore in 1880 with music composed by William Bradbury. Gilmore was a pastor in New Hampshire.)

He leadeth me, O blessed thought!
O words with heav'nly comfort fraught!
Whate'er I do, where'er I be
Still 'tis God's hand that leadeth me.

(Refrain)
He leadeth me, He leadeth me,
By His own hand He leadeth me;
His faithful follower I would be,
For by His hand He leadeth me.

Sometimes 'mid scenes of deepest gloom,
Sometimes where Eden's bowers bloom,
By waters still, o'er troubled sea,
Still 'tis His hand that leadeth me.

Lord, I would place my hand in Thine,
Nor ever murmur nor repine;
Content, whatever lot I see,
Since 'tis my God that leadeth me.

And when my task on earth is done,
When by Thy grace the vict'ry's won,
E'en death's cold wave I will not flee,
Since God through Jordan leadeth me.

Chapter 19
Earthquake Evangelism!
Acts 16:16-40

Charles E. Jefferson once described the difference between an audience and a church. He said, "An audience is a crowd. A church is a family. An audience is a gathering. A church is a fellowship. An audience is a collection. A church is an organism. An audience is a heap of stones. A church is a temple." And he concludes, "Preachers are ordained not to attract an audience, but to build a church."[67]

Acts 16 tells the story of the establishment of a new church at Philippi. It is to this church that Paul writes the epistle of Philippians.

'Church planting' is our modern missions' term for that which happened from the beginning of the expansion of the gospel throughout the world. God's ways of doing church planting are not always our ways. Nor, I am fearful, are our ways always His ways.

Often we go about church planting in such a way that we build something other than a solid biblical church.

At a riding stable, the following sign was posted. "We have fast horses for folks who like to ride fast. We have slow horses for folks who like to ride slow. We have big horses for big folks and little horses for little folks. And for those who have never ridden horses before, we have horses that have never been ridden."

Let me make it clear! I am not saying that all of our modern methods are wrong. What I fear is that we have often lost the

---

[67] What is a church? - Dynamic Preaching Magazine, May, 1994.

essentials for starting a true biblical church. There are some surprises in this chapter!

Let's consider **God's Strategic Plan.**

First of all, there seems to be **a 'key city' strategy** to the missionary movement as the gospel spreads to the Gentiles. You perhaps have observed that there is not a church established in every place where Paul and his co-workers preached. Troas, for example, nor does it seem that there was sufficient response in Athens for a church to be established. Paul and Silas had been forbidden by the Holy Spirit to go into regions of Asia Minor and had now been led by the Spirit to Macedonia, and specifically to the city of Philippi.

Acts 16:11-12 tells us *"Therefore, sailing from Troas, we ran a straight course to Samothrace, and the next day came to Neapolis, and from there to Philippi, which is the foremost city of that part of Macedonia, a colony. And we were staying in that city for some days."* The NIV translates 'foremost' as 'the leading city'. Philippi was a Roman Colony, which meant that it had special status with Rome. For example, it was exempt from taxes. It was a key city in which to establish a base of operations to reach out to other cities and towns of Macedonia.

Paul had a great burden and desire to go to Rome also. This was because Rome would be the center from which the whole empire would be assessable.

We also see that God's strategy was **the "changed life" strategy** rather than the "changed culture" strategy. Paul and Silas are followed by a demon possessed slave girl for many days. Verses 16-18. Verse 16 begins with *"Now it happened, as we went to prayer, a certain slave girl possessed of a spirit of divination met us . . ."* Followers of Jesus who are in touch with Jesus in their daily life will inevitably disrupt the corruption and evil of the culture around them. Paul's motivation for casting the evil spirit out of this enslaved girl was that he was *'greatly annoyed"* by her following them and proclaiming *"These men are the servants of the Most High God, who proclaim to us the way of salvation."*

You do not find Paul and Silas crusading against slavery even though Christian teaching is contrary to slavery. The strategy seems to be to reach people with the gospel and see them changed in their hearts through faith in Jesus Christ. Then the culture will be altered by the testimony and influence of many born again people in the society. However, believers in Jesus will automatically be standing against corruption and evil in the culture in which they live and they will be confronted and often attacked by Satan's forces.

In the case of this slave girl who was a fortune teller possessed by an evil spirit, there is no indication that she became a believer, although one would hope that she did. The casting out of a demon doesn't make one a born-again Christian. It was the fact that the demon that had been profiting her masters, and she was no longer of any use to them, that led to severe opposition from her masters. Their 'gold-mine' was destroyed when Paul cast the demon out of her. So this slave girl's masters *"seized Paul and Silas and dragged them into the marketplace to the authorities."* Verse 19. They brought charges against Paul and Silas. *"These men, being Jews, exceedingly trouble our city; and they teach customs which are not lawful for us, being Romans, to receive or observe."* Then the multitude (the whole city) *rose up against them; and the magistrates tore their clothes and commanded them to be beaten with rods. And when they had laid many stripes on them, they threw them into prison, commanding the jailer to keep them securely." Verses 20-23.* Drug traffickers, prostitution king-pins, abortion providers and all other evildoers in our society will be agitated by true Christians in their communities who stand for morality and righteousness which interferes with their business profits.

While the primary strategy is the "changed-life" through the new birth, believers must stand against evil in their culture and seek to make a difference in rooting out satanic activity. When governments are failing to guard their people against sin and evil, some believers will be called to run for office and to become 'salt and light' in our government. They will get involved in seeking to "drain the swamp."

William Wilberforce became an evangelical Christian in 1785, one year after he was elected to the British parliament. He headed the parliamentary campaign against the British slave trade for twenty years until the passage of the Slave Trade Act of 1807. Wilberforce was convinced of the importance of religion, morality and education. He championed causes and campaigns such as the Society for the Suppression of Vice, British missionary work in India, the creation of a free colony in Sierra Leone, the foundation of the Church Mission Society, and the Society for the Prevention of Cruelty to Animals.[68] It is my belief that Christians ought to be making a difference in working for a better culture even though our primary task is to proclaim the gospel that is the power of God unto salvation.

For example, we must do all we can to enact legislation to reverse Roe vs. Wade. However you are not likely to win a pro-choice person to Christ by attacking their position; you are more likely to be successful in changing their position by winning them to Christ through the gospel of the love of Jesus Christ, and then getting them involved in studying the Bible.

Next we see that the Lord's church at Philippi is composed of **God's Saved People.**

---

[68] Information gleaned from Wikipedia.

Churches are established as people are saved from their sin by trusting Jesus Christ and his death on the cross as their atonement. The true church is not just an organization, it is a living organism, made up of truly born again believers. Until you have those truly saved people, you do not have a church.

Paul was doing church planting in areas which were frontier areas as far as the gospel was concerned. He was preaching Christ where Christ had not yet been preached. He was not just appealing to dissatisfied Christians to come over to his congregation.

It is an admirable goal in our church planting efforts to reach 'non-churched Charlie.' The people God rescues from the dominion of darkness are not always the people we would choose. We want people who are prominent, influential people in the community, people with wealth and clout. But note who the people are who are reached at Philippi and become the core group for a wonderful church.

1) There is Lydia, (verses 13-15) a successful business woman, and others of her household. There were probably some other women who were her co-workers in her fabric and clothing business who became believers. Maybe even Syntyche and Euodia mentioned in Philippians 4 were among them. This was the beginning of the church in Philippi.

2) A slave girl, rescued from her demon possessed state. Verses 16-18. We are not specifically informed that she accepted Christ and was saved, but I think it was highly likely. She had a spirit of divination (NKJV) or a spirit by which she predicted the future (NIV). The Greek language tells us she literally had a *"spirit of Python"*. She was a fortune teller. Don't mess with astrology and fortune telling; not all of it is fakery; much of it is done through demons.

3) A jailor, a warden at the jail, who was not necessarily regarded as among the most highly influential of the community.

God chooses out his people in mysterious ways and often surprises us by His choices. 1 Corinthians 1:26-29 (NIV) reminds us, *"Brothers, think of what you were when you were called. Not many of you were wise by human standards; not many were influential; not many were of noble birth. But God chose the foolish things of the world to shame the wise; God chose the weak things of the world to shame the strong. He chose the lowly things of this world and the despised things-- and the things that are not--to nullify the things that are, so that no one may boast before him."*

Now let's consider **God's Spirit-Filled Preachers.**

This is not only for preachers and missionaries but for all believers.

1) Paul and Silas resist Satan's strategic attacks.

We see Satan seeking to make an alliance with the missionaries through this demon possessed slave girl. Our English translations make it sound like what she kept repeating is true, and her words seem to be right on the mark! Acts 16:17. *"This girl followed Paul and us, and cried out, saying, "These men are the servants of the Most High God, who proclaim to us the way of salvation."*

The demons often spoke the truth about Jesus when He confronted them. Note these examples. Mark 1:24 tells of a man in the synagogue at Capernaum, possessed by a demon. *"And he cried out, saying, "Let us alone! What have we to do with You, Jesus of Nazareth? Did You come to destroy us? I know who You are - the Holy One of God!"* In Mark 3:11, we read *"And the unclean spirits, whenever they saw Him, fell down before Him and cried out, saying, "You are the Son of God."* In Luke 8:28 we read about the demoniac living naked the cemetery. *"When he saw Jesus, he cried out, fell down before Him, and with a loud voice said, "What have I to do with You, Jesus, Son of the Most High God? I beg You, do not torment me!"*

Paul is clearly agitated, deeply troubled by this constant pursuit by this demon possessed girl. Neither Jesus Himself nor his apostles would accept the acknowledgement of who Jesus was from a demon.

But there is more behind this, as you examine the text closely.[69] A.T. Robertson and Charles Swindoll (and others) point out that this slave girl was not saying that Jesus was 'the' only way of salvation but merely 'a' way of salvation. Charles Williams in his translation of the New Testament translates it "a way of salvation." This slave girl, through the demon was teaching that there are many ways of salvation and Paul and Silas were teaching one of the ways to come to the Most High God. Throughout history, and even more prominently today, there is a movement termed 'eclecticism' that teaches that all religions believe in basically the same God and there are many ways of salvation.

2) Paul and Silas were rejoicing in suffering.

Paul and Silas end up in jail, having been severely beaten with rods. This was the maximum security part of the jail and they were in pain. Their response is amazing! Charles Swindoll writes, "How would you respond to such mistreatment?

---

[69] There is no article before `hodon soterias' (Note: it is not even in the Textus Receptus).

You've been lied about, beaten, thrown into a dungeon, and locked in stocks. Every breath painfully reminds you of your cracked ribs and bruised kidneys. Your back aches; your leg muscles cramp. Rats scurry across the floor in the dark. Feel like singing?"[70] Acts 16:25 gives this incredible response. *"But at midnight Paul and Silas were praying and singing hymns to God, and the prisoners were listening to them."* The other prisoners were attentively listening. You bet! When God's people pray and sing under such circumstances, you can be sure that it gets the attention of others.

Now let's give some attention to **God's Saving Power.**

The earthquake gets the jailer's attention. The jailer was sleeping and is awakened by the violent earthquake that shook the prison's foundations and loosed the chains of the prisoners and opened the locked prison doors.

Often God reaches unsaved people through the unusual and often tragic circumstances of life. An accident, cancer, or the loss of a dear loved one gets their attention as they have been drifting along in life.

The jailer's motive for repentance is fear. He is fearful of his fate. He is thinking that all the prisoners had escaped and he is about to commit suicide. Paul calls out to him, *"Do yourself no harm! We are all here!"* Verse 28. The most crucial question of all then comes from his lips. *"Sirs, what must I do to be saved?"*

The answer to every person is the same: "What shall I do?" There is nothing to do but *"Believe in the Lord Jesus Christ and you will be saved, and your household."* Verse 31.

---

[70] Charles Swindoll, Commentary on Acts, Volume 2, page 146.

We read that the jailer and his whole household were baptized. Verse 33. Some who believe in salvation of infants through baptism seek to use this passage to legitimize their practice. They argue that surely there must have been infants in this man's household. The text refutes this argument. Verse 32-33 tells us *"Then they spoke the word of the Lord to him and to all who were in his house. And he took them the same hour of the night and washed their stripes. And immediately he and all his family were baptized."* Clearly all of his household were old enough to hear and understand the spoken word and to believe. Verse 34 indicates that the jailer and all in his household believed in God.

The next day, the magistrates of the city instruct the jailer to let the prisoners, Paul and Silas go. They wanted them to depart quietly and forget about this whole indictment. Paul then lets them know that they are Roman citizens and therefore they had been illegally beaten and jailed. The magistrates, hearing this, panic and come pleading with them to leave their city quietly. After Paul and Silas visit Lydia again at her home, they journey on their way.

The story is told of a beggar who stopped a lawyer on the street in a large southern city and asked him for a quarter. Taking a long, hard look into the man's unshaven face, the attorney asked, "Don't I know you from somewhere?" "You should," came the reply. "I'm your former classmate. Remember second floor, Old Main Hall?" "Why, Sam, of course I know you!" Without further question the lawyer wrote a check for $100. "Here Sam, take this and get a new start. I don't care what happened in the past. It's the future that counts!" And with that he went on his way. Tears welled up in the man's eyes as he walked to a bank nearby. Stopping at the door, he saw through the glass the well-dressed tellers and the spotlessly clean interior. Then he looked at his filthy rags. "They won't take this from me. They'll swear I forged it!" he muttered as he wandered away. The next day the two men met again. "Why, Sam, what did you do with my check? Gamble it away? Drink it up?" No", said the beggar, as he pulled the check out of his dirty shirt pocket and told him why he hadn't cashed it. "Listen, friend," said the lawyer, "what makes the check good is not your clothes or appearance, but my signature. Go on, now, cash it!"[71]

The Bible says, *"Whosoever shall call on the name of the Lord shall be saved."* Cash the check by faith! Trust Christ Jesus who died for your sins. He will save you and give you eternal life!

Only Trust Him!
(Written by John Hart Stockton, a Methodist minister, who was born in 1813 and died in 1877.)[72]

Come, every soul by sin oppressed,
There's mercy with the Lord;
And he will surely give you rest,
By trusting in his Word.

(Refrain)
Only trust him, only trust him,
Only trust him now.

---

[71] Pulpit Helps, July, 1996.

[72] The original words and title were "Come to Jesus", as penned by John H. Stockton. In 1873, Ira D. Sankey seems to have secured a manuscript copy of this hymn and said: "One day in mid-ocean, as I was looking over a list of hymns in my scrapbook, I noticed one commencing, 'Come every soul by sin oppressed,' by the Rev John Stockton, with the familiar chorus, 'Come to Jesus.' Believing that these words had been so often sung that they were hackneyed, I decided to change them and tell how to come to Jesus by substituting the words, 'Only Trust Him.' In this form it was first published in Sacred Songs and Solos in London."

He will save you, he will save you,
He will save you now.

For Jesus shed his precious blood
Rich blessings to bestow;
Plunge now into the crimson flood
That washes white as snow.

Yes, Jesus is the truth the way
That leads you into rest;
Believe in him without delay,
And you are fully blest.

Come then and join this holy band,
And on to glory go,
To dwell in that celestial land
Where joys immortal flow.

Chapter 20
A Riot or a Revival!
Acts 17:1-15

Often some good comes out of some very bad situations. Most of you are familiar with the airlines' Frequent Flyer programs. A rather extreme example of going out of one's way to qualify for bonus coupons came when TWA flight 847 was hijacked in June, 1985, and was flown four times between Algeria and Beirut. Larry Hilliard, regional director of corporate communications for TWA, revealed that Deborah Toga, wife of one of the hostages, had inquired whether these hostage trips qualified under the airline's Frequent Flyer program. They did![73]

As Paul and his missionary team continue their work for the Lord, they are tenacious about sharing the message of Jesus Christ. Doctor Luke, it appears, stayed in Philippi to continue the work there. Verse 4 mentions only Paul and Silas at Thessalonica and verse 10 mentions only Paul and Silas as they are ushered off to Berea. Then we read that Timothy and Silas stayed at Berea while they ushered Paul off to Athens. Verse 14. Note also the personal pronoun change to *'they'* at the end of chapter 16 and also in 17:1. The writer, Luke, no longer is using the term *'we'*. Wherever they go, the gospel brings a reaction. It seems it is either a revival or a riot.

We also are to be involved in the work of sharing Jesus Christ with others. There are some lessons we can learn here about our faithful witnessing for our Lord.

---

[73] Peter Hay, The Book of Business Anecdotes, New York, Facts on File Publications, 1988.

Being a faithful witness for Christ involves **Continuous Effort to Share Christ.**

The focus of Paul's life was to be continually involved in sharing Jesus Christ with others. There are some places that it appears he just passed by, like Amphipolis and Appolonia. However his consuming passion, the purpose of his life, was to share Christ Jesus with a needy world. That ought to be our purpose also, if we are believers in Jesus Christ, who have been the recipients of His grace.

I had a conversation with a man who has had some struggles seeking to find the real purpose that the Lord has for his life. He had struggled with the feeling that his job is mundane and meaningless when it comes to the big picture of God's kingdom work. He finally came to the conclusion that his singular purpose is "to know Christ and to make Him known." What he does to pay the expenses is incidental to that.

If your life is not showing some consistency in godliness and the fruit of the Spirit, you are better off to keep your mouth shut. If you claim to be a Christian, and are living immorally, shut up about your faith in Christ. You'll do more damage than good if your life is not backing up your words. If you claim to know and love Christ and are harsh with your brothers and sisters in Christ, shut up about your faith. If you claim to know Christ and are always blowing up with others, then you might as well not talk. I'm not talking about perfection, I'm talking about some degree of consistency, and I'm talking about purity of heart.

2 Corinthians 2:14-16 talks about the aroma that we spread with our lives. *"Now thanks be to God who always leads us in triumph in Christ, and through us diffuses the fragrance of His knowledge in every place. For we are to God the fragrance of Christ among those who are being saved and among those*

who are perishing. To the one we are the aroma of death leading to death, and to the other the aroma of life leading to life. And who is sufficient for these things?" May your life be the 'fragrance of Christ' and not the 'stink of hypocrisy' . If people would say, "Your actions speak so loud that I can't hear a thing you are saying", then shut your mouth. Your words will do more harm than good.

But Paul does not allow any opposition to shut his mouth or make him cease his efforts to share the gospel of Christ. He and Silas go from the beatings and jail of Philippi to Thessalonica and they are right back at the task of sharing the gospel message. What does it take to shut our mouths? We face a little resistance and a little verbal abuse, and we decide to just be quiet about our faith.

Next we see the **Consistent Exposition of Scripture.**

Paul's approach seems to always be, to go to the Jews first. Every place he goes where there is a synagogue, he seeks to share the gospel as long as they will allow him to do so. Note Acts 17:2-3. *"Then Paul, as his custom was, went in to them,* (the synagogue) *and for three Sabbaths reasoned with them from the Scriptures, explaining and demonstrating that the Christ had to suffer and rise again from the dead, and saying, "This Jesus whom I preach to you is the Christ."*

Paul's approach in sharing the gospel is consistent with his audience. As he works with his Jewish audience, including God-fearing Greeks who had attached themselves to the synagogue, he begins with the Old Testament prophecies about the promised Messiah. His message was not his own ideas or his own gospel. Rather, Paul's message was *"this Jesus I am proclaiming to you is the Christ - the Messiah."* Paul *"reasoned with them from the Scriptures. . ."* Verses 2-3.

Paul based his teaching upon the authority and veracity of God's revelation in the sacred Scriptures.

This is a very good approach with any one, not just with someone from Jewish background. Are you studying the Scriptures so that you can reason with them, explaining and proving from Scripture who Jesus of Nazareth is? Now, don't be intimidated by that. Just be constantly seeking to improve your ability to understand and expose the Scripture to others. People were won to Christ, not by Paul's eloquence, but by Paul's exposition of Scripture. Remember that God promises to use his word to bring forth fruit.

Memorize this wonderful promise of God found in Isaiah 55:10-11: *"For as the rain comes down, and the snow from heaven, and do not return there, but water the earth, and make it bring forth and bud, that it may give seed to the sower and bread to the eater, so shall My word be that goes forth from My mouth; it shall not return to Me void, but it shall accomplish what I please, and it shall prosper in the thing for which I sent it."*

There was considerable success in Thessalonica as some Jews were persuaded but also a *"great multitude of the devout Greeks, and not a few of the leading women, joined Paul and Silas."* Verse 4. Verse 5-8 goes on to say, *"But the Jews who were not persuaded, becoming envious, took some of the evil men from the marketplace, and gathering a mob, set all the city in an uproar and attacked the house of Jason, and sought to bring them out to the people. But when they did not find them, they dragged Jason and some brethren to the rulers of the city, crying out, "These who have turned the world upside down have come here too. Jason has harbored them, and these are all acting contrary to the decrees of Caesar, saying there is another king - Jesus." And they troubled the crowd and the rulers of the city when they heard these things."* So in Thessalonica, we see both a revival and a riot.

Because of the rioting opposition of these envious Jews, and for safety sake, Paul and Silas, move on to Berea under the cover of night-time darkness. After arriving in Berea, Paul preached the gospel to the people there and got them into the word of God. Acts 17:10-11. *"Then the brethren immediately sent Paul and Silas away by night to Berea. When they arrived, they went into the synagogue of the Jews. These were more fair-minded than those in Thessalonica, in that they received the word with all readiness, and searched the Scriptures daily to find out whether these things were so."* Paul welcomed people to examine scripturally what he was preaching. The Bible can stand the test of any amount of critical examination. That is what we must seek to do - get people into studying the word of God for themselves.

It is through the study of the Bible, and reasoning from the Scriptures that people come to believe in Jesus Christ and are transformed by God's Spirit. Our family was vacationing in British Columbia in the 1970's while I was pastoring Lansdowne Baptist Church in Edmonton, Alberta, Canada. We stopped by a friend's place on the shores of Shuswap Lake and set up our camping trailer in their yard for the night. That evening, a couple from Edmonton stopped by to see them and we were able to meet John and Olive Coutts. While visiting, we found that they had been checking out the teachings of a cult group. Recognizing that these people were searching for the truth about God, I suggested to them that we would be happy to lead them in a Bible study in their home. They readily accepted and we began a study of the Gospel of John. Over the next few weeks, they came to believe in Jesus Christ, were baptized and became members of our church. They are now both home with the Lord in heaven, after serving Him faithfully and energetically for a couple of decades. This is simply one example of how getting a person into serious study of the Scriptures and reasoning with them as to who Jesus Christ really is, can lead them to being born-again by the Holy Spirit.

Next we see how Paul and Silas had a **Constant Expectation of Results.**

At Thessalonica, there was a riot (verse 5) stirred up by some jealous Jews, who were more concerned about losing their power than about doctrinal correctness. Here we see Jason, and some other brothers, standing firm even though they are dragged in front of the authorities. These are probably just new believers and apparently Jason had hosted Paul and Silas in his home.

At Berea, it seems more like a revival with eager response to the gospel. Whenever you are actively sharing the gospel with others, you will always get a reaction. It may be positive, with people seeking to know truth and resulting ultimately in faith in Christ. Or it may be hostility or indifference. Unless you deal with the issue of your response to hostility or indifference by many, you will never be involved in seeking to witness for Christ. You need to be willing to be thought a fool for Christ for that is exactly how the hostile crowd views you. Get over the need to be well thought of by everyone or the need to please everyone. We are here on this earth as God's redeemed people to please God above all else. Observe again the response of Peter and John as they were threatened in Acts 4:18-20. *"So they called them and commanded them not to speak at all nor teach in the name of Jesus. But Peter and John answered and said to them, "Whether it is right in the sight of God to listen to you more than to God, you judge. For we cannot but speak the things which we have seen and heard."* The recently disgraced Bill Cosby once said, "I don't know the key to success, but I do know the key to failure is to try to please everybody."[74]

When you look at this passage, you see that Paul and Silas left believers, Christ–followers, behind them in both Thessalonica and Berea. The positive results were the same in both places. Acts 17:4, 12. We need to also remember that even for those who rejected the gospel, there was an effective witness. They will never be able to stand in God's presence at the judgment and say, "No one ever told me the gospel!" Bill Bright of Campus Crusade has captured what successful witnessing is. "Successful witnessing is simply sharing Christ in the power of the Holy Spirit and leaving the results to God."

As we think about our responsibility to be a witness for our Lord, we need to think also about our motivation. Is it the passion of our lives "to know Him and to make Him known?" Have we become so in love with Jesus Christ, that we are motivated to share Him with others?

John B. Gordon, a respected Southern General, led the last official attack on the Union troops at Appomattox in April of 1865 when Lee surrendered to Grant. Later General Gordon became a candidate for the U.S. Senate. Angry over some political incident, a man who had served under Gordon in the Confederate Army, now a member of the legislature, vowed to see Gordon defeated. When the convention opened, he angrily stamped down the aisle with his anti-Gordon vote in hand. As he saw Gordon sitting on the platform, he noticed how the once handsome face was disfigured with the scars of battle. Overcome with emotion, he exclaimed, "It's no use; I can't do it. Here is my vote for John B. Gordon." Then turning to the

---

[74] Bill Cosby, quoted in Bottom Line "Tomorrow" magazine.

General, he said, "Forgive me, General; I had forgotten the scars."[75]

Has your devotion to Christ wavered and do you become annoyed that He asks you to take a stand for Him? Go back to the cross and remember the scars.

When I Survey the Wondrous Cross
(Written and published by Isaac Watts – 1707)

When I survey the wondrous cross
On which the Prince of glory died,
My richest gain I count but loss,
And pour contempt on all my pride.

Forbid it, Lord, that I should boast,
Save in the death of Christ my God!
All the vain things that charm me most,
I sacrifice them to His blood.

See from His head, His hands, His feet,
Sorrow and love flow mingled down!
Did e'er such love and sorrow meet,
Or thorns compose so rich a crown?

Were the whole realm of nature mine,
That were a present far too small;
Love so amazing, so divine,
Demands my soul, my life, my all.

---

[75] Larry Moyer, Evantell letter. Fall issue, 1992 .

Chapter 21
The Gospel and Intellectuals!
Acts 17:16-34

Athens was regarded as the cultural and intellectual center of the world. Socrates, Plato and many other intelligent philosophers had walked its streets and debated their philosophies in the Agora (marketplace) and at the Areopagus (Mars Hill) as many as 400 years before Paul came. In this encounter with the elite intelligentsia of the day, Paul is greatly distressed by what he sees, idols everywhere.

The Frenchman, Renan, said about Paul in Athens: "the ugly little Jew abused Greek art by describing the statues as idols." Athens had become the hub of culture and learning but they had not arrived at the truth. Even the philosophies of the day, the Epicureans and the Stoics had degenerated into systems that were politically correct, allowing for rampant sin without denunciation.

America today is facing similar problems where we are taught to be politically correct and tolerant of most anything.

Paul Harvey wrote the following in one of his columns printed in the Chicago Daily Herald, Feb. 27, 1996.

"Pastor Joe's Message Irks Kansas Legislators"

Man, oh, man! They won't invite Pastor Joe to the Kansas State Legislature again.
They invited Pastor Joe Wright of Wichita's Central Christian Church to deliver the invocation - and he told God on them.
Now, God knows what they've been up to.
No sooner had their guest chaplain concluded his prayer than three Democrats on the state Legislature were on their feet at microphones protesting, "He can't talk like that about us!" Rep.

Delbert Gross considered the invocation "divisive," "sanctimonious" and "overbearing."

Rep. David Haley called it "blasphemous and ignorant." Rep. Sabrina Standifer echoed the indignation.

What in the world did Pastor Joe say in Topeka that incited the righteous wrath of three Democrats from Hays and Kansas City?

I've secured the entire text of the invocation so you can evaluate it for yourself.

"Heavenly Father, we come before you today to ask Your forgiveness and seek Your direction and guidance.

"We know Your word says, `Woe to those who call evil good' but that is exactly what we have done. We have lost our spiritual equilibrium and inverted our values.

"We confess that we have ridiculed the absolute truth of Your word in the name of moral pluralism.

"We have worshipped other gods and called it 'multiculturalism.'

"We have endorsed perversion and called it 'an alternative lifestyle.'

"We have exploited the poor and called it 'a lottery.'

"We have neglected the needy and called it 'self-preservation.'

"We have rewarded laziness and called it 'welfare.'

"In the name of 'choice', we have killed our unborn.

"In the name of 'right to life', we have killed abortionists.

"We have neglected to discipline our children and called it 'building esteem.'

"We have abused power and called it 'political savvy.'

"We've coveted our neighbors' possessions and called it 'taxes.'

"We've polluted the air with profanity and pornography and called it 'freedom of expression.'

"We've ridiculed the time-honored values of our forefathers and called it 'enlightenment.'

"Search us, O God, and know our hearts today. Try us, and show us any wicked way in us. Cleanse us from every sin, and set us free.

"Guide and bless these men and women who have been sent here by the people of Kansas and who have been ordained by You to govern this great state.

"Grant them Your wisdom to rule, and may their decisions direct us to the center of Your will.

"I ask it in the name of Your Son, the living Savior, Jesus Christ.

Amen."[76]

Paul was waiting in Athens (Verse 16) but he got involved in sharing the gospel of Jesus Christ and speaking of His resurrection, during his wait for his companions. He approaches the intellectuals of Athens in some interesting ways.

As we study his approach, first we see **The Deficiency of Intellectualism and Philosophy**

We need to distinguish between intellect and intellectualism. I praise God for intelligence and for mental capability to whatever degree each of us has been gifted. Let's not be anti-education or be proud of ourselves when we cease to do hard thinking and learning. However let's not fall into the trap of intellectualism.

1. The problem of arrogance.

The truly educated person is humble, realizing that no matter how much a person knows, it is just a drop in the bucket of what there is to know. When you graduate with a degree, unless you realize how little you really know, you are not truly

[76] Paul Harvey column, Chicago Daily Herald, February 27, 1996.

educated. Verse 18 (NIV) says that a group of Epicurean and Stoic philosophers began to *"dispute"* with him. This word 'dispute' is used in Acts 18:27 and is translated 'help'. These arrogant philosophers were trying to help this poor man, Paul, come into the light from his nonsensical ideas.

John Phillips says, the Epicureans held that "indulgence was the key to life and that pleasure was the highest good." The Stoics were fatalists and pantheists believing that "God was the world soul and the world was God's body. Indifference was the key to life and suicide was a high virtue."[77] Arrogant intellectualism cannot be taught anything because it is convinced that it knows everything worth knowing already.

A young man who had been hired by the personnel department of a large supermarket chain reported to work at one of the stores. The manager greeted him with a warm handshake and a smile, handed him a broom and said, "Your first job will be to sweep out the store." "But," the young man said, "I'm a college graduate." "I'm sorry," the manager said. "I didn't know that. Here, give me the broom and I'll show you how."[78]

God hides His truth from the arrogant and proud intellectual. In Matthew 11:25-26, we read, *"At that time Jesus answered and said, "I thank You, Father, Lord of heaven and earth, that You have hidden these things from the wise and prudent and have revealed them to babes. Even so, Father, for so it seemed good in Your sight."* Eugene Peterson, in his paraphrase, The Message, says it this way. *"Thank you, Father, Lord of heaven and earth. You've concealed your ways from sophisticates and know-it-alls, but spelled them out clearly to ordinary people."*

---

[77] Gleaned from commentaries on Acts by John Phillips and G. Campbell Morgan.

[78] From my personal Illustration files, accumulated over the years.

2. The problem of a condescending attitude.

These philosophers call Paul a *"babbler"*, which is from a word (spermalogos) which means 'a seed picker'. This was a derogatory term meaning that you have no "original thoughts". You just run around like a bird picking up a seed here and a seed there. Acts 17:18 (NIV) says, *"A group of Epicurean and Stoic philosophers began to dispute with him. Some of them asked, "What is this babbler trying to say?" Others remarked, "He seems to be advocating foreign gods." They said this because Paul was preaching the good news about Jesus and the resurrection."* The word in the original Greek for *"foreign gods"* is from "daimonion" or "demons".

Listen to the media closely and see how frequently anyone who is a conservative Christian is treated with a condescending attitude. We are referred to as the 'right wing radicals' or the 'extremists'. Some even go so far as to speak of Christians as the dangerous element of our society, as if all of us reason the same as Paul Hill who killed an abortion doctor and justified his actions.[79]

3. The problem of blindness to truth.

Philosophers are often more intrigued with the journey than they are with the destination. Philosophy is technically the 'search for truth' but if you find the truth, there is no more search.

Another problem in intellectualism is that the arrogant intellectual is convinced that he has found the truth even

---

[79] Paul Hill was a pro-lifer who believed God was telling him to save babies by shooting and killing a doctor who performed abortions. This happened in the mid 1990's.

though he may be far from the truth. Carl Sagan[80] was a very intelligent man but he was dead wrong when he pontificated about the origin of the universe and how it came into being. I am certain he was absolutely sure he was speaking truth when he asserted with such authority that the universe was born in a big explosion of cosmic gases some 2 billion years ago. 2 Corinthians 4:3-4 declares that *"But even if our gospel is veiled, it is veiled to those who are perishing, whose minds the god of this age has blinded, who do not believe, lest the light of the gospel of the glory of Christ, who is the image of God, should shine on them."*

The Athenians were blinded in their idolatry. Their own poets said, "We are his offspring", and yet they worshiped gods made by the offspring of God. How much more can one contradict his beliefs by his practice?

When you write about the abortion issue to your senators, you will get a letter back that will say something like this. In 1996, Illinois Senator Carol Mosely Braun replied to my letter in part in this way: "I understand the concerns that many have about late term abortions. I do not believe in abortion as a method of birth control. My own religious beliefs hold life dear, and I would prefer that every potential child have a chance to be born. However, I believe that this decision must be left to women, their families, and their doctors, not government officials."[81]

Do you see the blindness in those statements? Note that she refers to the aborted baby as a 'potential child'. Apparently she doesn't believe it is a child until it exits its mother's womb.

---

[80] Carl Sagan died in 1996, but was still alive when I preached this series of sermons.

[81] From a response to my letter to Illinois Senator Mosely Braun protesting the veto of the President Clinton and her vote against the bill banning partial birth abortions.

Carol Mosely Braun and President Clinton would not take that position if day old babies outside the womb were being murdered by their mothers and their doctors. Government would get involved and they would be found guilty of murder.[82] If they believe that it should be left to the woman's decision, would they argue the same about a mother of infants or small children already born. Should it be left to the decision of the mother as to whether or not she feels that she can care for them? If it is murder to take the infant's life after it is born, then why is it OK to take the baby's life before it is born?

Now let's study Paul's **Approach to the Intellectual.**

Note Paul's bridge that he uses to get their attention. Acts 17:22-23. *"Then Paul stood in the midst of the Areopagus and said, "Men of Athens, I perceive that in all things you are very religious; for as I was passing through and considering the objects of your worship, I even found an altar with this inscription: TO THE UNKNOWN GOD. Therefore, the One whom you worship without knowing, Him I proclaim to you . . . ."*

The altar to "the Unknown God" describes much of the religious culture of America today. A 1996 Gallup poll showed that over 90% of Americans believe in God but fewer are attending church with any degree of regularity. As I recall, the survey said something like 41%. In 2019, as I write this, the numbers have shrunk dramatically.

But what kind of god do Americans believe in? The god of the millions of Mohammedans is Allah. The million gods of the pantheon are the gods of the growing number of Hindus. Then

---

[82] Now in this year, 2019, some governors are even approving infanticide, allowing mothers to choose to allow their babies to die, after they are born alive. Who would have thought America would ever be so decadent?

there is the god of the New-Agers, who believe in "the force be with you." How many believe in the only true God revealed in Scripture?

1. God is the Infinite Creator God. Verse 24.

Paul begins with a strong statement about the Creator God. He is the maker of everything. He is Infinite in His being and cannot be contained in man-made temples. *"God, who made the world and everything in it, since He is Lord of heaven and earth, does not dwell in temples made with hands."*

Begin your witness to the lost intellectual talking about the God who created everything. If you don't believe in the Creator, then where and how did it all begin? If the Creator God does not exist, then there is no plausible explanation for the existence of everything. God, the Creator of everything is the Designer God. John 1:1-3 declares that Jesus (the Word) is the Creator of everything. *"In the beginning was the Word, and the Word was with God, and the Word was God. He was in the beginning with God. All things were made through Him, and without Him nothing was made that was made."* He is *"Lord of heaven and earth."*

2. God is the Independent God. Verses 24-25.

The true God is not dependent upon human beings for anything. We also need to remember that we need God, God does not need us. John Phillips writes, "God is independent of sacrifices, sanctuaries, and service alike. It is not the work of men's hands God wants, it is the worship of men's hearts. It is impossible either to corner God in a temple or to conceptualize Him with an idol."[83]

---

[83] John Phillips, Exploring Acts, Commentary on Acts, Kregel Publications, Grand Rapids, MI; page 123.

Much of modern evangelicalism has fallen into the trap of preaching a distorted gospel that presents God as a God who exists to serve us, to be a kind of celestial errand boy for us.

3. God is the Sovereign God. Verse 26.

Paul teaches the Athenian philosophers that God is in control of all things. All nations come from the same one man, Adam, and the boundaries of the nations are controlled by God. The Greeks thought themselves to be the superior race and all others were considered "barbarians". But Paul leaves no room for a 'Master race' philosophy as he points out that we all have the same origin in Adam. Hitler's Aryan supremacy and the Bosnian Serbian ethnic cleansing or the Ku Klux Klan white superiority, and any other superior ethnic philosophy, are all swept aside here.

The affairs of mankind are not controlled by their many gods, nor by their sacrifices offered to those gods, but by the Sovereign Creator God.

4. God is the Knowable God. Verses 27-28.

In verses 27-28 Paul declares that everyone from every nation on earth can know the true God and ought to seek to know this true God. *". . .so that they should seek the Lord, in the hope that they might grope for Him and find Him, though He is not far from each one of us; for in Him we live and move and have our being, as also some of your own poets have said, 'For we are also His offspring.'"*

The word "reach out" (NIV) and "feel for" (KJV) is the idea of "groping for" (NKJV). Through what God has revealed in nature, man can grope for and discover that God is the Creator of all. It is not difficult to see that it is God who gives us the very breath we breathe and keeps our hearts beating. He is the God who is very near us all the time. As Paul states it, *"in him we live and move and have our being"*, our very existence.

The true God is not far from us. 'Agnostos', in the Greek language, *"The unknown god"* is the word from which we get 'agnostic', which refers to one who doesn't know if there is a God. Paul is declaring to them that the true God is knowable.

5. God is the Transcendent God. Verse 29.

The true God, even though he is near and knowable, is also transcendent or completely separate from us. *"Therefore, since we are the offspring of God, we ought not to think that the Divine Nature is like gold or silver or stone, something shaped by art and man's devising."* Verse 29. Therefore you can't represent God by some created idol. We are made in God's image but we are not to make God in our image. God is not material, nor is He contained in His creation. He is the Creator and yet completely separate from His creation.

6. God is the Judging God. Verses 30-31.

A future judgment day was totally foreign to the thinking of the Greek philosophers. Paul proclaims a future judgment day, a day of accountability to the true God. *"Truly, these times of ignorance God overlooked, but now commands all men everywhere to repent, because He has appointed a day on which He will judge the world in righteousness by the Man whom He has ordained. He has given assurance of this to all by raising Him from the dead."* Verses 30-31. The man appointed by God as the supreme Judge is Jesus Christ.

God has commanded that all men everywhere repent. Verse 30. The word *'repent'* literally means 'to change your mind'. All men are commanded to turn from our independence and our sin of ignoring God. We are to turn from our unbelief to trust Jesus Christ as our Savior and Lord. Do not delay! Repent today! Tomorrow may be judgment day!

7. God is the Living God. Verse 31.

This is all proven true because Jesus Christ is alive. He has been raised up from the dead. To these Greek philosophers, this matter of a physical resurrection was certainly a new thing and an absurd idea. These Grecian philosophers thought that anything physical was evil and corrupt and reality was grounded in the metaphysical. This is the crucial point in true Christianity! Christ Jesus is risen from the dead!

The response of the Athenians was primarily sneering and procrastination. Either they rejected it or they were sufficiently fascinated with these new concepts that they wanted to hear more. *"And when they heard of the resurrection of the dead, some mocked, while others said, "We will hear you again on this matter." So Paul departed from among them."* Verses 32-33. However a few believed the message and followed. Some men, among them, Dionysius, a member of the court of the Areopagus, and a woman named Damaris, and a number of other women believed and joined with Paul. Verse 34.

A person will never come to believe in Christ Jesus if he depends entirely upon his intellect, his reasoning power. Through your observation of what God has made, and proper reasoning, you ought to come to believe in God's existence and power. Romans 1:20 tells us this. *"For since the creation of the world His invisible attributes are clearly seen, being understood by the things that are made, even His eternal power and Godhead, so that they are without excuse . . ."*

The message of the gospel, that Christ Jesus died for our sins upon the cross, that God the Father has set forth this way of salvation through the blood of Christ shed for us, is only known through the revelation of Scripture. You will never come to repent and believe unless you accept the truth of this gospel revealed in Scripture, because God's love revealed in this way is beyond our discovery merely through our human reason. *"For the message of the cross is foolishness to those who are perishing, but to us who are being saved it is the power of God. For it is written: "I will destroy the wisdom of the wise, and bring to nothing the understanding of the prudent." Where is the wise? Where is the scribe? Where is the disputer of this age? Has not God made foolish the wisdom of this world? Since, in the wisdom of God, the world through wisdom did not know God, it pleased God through the foolishness of the message preached to save those who believe."* 1 Corinthians 1:18-21.

God commands people everywhere to repent and believe the good news. Turn from your wicked ways, your arrogance and your pride, and trust Jesus Christ and His shed blood on the cross as your means of salvation. Do not delay!

Fairest Lord Jesus!

(It was first published in a German Roman Catholic publication in 1677, without any author's name. A modern translation was published in 1842.)

Fairest Lord Jesus, Ruler of all nature,
O Thou of God and man the Son,
Thee will I cherish, Thee will I honor,
Thou, my soul's glory, joy and crown.

Fair are the meadows, fairer still the woodlands,
Robed in the blooming garb of spring;
Jesus is fairer, Jesus is purer,
Who makes the woeful heart to sing.

Fair is the sunshine, fairer still the moonlight,
And all the twinkling starry host;
Jesus shines brighter, Jesus shines purer
Than all the angels heav'n can boast.

All fairest beauty, heavenly and earthly,
Wondrously, Jesus, is found in Thee;
None can be nearer, fairer or dearer,
Than Thou, my Savior, art to me.

Beautiful Savior! Lord of all the nations!
Son of God and Son of Man!
Glory and honor, praise, adoration,
Now and forevermore be Thine.

Chapter 22
Getting Beyond The Porch!
Acts 19:1-7

I remember my first trip to the Roanoke, Virginia area and driving on some of the narrow back country roads of the beautiful Shenandoah Valley. As we drove down the road, we would pass homes with porches on which you would see people rocking away in their chairs on the porch, enjoying the coolness and beauty of the evening. It is a different way of life that has much appeal. However, it would be tragic for that family if they had to live their whole life never getting beyond the porch and into the home.

Many church members today across denominational lines are sincere about serving God but they have only gotten as far as the porch and have never entered into the 'household' or family of God. They are like those disciples of John, the Baptist, who because of their ignorance of Christ and the gospel had not yet been born into God's redeemed family. They were sincere seekers who had only gotten onto the porch.

While this group of disciples of John, the Baptist, is a unique situation, that occurred in the transition period between John, the Baptist and Jesus Christ, it has application to many today who claim to be Christian but do not understand the truth of the gospel. They believe in God in a general sense, attend church at least occasionally and are seeking to be good people. They are sincere but are not born again by the Holy Spirit. They are still rocking on the porch of salvation but have not entered into the household of faith.

Let's carefully interpret this passage or we will fall into traps of doctrinal error as many already have done. How does a person get beyond the porch as a seeker of God to truly be saved and a genuine part of God's family?

First we need to **Recognize That Sincerity Without Truth Is Inadequate.**

We need to understand who this small group of disciples were. According to Acts 19:7, they were *"about twelve in all"*. Apollos had been in Ephesus before Paul but had apparently not had contact with these people. Acts 18:24-28 tells us that Apollos also was lacking in his knowledge of the truth of the gospel, however, he was a born again believer and a gifted preacher. Apollos was preaching in the synagogue, declaring that Jesus is the Christ.[84] Apollos was *"mighty in the Scriptures"* (primarily the Old Testament at that point of church history) and *"had been instructed in the way of the Lord"*. Acts 18:24-25. Verse 25 also makes the point that Apollos only knew the baptism of John. In other words, he was not instructed in the baptism in the name of Jesus Christ, or Christian baptism. Priscilla and Aquila took him aside and helped him. They *"explained to him the way of God more accurately."* Acts 18:26.

These disciples of John, the Baptist, were more seriously deficient than Apollos in their knowledge of the truth of the gospel. They seemed to be very sincere men who were repentant toward God, but they had just gotten onto the porch as seekers of God. Paul sensed that they were not really saved people and he checked them out to find out where they stood.

Here we must deal with some very important textual and interpretative issues so that we do not go astray. Paul's question in Acts 19:2 is designed to understand whether or not these men were born again by the Holy Spirit. The KJV and the NKJV are poor translations at this point, *"Have you*

---

[84] 'Christ' is the Greek equivalent of the Hebrew word for 'Messiah', meaning 'anointed one'.

received the Holy Spirit since you believed?" Pentecostals and other charismatics have used this verse to teach that the receiving of the Holy Spirit is a separate experience from the new birth, or a 'second blessing'. The NIV is a better translation here - *"Did you receive the H.S. when you believed?"* In other words, if you have truly understood the gospel and trusted Christ as Savior, you would have received the Holy Spirit at that time. Note the response of these men. Verse 2b. *"We have not so much as heard whether there is a Holy Spirit."* In the Greek language, it is literally, *"we did not so much as hear whether the Holy Spirit was."* Most likely what they were saying was that they had no knowledge of the Holy Spirit having come. As Jews, they certainly would have known of the Holy Spirit with any knowledge of the Old Testament. Also, being they were disciples of John, the Baptist, they had heard him speak prophetically of the coming of the Messiah who would baptize with the Holy Spirit. Matthew 3:11 gives John's words at the time of Jesus' baptism in the Jordan River. *"I indeed baptize you with water unto repentance, but He who is coming after me is mightier than I, whose sandals I am not worthy to carry. He will baptize you with the Holy Spirit and with fire."*

These disciples of John the Baptist, who had submitted to the baptism of repentance under John, had apparently left Israel soon after that and had not heard the gospel of the Christ who died and rose again. Therefore they were still on the porch and had not entered into salvation through faith in Jesus Christ.

There are countless members of churches across all denominational lines who are on the porch but are not saved. They are sincere but have believed some false doctrine about how God's grace comes to us. Countless people have been taught and believe that their baptism as infants conveyed the grace of God's forgiveness to them and brought them into a covenant relationship with God. No matter how sincere they are, this is not true. They believe that salvation is something they possess because of their baptism as an infant, even though there has been no changed heart and life by the power of the Holy Spirit. Perhaps as you read this, you find yourself in this condition. You are still out on the porch.

Secondly, **Realize That Faith In Jesus Christ Saves Us.**

Paul's message to these twelve men is summarized in Acts 19:4. *"Then Paul said, "John indeed baptized with a baptism of repentance, saying to the people that they should believe on Him who would come after him, that is, on Christ Jesus."* We ought not to assume that these are the only words that Paul said, but this is the essence of the message he gave to them. He was pointing out to them that they had not followed the message of John, the Baptist. His baptism was a baptism of repentance, preparing for the coming Messiah. John was telling the people to believe in the one coming after him, namely Jesus.

Here is an interesting side issue. The name "Joshua", or "Jeshua", and "Jesus" are the same name, only in different languages, both with the meaning "God is salvation". That is, the name "Jesus" is a Latinization of the Aramaic 'Jeshua' or 'Yeshua', which is in turn taken from the Hebrew 'Yehoshua', or 'Joshua'. In Hebrews 4:8, the writer of Hebrews makes the point that Joshua was not able to lead the people of Israel into a permanent rest. He teaches that the permanent future rest is for those who trust in Jesus and cease from their works, or cease from depending upon their works to enter heaven's rest. Hebrews 4:10. Note also that Moses, representing the Law of God, died on Mount Nebo and could not lead the people into the Promised Land. Joshua (God is salvation) was the new leader who would lead them across Jordan into the Promised Land. Jesus is the only One through whom we as believers in Him can find mercy and grace to enter the eternal rest.

Therefore don't miss Paul's message here in Acts 19. Again, he was clearly preaching that we are saved only through faith in Jesus Christ. These sincere seekers who were still on the porch, immediately responded to the truth about Jesus Christ, and are baptized into the name of the Lord Jesus.

Here is a case of people being baptized twice. Their first baptism, immersion in water, was a transitional baptism historically, a baptism of repentance showing their prepared hearts for the coming Messiah Savior. Now that they had heard the gospel of Christ, knew of His death and resurrection, His ascension and the subsequent coming of the Holy Spirit, they responded in faith and were immersed into the name of the Lord Jesus Christ. It is not their baptism that saved them but their faith in Christ that saved them. A. T. Robertson clearly explains, "Luke simply explains that now these men had a proper object of faith (Jesus) and now were really baptized. This baptism in water did not "convey" the Holy Spirit nor forgiveness of sins. Paul was not a sacra- mentalist."[85]

How about doing an examination of yourself and your standing with God? Are you truly saved? Have you repented of your sins and trusted Christ alone and His finished work of redemption on the cross of Calvary for your salvation? Until you have proper knowledge of the gospel (good news) of forgiveness of sins that has been purchased for us by Jesus Christ, God's Son, and until you have responded to turn to Christ and trust Him as the only Savior, you are not saved. Until then, no matter how sincere you are, you are still on the porch and are not on your way to heaven.

---

[85] A. T. Robertson, IBID, page 313.

It is also true that once you have trusted Christ as your Savior, you are commanded by Christ to be baptized (immersed)[86] as a proclamation of your identification with Christ in his death, burial and resurrection. Matthew 28:16-20. John Phillips writes, "They knew Jesus, but they only knew Jesus as preached by John. They obeyed the light they had and had been baptized by John. Now God gave them more light, and immediately they responded to that. In his conversation with them, Paul discovered at once that their knowledge of Christ was deficient. John's baptism pointed forward to the One who was coming; Christian baptism points back to the One who has come. John's baptism was linked to repentance. "I am repentant, therefore I submit to this baptism; it is the public expression of a personal expectation of the soon-coming Christ." Christian baptism is linked to regeneration. "I have been regenerated; therefore I submit to this baptism; it is the public expression of my personal experience of an indwelling Christ." . . . Moreover, John's water baptism pointed to a promised baptism of the Spirit - it predicted the day of Pentecost. Christian baptism points to a present baptism of the Spirit - it proclaims the day of Pentecost.

"John's baptism said, "There is going to be a change in the dispensations; the Holy Spirit is going to come into the world." Christian baptism not only demonstrates that has happened, it says, "There is a change in my disposition; the Holy Spirit has come into my heart." . . . (The person who is baptized) is publicly identified, by his baptism, with something far greater than his nationality; he is identified with the church. His baptism does not make him a Christian, but it proclaims him a Christian; it does not put him in the church, but it announces that he is in the church."[87]

This is a transliteration rather than a translation of the word. A literal translation of "baptizo" is "immerse or dip".

[87] John Phillips, Commentary on Acts, Moody Press, Chicago, IL, pages 150,151.

Now let's **Rest In The Reality of The Holy Spirit.**

There are many erroneous teachings and beliefs about the Holy Spirit that are present today that have led to confusion and also the disillusionment of many. The popular but false teaching in some quarters is that believers must ask God to give the Holy Spirit to them. The gift of the Spirit is one of the benefits bestowed upon a believer at the moment of his conversion. Romans 8:9 says, *". . . if anyone does not have the Spirit of Christ, he is not His."* Either one has the Holy Spirit, in which case he belongs to Christ and is saved, or else one does not have the Holy Spirit, in which case he is not saved.

"It is wrong to ask God to give us something He has already given to us. The baptism of the Spirit and the gift of the Spirit are inter-related. The baptism put me in Christ; the gift puts Christ in me. The one makes me a member of his mystical Body, the church; the other makes my material body the Holy Spirit's temple."[88] The heavenly Father already gave the Holy Spirit at Pentecost.)

Here are some **other unwarranted and false conclusions** from verse 6.

1) The laying on of hands by an apostle or a pastor is necessary to receive the Holy Spirit.

The laying on of hands is simply an endorsement by them and a warm expression of welcome into the family. It is mentioned infrequently in Scripture and in Acts 10, the Holy Spirit comes upon Cornelius and his family while Peter was still speaking. It is not by the power or authority of Peter or Paul or a pastor laying on his hands that the Spirit comes and regenerates us; it

---

[88]   John Phillips, IBID, page 149.

is the power of God sending His Holy Spirit into the life of the repentant believer that brings salvation.

2) Speaking in tongues and prophesying are the signs of the Holy Spirit's coming. This teaching says unless you speak in tongues and prophecy, you aren't baptized by the Spirit. I will not get deeply into this issue here. Let it be sufficient to point out that only three times in the book of Acts are 'tongues' mentioned. They are Acts 2 – the original coming of the Holy Spirit to indwell Jewish believers; Acts 10 – the expansion of the gospel to the Gentiles; and Acts 19 – this group of twelve disciples of John who had not yet heard of Christ's death and resurrection. These are all transitional phases of the expansion of the grace revolution. Therefore, to conclude that tongues speaking (other languages spoken in this world, or as some interpret, a heavenly angelic language) is a necessary sign of the baptism or filling of the Holy Spirit is a false conclusion.

These gifts of tongues (the ability to speak in another language without having learned that language) and prophecy (the receiving of God's message to the church) were necessary before the completion of the New Testament. I believe that the equivalent of the gift of prophecy today, now that we have the completed Scriptures, is the gift of preaching the word of God.

If you are saved, the Holy Spirit has come into your life, giving you the life of Christ in you. You have all of the Holy Spirit, so don't be asking for more of the Holy Spirit. Seek rather to be filled or controlled by the Holy Spirit. Ephesians 5:18-20. The filling of the Holy Spirit is not a matter of having more of the Holy Spirit but of the Holy Spirit having more (all) of you. If you are truly saved, the Holy Spirit is in your life and will bear witness with your spirit that indeed you are a child of God. Romans 8:16 assures us, *"The Spirit Himself bears witness with our spirit that we are children of God."*

Don't be seeking for the spectacular; rest in the presence and power of the Holy Spirit in your life. Seek to be under the control of the Holy Spirit and depend upon God, the Spirit, to produce the fruit of the Spirit in your life.

Are you still on the porch today? You have been sincere but you have not understood until today that trusting Jesus Christ is the only way to be saved. There is no other Savior but Christ Jesus! Receiving Jesus Christ as your personal Savior and Lord is the only way to enter the household of God and become a member of His redeemed family. Let Him come into your life and give you the Holy Spirit who will make you alive spiritually. Right now, He will forgive you for all your sin and the Spirit of God will come to live in you and will make you a redeemed child of God. From this moment on, you will be placed on the road to heaven. God will write your name in His Book of Life and you will be assured of a place in heaven. On Judgment Day, you will not be out on the porch and hear those awful words, "Depart from me, I never knew you!"

Jesus, I Come to Thee!
(Written and published by William J. Sleeper, 1887)

Out of my bondage, sorrow, and night,
Jesus, I come! Jesus, I come!
Into Thy freedom, gladness, and light,
Jesus, I come to Thee!
Out of my sickness into Thy health,
Out of my want and into Thy wealth,
Out of my sin and into Thyself,
Jesus, I come to Thee!

Out of my shameful failure and loss,
Jesus, I come! Jesus, I come!
Into the glorious gain of Thy cross,

Jesus, I come to Thee!
Out of earth's sorrows into Thy balm,
Out of life's storm and into Thy calm,
Out of distress to jubilant psalm,
Jesus, I come to Thee!

Out of unrest and arrogant pride,
Jesus, I come! Jesus, I come!
Into Thy blessed will to abide,
Jesus, I come to Thee!
Out of myself to dwell in Thy love,
Out of despair into raptures above,
Upward for aye on wings like a dove,
Jesus, I come to Thee!

Out of the fear and dread of the tomb,
Jesus, I come! Jesus, I come!
Into the joy and pleasure, Thine own,
Jesus, I come to Thee!
Out of the depths of ruin untold,
Into the flock Thy love doth enfold,
Ever Thy glorious face to behold,
Jesus, I come to Thee!

Chapter 23
Avoiding Religious Hocus Pocus!
Acts 19:8-20

Hank Hanegraaff tells about a letter "of personal testimony" he received from a woman who had been blind from birth. After coming to faith in Christ, she joined a church that had been infiltrated by the Faith movement. It wasn't long before they were instructing her to confess perfect sight and commanding God to honor His word.

When nothing happened, they began to denounce this woman for her lack of faith. They told her that there was "something in my life that hindered God's will," she wrote. "God", they said, "was held up because of some point of sin or disobedience that He just couldn't get around until I straightened up."

This dear lady writes, "I spent hours, sleepless nights, agonizing over the issue. I became depressed and began to lose my joy. I even quit praying. Some Sundays I simply couldn't stand church because I felt like an outsider in God's family, watching his pet children get 'blessed' because of their `faith.

Finally she was properly instructed in the word of God, and was delivered from this kind of hocus pocus Christianity.[89]

I realize that I am now tampering with a national icon in some people's minds, but some things that Pat Robertson teaches on the 700 Club are in the same category. "Poverty is a curse," Pat Robertson states. He goes on to say that one cause of poverty is "a lack of knowledge of God's principles of blessing." After all, the Laws of Miracles work as predictably as the Law of

---

[89] Hank Hanegraaff, Christianity in Crisis, Harvest House Publishers, Irvine, CA, 1993, page 261.

Gravitation or any other natural law. Although he denies a "mind over matter" philosophy, Robertson argues that positive confessions are "the master key to miracles": "Do not ask the storm to stop. Tell it to stop!! . . . There cannot be doubt in the inner man in the heart . . . you know without question the storm is going to be stopped. You know the finances are going to be provided . . . Begin to possess it."[90]

Kenneth Copeland says, "When are we all going to wake up and learn God didn't allow the Devil to get on Job. Job allowed the Devil to get on Job. . . All God did was maintain His confession of faith about that man. He said, 'that man is upright in the earth.' But Job said he was not upright in the earth. He said, 'I'm miserable. My tongue is disobedient.'" . . . Benny Hinn calls Job a "carnal bad boy" and Fred Price calls him a "Big Mouth".[91]

Much of what flies under the name of Christianity today is a far cry from it! The television evangelists who practice their "snake oil" remedies and promise God's prosperity and power in response to your generous donations for the ministry are numerous.

But it is not new, is it? Paul faced it at Ephesus as many sought to emulate God's power without knowing or submitting to Jesus Christ. So let's heed the warnings that surface as we examine this passage of Scripture.

First there is **A Warning Against Hardening Your Heart. Acts 19:8-10.**

---

[90] Pat Robertson, quoted by Michael S. Horton, Beyond Culture Wars, Is America a Mission Field or Battlefield? Moody Press, Chicago, IL, page 192.

[91] Kenneth Copeland – as quoted by Hank Hanegraaff, Christianity in Crisis, IBID p. 263.

Paul went to the synagogue at Ephesus and for three months *"spoke boldly for three month reasoning and persuading concerning the things of the kingdom of God."* Verse 8. Verse 9 says *"some were hardened and did not believe, but spoke evil of the Way before the multitude . . ."* The word *'hardened'* in the NKJV is translated by the NIV with the word *"obstinate"*. It means 'hard, rough or harsh; calloused'. It is the same word used in Romans 9:18, speaking of Pharaoh; and in Hebrews 3:8, describing Israel. Hebrews 3:8 says, *". . . do not harden your hearts as in the rebellion, in the day of trial in the wilderness . . ."*

They began to get nasty in their references to the gospel they were hearing. 'The kingdom of God' was his message which is a message that revolves around the King. Verse 8. Paul was proclaiming that this Jesus was indeed the Christ and that he is the King, the Lord.

As you study the Scriptures, John 3 for example, you see that in order to enter the kingdom of God, you must be born again. The unbelieving, hard-hearted Jews in the synagogue at Ephesus *"spoke evil of the Way before the multitude"*, (verse 9) as they referred to Christianity, because Paul was declaring that Jesus indeed is the only way to heaven and to the Father.

Paul does not stay there when the Jews begin to get abusive but removes himself and those who had come to believe and for two years he teaches in the lecture hall of Tyrannus, which means 'the tyrant'. 'Tyrant' - what a name for a teacher! Paul taught for probably three hours every day with the result reported in Acts 19:10. *"And this continued for two years, so that all who dwelt in Asia heard the word of the Lord Jesus, both Jews and Greeks."*

Jesus told his disciples not to cast their pearls before swine. In his instructions to the twelve as they were sent out to preach the kingdom of God to the Jews, Jesus told them, *"And whoever will not receive you nor hear your words, when you depart from that house or city, shake off the dust from your feet. Assuredly, I say to you, it will be more tolerable for the land of Sodom and Gomorrah in the day of judgment than for that city!"* Matthew 10:14-15.

Here is our warning! There is great danger in hardening your heart and becoming increasingly calloused to God's message of salvation. You eventually begin to develop a cynicism and you are in danger of refusing to believe. There is the danger also that God will move His messengers on to others and you will no longer hear the offer of salvation.

Secondly there is **A Warning Against Religious Chicanery. Acts 19:11-12.**

Now we come to the only place in the Bible where handkerchiefs and aprons were taken from Paul and given to sick people and demon possessed people and they were healed. Today we have these television healers, many of whom have been proven by investigative reporters to be frauds, who send out their anointed prayer cloths and their bottles of anointing oil that has been blessed with healing power by the evangelist, all for a generous donation to their ministry. They are like 'snake-oil salesmen' who offer some scam 'witch-craft- like' healing to the unsuspecting and vulnerable.

However, we need to deal with the question, "How should we interpret this Scripture?"

First, we need to understand these items that are mentioned which brought healing to sick people. The word for "handkerchiefs" refers to "sweat cloths" used to wipe away the perspiration and dirt as he worked in his trade, and the "aprons" were the work aprons worn by Paul in his tent making work.[92] They were not some patches of material prepared by Paul and prayed over and dispatched to the sick for healing. Some treated Peter in a similar way. Acts 5:15. *". . . they brought the sick out into the streets and laid them on beds and couches, that at least the shadow of Peter passing by might fall on some of them."* While God healed some people through these methods, this fact does not mean that this should be a prescription for today. In other words, we should not conclude that because God worked this way once, He wants us to emulate this practice forever.

Paul did not initiate this magical practice. This is something that probably was done by new believers who were still entangled in the magical, superstitious culture of Ephesus. Nevertheless, God was healing people through this practice, according to verse 12. Charles John Ellicott and other scholars intimate that this occurrence of healing through these aprons and sweat-cloths belonging to Paul were God's way of saying to these people of Ephesus that were following satanically controlled practitioners of witchcraft like the seven sons of Sceva, "God's power to heal is in the person of Jesus Christ, whom Paul preaches." God was authenticating His truth

---

[92] Handkerchiefs -The word used here σουδάρια, 'soudariais' of Latin origin, and properly denotes "a piece of linen" with which sweat was wiped from the face; and then "any piece of linen used for tying up or containing anything." In Luke 19:20, it denotes the "napkin" in which the talent of the unprofitable servant was concealed; in John 11:44; John 20:7, the "napkin" which was used to bind up the face of the dead applied to Lazarus and to our Savior.
Or aprons - 'simikinthia' - This is also a Latin word, and means literally a half girdle, or covering half the person a piece of cloth which was girded round the waist to preserve the clothes of those who were engaged in any kind of work. The word "aprons" expresses the idea. Barnes, Albert. "Commentary on Acts 19:12". "Barnes' Notes on the Whole Bible".
https:https://www.studylight.org/commentaries/bnb/acts-19.html. 1870.

preached by His servant, Paul.[93] The Jameison-Faussett-Brown Commentary observes, "So that from his body were brought unto the sick handkerchiefs or aprons, etc. - Compare Acts 5:15, Acts 5:16, very different from the magical acts practiced at Ephesus. "God wrought these miracles" merely "by the hands of Paul"; and the very exorcists (Acts 19:13), observing that the name of Jesus was the secret of all his miracles, hoped, by aping him in this, to be equally successful; while the result of all in the "magnifying of the Lord Jesus" (Acts 19:17) showed that in working them the apostle took care to hold up Him whom he preached as the source of all the miracles which he wrought."[94]

The seven sons of Sceva were Jews, sons of a '*Jewish chief priest*', (verse 14) who were practicing sorcery, seeking to drive out evil spirits by use of some magical mantra. Verse 13 mentions other exorcists who also "*. . . took it upon themselves to call the name of the Lord Jesus over those who had evil spirits, saying, "We exorcise you by the Jesus whom Paul preaches."* This practice is strictly forbidden by God in Moses's writings. These people saw the power of Paul to bring healing and so they sought to profit from this new power as Satan's servants.

This incident of healing in this way by God, through His servant Paul is similar to Moses' performance of miracles before Pharaoh. Some of the miracles that Moses did, such as throwing down his staff and it became a snake, were duplicated by the magicians of Egypt, who were operating

---

[93] "It was something for them to learn that the prayer of faith and the handkerchief that had touched the Apostle's skin had a greater power to heal than the charms in which they had previously trusted." Ellicott, Charles John. "Commentary on Acts 19:12". "Ellicott's Commentary for English Readers".
[94] Jamieson, Robert, D.D.; Faussett, A. R.; Brown, David. "Commentary on Acts 19:12"

through satanic power. However, Moses's snake swallowed up their snakes, indicating that Jehovah alone was the true God.

God did many "extraordinary miracles" through Paul. It was necessary, as the word of God was being finalized to authenticate his primary messengers, Peter and Paul, through miracles that God worked through them. The Zondervan Topical Study Bible says, "The mission story of Acts revolves around two missionaries, Peter and Paul. Perhaps because Paul was a controversial figure in the early church, Luke recorded an amazing number of parallel events involving both Peter and Paul, demonstrating that they were of equal status and importance."[95]

This article then proceeds to outline the very similar record that Luke has included about Peter and Paul. By definition, miracles are unusual, extraordinary occurrences. There are three major periods of time in biblical history when miracles abound. 1) Moses and the Exodus and the entrance to Promised Land; 2) Elijah and Elisha – the time of the kingdom crisis in Israel and Judah; 3) The time of incarnation of the Messiah and early formation of the church, and the finalization of the Scriptures. As Michael Horton says, "Miracles cannot be "expected" or "demanded", for they are by definition divine surprises. A miracle astonishes, as Simon Peter was astonished. A miracle contradicts laws of nature as well as our expectations of the way things should happen, rather than conforming to them. Nothing makes a miracle happen but the sovereign will of a loving heavenly Father. He may use our prayers, but there is absolutely no causal necessity involved."[96]

---

95 The Zondervan Topical Study Bible, page 1225.
96 Michael S. Horton, Beyond Culture Wars, Is America a Mission Field or Battlefield? Moody Press, Chicago, IL, page 192.

Next we consider **A Warning Against Seeking Power Substitutes. Acts 19:13-16.**

The sons of Sceva aren't interested in knowing Jesus, but they are interested in possessing power. Other itinerant Jewish exorcists also did this according to verse 13, and apparently with some success. So they continue their sorcery but they sought to use the name of Jesus, whom Paul preached, to drive out demons.

One day, one of the demons, speaks (verse 15) and the man who had the evil spirit beats them up and literally *"masters them"*, ("overpowered them" – NKJV, NIV) and they ran away naked and bleeding. As Charles Swindoll says, ". . . even demons knew a cheap imitation when they saw one - or seven of them in this case."[97]

There are lots of people who want what Jesus can give them but they don't want Jesus. They see God as existing to serve their needs rather than them existing to glorify God. They seek to use God as their own personal errand-boy!

But, you ask, "Isn't God interested in our needs?" Certainly, for He knows what we have need of even before we ask Him. The main issue for God is to rescue us from our sin and our self- centeredness. It is the issue of the kingdom of God. Who will reign over us?

Secularism has invaded so much of what is called Christianity today. Commenting on the Lord's Prayer, Michael Horton says, "Heaven and earth have never been so separated in our minds. What we consider practical is not the study of God, but the study of how we can be happier and more fulfilled, and

---

[97] Charles Swindoll, Commentary on Acts, Volume 2, page 31.

even our moral campaigns are pitched in self-fulfillment, instead of justice and duty. But here, Jesus insists that we be chiefly concerned with the glory of God and the holiness of His name and only secondarily concerned about our own needs, whether real or felt."[98]

Don't seek to know power, seek to know God. Don't seek prosperity, seek to allow Jesus Christ to reign supremely in your life.

Now let's note **A Warning Against Worldly Concessions. Acts 19:17-20.**

"This became known both to all Jews and Greeks dwelling in Ephesus; and fear fell on them all, and the name of the Lord Jesus was magnified." Verse 17.

Some became believers and they held a million dollar bonfire as they brought their sorcery scrolls and got rid of them.

Many Christians today are still making concessions to the world. G. Campbell Morgan wrote, "That sacrificial fire - that burning of the books of magic (sorcery) was not the burning of books belonging to the Ephesians still remaining in idolatry. They were books belonging to the people in the church."[99]

We make concessions to the old nature, or make provision for the old nature to continue to thrive. When we as believers get serious about 'burning' our connections with the world that we so dearly hold onto, then the results will be as they were in Ephesus and the region around. Acts 19:20 says, *"So the word of the Lord grew mightily and prevailed."*

---

98 Michael Horton, Beyond Culture Wars, Is America a Mission Field or Battlefield? Moody Press, Chicago, IL, page 188 .
99 G. Campbell Morgan, IBID, p. 456.

How about those books, magazines, pornographic or borderline, which are stored away or openly displayed in the homes of professing believers? Videos, movies, R-rated or not, that distort or destroy our moral values and fuel the sinful old-nature desires, must be avoided like the plague. The tapes of secular music that comes from the lips of people who are opposed to what Jesus teaches us, both in their life style and in their lyrics must not feed our minds.

How about having a bonfire for books of false teachers with whom you have been intrigued that keep drawing you away to seeking power instead of Providence; that keep you searching for prosperity instead of serving and trusting God, the Provider? Wherever we make a concession to the world, we contaminate our relationship with our Lord and Savior, Jesus Christ and destroy our witness to a watching world.

I heard on a news report in 1996 that as high as 30% of abortions in America are performed on women who profess to be born again. I don't know the recent stats. There is often a big gap between what we profess to believe and our practice.

What bonfire is the Lord asking you to light, either literally in burning of books and CD's, but also figuratively in forsaking some evil practice? How about disciplining ourselves in what we allow ourselves to watch in the movies and on the TV? Let's not just hear the warnings but heed them in taking some kind of obedient action as the Holy Spirit prods each of us.

Larry Crabb in his book, 'Inside Out' says "We as Christians need to "live life more honestly". The pathway to change is more often discussed and debated than displayed. . . . The more deeply we sense our thirst, the more passionately we'll pursue water. And the more clearly we recognize how we dig our own wells in search of water, the more fully we can repent of our self-sufficiency and turn to God in obedient trust."[100] We need to focus in on our relationship with God, knowing Him more intimately, loving Him more passionately and then serving him more purely.

Higher Ground!
(Written by Johnson Oatman, Jr., 1898)

I'm pressing on the upward way,
New heights I'm gaining every day;
Still praying as I'm onward bound,
"Lord, plant my feet on higher ground."

(Refrain)
Lord, lift me up and let me stand,
By faith, on Heaven's tableland,
A higher plane than I have found;
Lord, plant my feet on higher ground.

My heart has no desire to stay
Where doubts arise and fears dismay;
Though some may dwell where those abound,
My prayer, my aim, is higher ground.

I want to live above the world,
Though Satan's darts at me are hurled;
For faith has caught the joyful sound,
The song of saints on higher ground.

I want to scale the utmost height
And catch a gleam of glory bright;
But still I'll pray till heav'n I've found,
"Lord, plant my feet on higher ground."

---

[100] Larry Crabb, Inside Out, Nav Press, pages 202,219-220.

Chapter 24
Stepping Out of the Limelight!
Acts 18:18-23

Humility is difficult to achieve. When you think you have attained it, it is a sure sign you have lost it. You've heard the story about the book "Humility and How I Attained It!" In promoting it, the author wrote, "The first 38 chapters are about me; and the last chapter is how you can be like me!" Just in case you didn't get it, that is a fictitious story.

I recall the story of the Dominican monk who said that, "The Jesuits are known for their learning, and the Franciscans for their piety and good works, but when it comes to humility, we're tops!"

Paul was a leader who stepped into many situations and served the Lord with enthusiasm and vigor. Most of the time, we see Paul as a "Take charge and let's get it done" kind of person. He was task-oriented. When he split with Barnabas over the matter of allowing John Mark, the deserter, to accompany them on the second missionary journey, Paul was deeply concerned that he might desert them again and interfere with their success in extending the gospel outreach.

However Paul was also a humble servant who knew how to step aside and allow others to serve the Lord. Paul knew that he was appointed by the Lord as an apostle and he exercised his authority in fulfilling God's will. However, he was always deeply aware of his unworthiness and that he was saved and called to preach the gospel through the grace and mercy of God. He never forgot from whence he had come. He was a persecutor of the church and had been instrumental in the death of some of the Lord's redeemed people. He certainly had a checkered past and that had made the followers of Jesus suspicious and wary of him.

Paul exemplifies the truth taught by our Lord that greatness comes in being the servant of all. In Mark 10:35-45, James and John, the sons of Zebedee, are seeking places of prominence in the Lord's kingdom. They requested that one could sit on the Lord's right hand, and the other on His left, when He would come in His glory. Jesus teaches them what greatness is all about in verses 42-45. *"But Jesus called them to Himself and said to them, "You know that those who are considered rulers over the Gentiles lord it over them, and their great ones exercise authority over them. Yet it shall not be so among you; but whoever desires to become great among you shall be your servant. And whoever of you desires to be first shall be slave of all. For even the Son of Man did not come to be served, but to serve, and to give His life a ransom for many."*

Let's take a look at several examples of Paul's humility and servanthood.

First of all, **Paul Practiced Personal Integrity. Acts 18:18.**

For some unknown reason Paul had taken a vow during his time of ministry at Corinth. We do not know the reason, but commentators speculate about it. Was it a Nazarite vow as outlined in Numbers 6:1-21?

John Stott and many others conclude that it probably was a Nazarite vow. John Stott comments, "The reference to his hair makes it almost certain that it was a Nazarite vow, which involved abstinence from drinking wine and from cutting one's hair, at the end the hair was first cut and then burned, along with other sacrifices, as a symbol of self-offering to God."[101]

---

101 John Stott, The Spirit, The Church and the World: The Message of Acts, Inter-Varsity Press, pages 300-301.

The old Jamieson, Fausset and Brown commentary disagrees, claiming it was not likely a Nazarite vow. "That it was the Nazarite vow (Numbers 6:1-27) is not likely. It was probably one made in one of his seasons of difficulty or danger, in prosecution of which he cuts off his hair and hastens to Jerusalem to offer the requisite sacrifice within the prescribed thirty days [Josephus, Wars of the Jews, 2.15.1]. This explains the haste with which he leaves Ephesus (Acts 18:21), and the subsequent observance, on the recommendation of the brethren, of a similar vow (Acts 21:24). This one at Corinth was voluntary, and shows that even in heathen countries he systematically studied the prejudices of his Jewish brethren."[102]

John Phillips suggests three possible reasons for the vow. 1) "Perhaps it was Paul's way of becoming more effective with the Jews in reaching them with the gospel. 2) Or perhaps it was a way of showing the Lord how desirous he was of being used by God in the Jewish community there. 3) Or perhaps it was just a voluntary self-discipline imposed to deepen his spiritual commitment."[103]

It is most likely that Paul's motive for his vow was connected with an accusation which the Jews had made toward Paul. Although the Bible doesn't say why he chose to follow the Jewish practice for this particular vow, I think it is a reasonable assumption that it had something to do with Paul's desire to be a witness to the unbelieving Jews. We know that his destination at this point was to be in Jerusalem for a certain feast. Acts 18:21. In Acts 21:20-21, Paul had arrived in Jerusalem and had reported to James and the elders on the

---

[102] Jamieson, Robert, D.D.; Fausset, A. R.; Brown, David. "Commentary on Acts 18:18". "Commentary Critical and Explanatory on the Whole Bible".
[103] John Phillips, Commentary on Acts, Moody Press, Chicago, IL

results of his preaching the gospel to the Gentiles causing great rejoicing. But there was an issue with Paul amongst the Jewish believers who still had great respect for Moses and the law. The elders in the Jerusalem church said to him, *"You see, brother, how many myriads of Jews there are who have believed, and they are all zealous for the law; but they have been informed about you that you teach all the Jews who are among the Gentiles to forsake Moses, saying that they ought not to circumcise their children nor to walk according to the customs."*

James and elders of the church in Jerusalem then give Paul advice to seek to refute their accusations. Now that he had reached Jerusalem, they advised him to take another vow of purification to demonstrate that he was not guilty, as they had charged, of despising Moses and the Law. Acts 21:22-26. *"What then? The assembly must certainly meet, for they will hear that you have come. Therefore do what we tell you: We have four men who have taken a vow. Take them and be purified with them, and pay their expenses so that they may shave their heads, and that all may know that those things of which they were informed concerning you are nothing, but that you yourself also walk orderly and keep the law. But concerning the Gentiles who believe, we have written and decided that they should observe no such thing, except that they should keep themselves from things offered to idols, from blood, from things strangled, and from sexual immorality."* *Then Paul took the men, and the next day, having been purified with them, entered the temple to announce the expiration of the days of purification, at which time an offering should be made for each one of them."*

Paul maintained his integrity in seeking to reach both Jews and Gentiles. He refused to bend whenever the keeping of the Mosaic Law was held to be an essential for salvation. This was the issue at the Council in Jerusalem in Acts 15.

However, whenever he could, he would submit to the practice of the Jews if it did not compromise the gospel of grace. Paul had the Gentile, Timothy, circumcised when he accompanied Paul to Jerusalem, so that this would not be a stumbling block to the Jews. Timothy was not circumcised as a necessary additional requirement for his salvation. Rather, he was circumcised so he would not be a stumbling block to the Jews.

Paul took these vows in order to seek to reach his Jewish audience. In 1 Corinthians 9:19-21, Paul lays out this principle of his evangelistic outreach. *"For though I am free from all men, I have made myself a servant to all, that I might win the more; and to the Jews I became as a Jew, that I might win Jews; to those who are under the law, as under the law, that I might win those who are under the law; to those who are without law, as without law (not being without law toward God, but under law toward Christ), that I might win those who are without law; . . ."[104]*

John G. Butler expressed his opinion that the elders in the church in Jerusalem were negligent in their duty to resist the Jewish believers who still insisted on following the Mosaic law. "This zeal should have been rebuked instead of respected by the church leaders in Jerusalem. Law and grace do not mix (Galatians 3:11-12). When the substance (Christ) has come, there is no need for the shadow (law observance)."[105] This weakness of leadership by the elders in Jerusalem appears to lead to the ensuing trouble for Paul, leading to his arrest and trial before Festus and King Agrippa.

---

[104] For further study of this topic, refer to Romans 14, where Paul deals with the principles of questionable things, and the avoidance of being a stumbling block to others.

[105] John G. Butler, Analytical Bible Expositor, Volume 12, LCB Publications, Clinton, Iowa, 2009, page261.

Whatever the reason, why does Luke mention Paul's visit to a small town barbershop? Acts 18:18. It wasn't because his hair was touching his collar or covering his ears and the code of the Christians was men had to have their hair short. It is clear that Paul was concerned about his personal integrity. When you make a vow, do not fail to keep it. Ecclesiastes 5:4-5 says, *"When you make a vow to God, do not delay to pay it; For He has no pleasure in fools. Pay what you have vowed - Better not to vow than to vow and not pay."*

Humble servanthood stands first and foremost upon personal integrity. Do you keep your word? Do you faithfully discharge your duties as you have vowed to do? As you maintain your integrity, do you do your utmost to reach all people with the gospel?

Secondly **Paul Promoted His Co-Workers. Acts 18:18-26.**

Paul took Priscilla and Aquila along with him as he left Corinth and went to Ephesus. Paul left Priscilla and Aquila at Ephesus to minister to the growing church there. It seems that Paul gets out of their way so that he would not be interfering with them in their ministry. Paul goes off to the synagogue to carry on his ministry with the Jews. Then verses 20-21 tell us that, even though they begged him to stay a longer time, he did not consent, but he left Ephesus. Paul's publicly stated reason for not staying on in Ephesus was that he wanted to get to the up-coming feast in Jerusalem. However, I think that he was aware that these two capable Bible teachers were there in Ephesus and he did not want to overshadow their work of equipping the saints.

Priscilla and Aquila are also a wonderful example of promoting your co-workers as they work with Apollos. Acts 18:24-26. *"Now a certain Jew named Apollos, born at Alexandria, an eloquent man and mighty in the Scriptures, came to Ephesus. This man had been instructed in the way of the Lord; and being fervent in spirit, he spoke and taught accurately the things of the Lord, though he knew only the baptism of John. So he began to speak boldly in the synagogue. When Aquila and Priscilla heard him, they took him aside and explained to him the way of God more accurately."* Aquila and Priscilla, this husband-wife team of the Lord's servants, do not put Apollos down in public by telling him that his understanding of theology is deficient. They take him to their home and there they instruct him more adequately in the things of God. Verse 26.

There are times when a pastor must lead, and not to do so is to shirk his responsibility. But there are also times when he must let others minister as he is equipping them for ministry. The Lord's work is carried on by many servants doing their jobs well within the body.

I don't know how well that I have learned to do this yet, but my philosophy with my co-workers is that I want to do everything possible to see that each one is as effective and as successful as he or she can be in serving the Lord.

When you help someone come up with a good idea or a good ministry plan, and he or she goes ahead with it, can you resist saying, "Well, that really was my idea!" Our goal must not be to advance ourselves, but to always humbly advance Jesus Christ and His kingdom through equipping others to do the work of the ministry. Why should it matter who gets the credit?

1 Corinthians 3:1-9 teaches this principle. *"And I, brethren, could not speak to you as to spiritual people but as to carnal, as to babes in Christ. I fed you with milk and not with solid food; for until now you were not able to receive it, and even now you are still not able; for you are still carnal. For where*

there are envy, strife, and divisions among you, are you not carnal and behaving like mere men? For when one says, "I am of Paul," and another, "I am of Apollos," are you not carnal? Who then is Paul, and who is Apollos, but ministers through whom you believed, as the Lord gave to each one? I planted, Apollos watered, but God gave the increase. So then neither he who plants is anything, nor he who waters, but God who gives the increase. Now he who plants and he who waters are one, and each one will receive his own reward according to his own labor. For we are God's fellow workers; you are God's field, you are God's building."

Next we see that Paul Resisted Popular Appeal. Acts 18:19b-20.

Paul came into Ephesus, accompanied by Priscilla and Aquila. Paul has been starting churches in many places as he has journeyed for several years now, preaching the gospel to Jews and Gentiles. He, by this time, had become well known in the churches and was no doubt regarded by many as the "superstar" of the early church.

As he came to Ephesus, he could have come, expecting to take over the ministry there and expecting Priscilla and Aquila to just move aside. But it seems that Paul decided to let them have a ministry there in Ephesus, and he moved on to minister for a while in the synagogue. Then he left to return to Caesarea and Antioch. Charles Swindoll comments, "Paul was not showy or slick, putting himself on a pedestal. Instead he was like an unobtrusive support column, always there holding others up."[106]

If we are to serve the Lord effectively, we do not respond only to the popular appeal of others. We don't need the acclamation

---

[106] Charles Swindoll, Commentary on Acts, Volume 3, page 14.

of others in order to be faithful in our service. Some believers quit serving because they say, "Nobody even noticed what I did! Maybe they'll notice if I don't do my job anymore!" The fact that we need approval means that our motives for serving are suspect. The only thing that really matters is that the Lord sees our work and He also knows our motives for which we do our work.

Further, **Paul Served Regardless Of Prominence. Acts 18:19-21.**

It is important to recognize that serving the Lord can deteriorate into mere performance of duty. We can fall into the trap of doing our work for the Lord in order to be seen of men or in order to be well thought of by others. Oswald Chambers once wrote, "Christian service is not our work; loyalty to Jesus is our work."[107] Charles Swindoll says, ". . . we can build houses for the poor, visit the sick, or comfort the grieving, but if we do so without an inner, driving loyalty to Jesus, we are performing, not serving."[108]

Humble service is being willing to faithfully do our work for the Lord without needing to be recognized or acknowledged by others. In fact it is the time of popularity and praise that becomes a danger to us. Proverbs 27:21 (NIV) tells us, *"The crucible for silver and the furnace for gold, but man is tested by the praise he receives."*

Humble service is not saying, "I am nothing and I can do nothing." Rather, it is recognizing that God has gifted each one of us in certain ways and therefore each of us must use our gifts to serve each other and to glorify the Lord.

---

[107] Oswald Chambers, The Best from All His Books, page 319.
[108] Chuck Swindoll, Commentary on Acts, Volume 3, page 17.

Lindsay Brown, president of International Fellowship of Evangelical Students, shared this account of mission activity in South America. A small group of IFES Christians at a South American university were intent on serving the Lord by serving the university. They met with the president of the university, asking him to please tell them what they could do to help the university and him. After thinking for a moment, the president replied, "You know, we have a difficult time keeping the toilets on campus clean. You could clean the toilets for us."

A little taken aback, but still determined, the Christian students took up the challenge. From then on, those campus toilets sparkled! The squeaky clean bathrooms also brought these Christian students opportunities to witness for Christ to amazed fellow-students. In fact, the president was so thrilled by their service that he insisted on every faculty member coming to view the students' careful work.

The upshot? The president ended up assigning the professors at his university a new task: to join the students in cleaning the toilets. In the course of the clean-up, the Christians were able to engage these professors in conversations centering on Christ. The IFES students rejoiced that through their humble service to the university, they've been able to tell both students and now professors the Good News of Jesus Christ.[109]

Howard Snyder writes, "We depend on our structures and our superstars. And we know the system works - just look what the superstars are doing in their super churches! We have the statistics and the buildings and the budgets to prove it. There is only one problem. There are not enough superstars to go around. Thousands of churches and only hundreds of

---

[109] Lindsay Brown, president of International Fellowship of Evangelical Students, Newsletter in June of 1996.

superstars. The church of Jesus Christ cannot run on superstars, and God never intended that it should. God does not promise the church an affluence of superstars. But he does promise to provide the necessary leadership through the gifts of the Spirit. Ephesians 4:1-16."[110]

The apostle Paul, inspired by the Holy Spirit, talks about the gifts of the Spirit and illustrates them by the human body. Just as there are many parts to the body, there are many gifts given to the body of Christ. Some parts are more prominent than others and get lots of attention and are noticed. But all parts are essential and needed. All parts are of the body are to serve each other and to honor each other, so that *"there should be no schism in the body, but that the members should have the same care for one another." 1 Corinthians 12:25.* The body will be unified and of honor to the head, Jesus Christ, as each believer gets involved and serves where he or she can, with the gifts that the Holy Spirit has given each one.

We have a bathroom scale that has a coin shaped battery in it. The scale is made up of many parts skillfully designed to give an accurate weight. We have had that scale for a couple of decades and it has always functioned well. However, the other day, I got on the scale and nothing showed on the read-out screen. The battery had died and I had to purchase and install a new battery before the scale was of any good. The church of Jesus Christ is like that scale. All of us are placed in the body of Christ with appropriate gifts, assigned by the Designer of the church. However, the absolute essential to make the church function in unity and harmony is the battery – the Holy Spirit. Each of us must be drawing our power from the indwelling Holy Spirit in order for each of us to fulfill our purpose in the body.

---

[110] Howard Snyder, The Problem of Wineskins, Church Structure in a Technological Age, IVP, 1975, pages 83-84.

I think about some of the behind the scenes, less noticed people, who have been key servants in the body of Christ. I think of Laverne, a single lady in a former church, who was faithful in cleaning the church kitchen every other Saturday, mostly unnoticed by others. I think of Keith, a life-time janitor at Bethel College in St. Paul, Minnesota, who would always be joyfully doing his job. He always had a smile and a greeting for student or professor alike. So liked was he that one year the student body dedicated their yearbook to him. I think of Pat who taught and loved on the two's and three's Sunday school class for probably three decades or more. One of my daughters, Cyndi, became her assistant and took over when Pat was no longer able to continue her role. On and on, I could go, in mentioning these unsung gems in the churches.

The role of apostles, prophets, evangelists and pastor/teachers is to be *"equipping the saints for the work of the ministry. For the edifying of the body of Christ . . . from which the whole body, joined and knit together by what every joint supplies, according to the effective working by which every part does its share, causes growth of the body for the edifying of itself in love."* Ephesians 4:11-16. So, may I encourage you, if you are in a leadership ministry in your church, follow the example of the apostle Paul, who equipped others to lead these new churches formed as a result of the grace revolution. Others were appointed as pastor/elders in order to equip the saints and to enable them to serve and use their gifts under the power of the Holy Spirit. Pastor, remember that you are there to equip the Lord's flock to do the work of the ministry with you. Don't succumb to doing everything yourself. Get everyone involved in serving the Lord with joy and gladness.

The Family of God!
(Written and published by William and Gloria Gaither)

You will notice we say "brother
And sister" 'round here-
It's because we're a family
And these folks are so near;
When one has a heartache
We all share the tears,
And rejoice in each victory
In this family so dear.

(Refrain)
I'm so glad I'm a part
Of the family of God-
I've been washed in the fountain,
Cleansed by His blood!
Joint heirs with Jesus
As we travel this sod,
For I'm part of the family,
The family of God.

From the door of an orphanage
To the house of the King-
No longer an outcast,
A new song I sing;
From rags unto riches,
From the weak to the strong,
I'm not worthy to be here,
But, praise God, I belong!

(Repeat Refrain)

Chapter 25
Beware Of Dozing Off In Church!
Acts 20:1-16

Sleeping in church can be embarrassing. When I was still in Seminary, I pastored a small church in Elk River, Minnesota. A deacon who was a farmer would sit at the back of the church on a chair, put his head back against the wall and often go to sleep. To be fair to him, he would have been up by four in the morning, to milk the cows in his dairy herd. It was warm in the church building and he could not stay awake. One Sunday, another deacon had to wake him when it was time to come and assist with the Lord's Supper.

A little boy went to church with his grandparents. His grandmother sat in the choir. It really disturbed her to see his grandfather nod off to sleep every Sunday in the middle of the sermon. Finally, she decided on a plan. She gave her little grandson fifty cents each Sunday morning to poke grandpa in the ribs whenever he fell asleep. This plan worked until Easter Sunday morning. The church was packed. Grandmother was sitting in the choir. She noticed grandfather nodding off. However, Tommy made no effort to wake him. Grandfather even started snoring right there in the crowded Easter service. Still Tommy did nothing. After the service grandmother was quite disturbed. She said, "Tommy what happened? You knew I would pay you fifty cents after the service if you kept grandfather awake." Tommy said, "Yes grandma, but grandpa offered me a dollar if I would let him sleep."

But sleeping in church can also be hazardous. Young Eutychus dozed off during Paul's long sermon. He fell from the third floor window ledge where he was sitting and was killed, but he was raised to life again. He is a symbol of us as believers who tend to doze off in life, not just during a sermon.

Paul, writing his letter to the Romans, speaks to our problem when he tells us to wake up from our slumbering. Romans 13:11-14. *"And do this, knowing the time, that now it is high time to awake out of sleep; for now our salvation is nearer than when we first believed. The night is far spent, the day is at hand. Therefore let us cast off the works of darkness, and let us put on the armor of light. Let us walk properly, as in the day, not in revelry and drunkenness, not in lewdness and lust, not in strife and envy. But put on the Lord Jesus Christ, and make no provision for the flesh, to fulfill its lusts."*

As believers, we need to **Wake Up to the Enemy's Traps. Acts 20:1-6.**

When we as believers in Christ are actively seeking to serve the Lord and to share the good news of Christ, we can expect Satan to do everything possible to defeat our lives and our efforts.

Verse 1 says, *"After the uproar had ceased. . ."* In chapter 19, a horrendous public riot had happened in Ephesus when Demetrius, the silversmith, stirred up his fellow-tradesmen and the public over the job loss and the economic loss resulting from this new "Way" preached by Paul. So another attack by the enemy is thwarted. But don't relax when one victory is won; another wave of Satanic attacks will not be far behind. Believers must always stay alert!

a. His plot to destroy. Verse 3.

Satan is the destroyer, and we see him coming at Paul again in Verse 3. Paul had journeyed again through Macedonia, visiting and encouraging the churches, for probably close to a year. Then he spent three months in Greece. By the way, it is during these three months that Paul wrote his letter to the Romans, most likely in A.D. 57.

Paul's plan was to sail from Greece to Syria, and then make his way to Jerusalem, hoping to reach there by Pentecost. Verse 16. Paul discovered the plot of the Jews to kill him, probably as he boarded the ship or to kill him at sea, and dispose of his body at sea. So Paul made other plans and went back around the land route through Macedonia, ultimately arriving at Philippi, and then sailing to Troas, where he links up with his companions. Does Paul not trust God to protect him? Certainly, but remember that God can protect you by informing you of the plots of evil men, enabling you to take evasive action.

Are you, as a believer, alert to Satan's attempts to destroy you, to defeat your family, and to defeat the church? In I Corinthians 10, Paul warns against specific things as he writes about the nation of Israel in the wilderness wanderings and he says, "... *these things were written about them to be examples for us."* The Israelites were griping and complaining and grumbling! They had a negative outlook of unbelief rather than faith in God. They complained that Moses brought them to the wilderness to die there. They practiced idolatry, and all the high revelry and drinking associated with it. They were guilty of sexual immorality. Paul warns in 1 Corinthians 10:12 *"Therefore let him who thinks he stands take heed lest he fall."* We must be alert to Satan's plot to destroy us and take evasive action.

b. The opportunity to Accuse. Verse 4.

We see that Paul had several traveling companions that are all named here. They were traveling with Paul to take the special offerings from the churches of Macedonia to the saints in Jerusalem. Why are all of these people making this trip with Paul? Because Paul foresaw the opportunity that Satan could take to accuse him of impropriety; of misappropriating funds and using them for himself.

We must be wise as believers. Make every effort to avoid any opportunity that Satan might be able to use to accuse us of wrong doing. Corporately as a church, we may get irritated at times with policies for our nursery, our child abuse policy, our policy as to how offerings are counted and handled, and other policies. These things are done to, as much as possible, prevent Satan from an opportunity. We need to handle our personal and family lives in the same cautionary manner.

Vice president Mike Pence and his wife, Karen, are followers of Jesus Christ. He has recently been criticized for his policy of not eating lunch or traveling in a car alone with a woman other than his wife. However, this is a wise precautionary policy that his wife and he have followed since their marriage to avoid any unnecessary accusations of impropriety.

Secondly, we need to **Wake Up To Corporate Worship. Acts 20:7-12.**

Eutychus, the young man who fell asleep sitting in the window, and fell three stories to the ground and died, is just a symbol here for us. He is a real young man, who for whatever reason, is tired and just can't keep his eyes open any longer. However, he was faithfully gathering with the local church disciples for their regular worship services.

Who hasn't wrestled with the same problem at some time in your church attendance history? The larger question is "How awake are we when it comes to our worship habits?"

a. The Sunday habit. Verse 7.

"Now on the first day of the week, when the disciples came together . . ." The keeping of the Sabbath on the seventh day was disappearing except amongst the Jews and the Judaizers, who insisted upon Gentile believers keeping the Jewish Sabbath laws and the circumcision laws. Christians, following the resurrection of Christ on the first day of the week, began to meet on that day to worship and to celebrate the living Christ. It is clear in 1 Corinthians 16:2 that Christians met on the first day of the week. However some were neglecting the habit as we see in Hebrews 10:23-25. *"Let us hold fast the confession of our hope without wavering, for He who promised is faithful. And let us consider one another in order to stir up love and good works, not forsaking the assembling of ourselves together, as is the manner of some, but exhorting one another, and so much the more as you see the Day approaching."* Regular attendance at the gathered meetings of the church is crucial.

I don't think it is possible to be a vibrant, alive, on the ball Christian when you neglect the Sunday habit. In fact, I will be bold enough to say, you will be a stronger Christian if you will make the effort to be here on Sunday evenings also. We come up with a lot of feeble excuses as to why we miss a Sunday. "It is too hot or too cold. It snowed or rained last night. I'm tired and it is the only day I can sleep in. We had company from out of town." Apparently aspirin doesn't work on Sundays!

Someone wrote this bit of humorous verse. "Whenever I go past our church, I stop and make a visit, For fear that, when I'm carried in, The Lord might say, "Who is it?"

b. The Lord's Supper habit. Verse 7.

Luke says, *". . . the disciples gathered together to break bread . . ."* This is no doubt a reference to sharing the Lord's Supper together, perhaps as the concluding part of their love feast or "fellowship pot-luck". Probably the early church had the Lord's Supper every Sunday, but we are not certain. Paul says, in I Cor. 11:26, *"For as often as you eat this bread and drink this cup . . ."* We are not to neglect coming to the Lord's Table as believers. It is to be a regular time of examining ourselves, checking up on our relationship with the Lord and with each other.

Are you awake and alert spiritually? Do you care about the condition of your relationship with the Lord and with other brothers and sisters in Christ?

c. The biblical preaching habit. Verse 7ff.

John Ruskin once defined a sermon as "thirty minutes in which to raise the dead." Henry Ward Beecher once said, "If anyone falls asleep in church, I have given the ushers permission to wake up the preacher!"

Paul's sermon was unusually long. Verse 7 tells us that he *"spoke to them and continued his message until midnight."* Verse 9 (NIV) informs us that *"Seated in a window was a young man\ named Eutychus, who was sinking into a deep sleep as Paul talked on and on."* He fell to the ground from the third story window ledge and was picked up dead. Paul rushed down and raised him from the dead. Then after Eutychus was raised from death, we read in Verse 11, Paul went upstairs and talked until daylight. You think I am 'long-winded'. Now I'm long folks, but not winded. And I'm not that long!

The critical question for each of us is, "Do you regard biblical preaching and teaching as essential to your Christian life?" If you do not, then you are sleeping, slumbering along toward the second coming of Christ!

We are in a critical day and age in this regard! We are in a media age of sound bites and showmanship. Even the news is projected in that way! The political conventions are managed that way. Marshall McLuhan was prophetically accurate when he talked about the medium being the message.

Preaching of the word of God has fallen into the same trap today in my opinion. People want entertainment more than truth. Many preachers are caving into preaching little sermonettes of 10 minutes in length because they fear that people will not endure longer sermons. Many are taking their cues about what to preach about by the market surveys of baby boomers, rather than from the Holy Spirit of God. Charles Swindoll writes, "The final glimpse of church life Luke shows us is the presence of biblical teaching. "Paul began talking to them," and he talked and talked and talked! In fact, he kept teaching until midnight - showing us that an adequate feeding of the saints requires a significant period of time to properly unfold the truth."[111]

This is no justification for being dull and boring as preachers. Give me a preacher who has spent enough time in the study to know the word of God, and enough time on his knees to know the God of the word. Give me a preacher who humbly depends upon the Holy Spirit to light the fire in his heart. Give me a preacher who has been in the presence of Jesus and will also light a fire in my heart.

Thirdly, we need to **Wake Up Our Relationship With The Lord. Verse 13.**

Verse 13 adds this little insight. *"Then we went ahead to the ship and sailed to Assos, there intending to take Paul on board; for so he had given orders, intending himself to go on*

---

[111] Charles Swindoll, Commentary on Acts, Volume 3, page 48.

foot." Paul chooses not to go with the others on the ship but to walk from Troas to Assos, a distance of about 20 miles. Why does Luke put this little gem in here? I think there would be no other reason than Paul needed time alone with the Lord, to refresh and revive his intimacy with the Lord.

One of the problems we all face is, **a. Ministry from an empty tank.**

Serving the Lord, being involved in the ministry of the word, whether for preachers or lay people, is demanding. It takes time and energy in the midst of a busy, demanding world. "Burn-out" comes when you feel that your tank is empty and you can't give anymore. You feel like a sponge, all wrung out and too long removed from Christ, the water of life.

b. A quiet time alone with the Lord.

Paul needed this refreshment to his soul so that he could face the future ministry and future challenges ahead of him with the strength that the Lord gives. We are weak in ourselves and Christ is our strength! Even Jesus Christ himself often withdrew into a solitary place to pray, where he could spend time in intimate fellowship with the Father. He often called his disciples away from the crowds to spend close fellowship with Him and to be refreshed with rest from the demands of life. Mark 6:31 says, *"And He said to them, "Come aside by yourselves to a deserted place and rest a while." For there were many coming and going, and they did not even have time to eat."*

Are you a slumbering saint? Have you grown weary in well doing and so you've just quit doing anything for the Lord anymore? Has your relationship with the Lord grown stale? Is your commitment and excitement of being with the people of

God, worshipping the Lord, no longer vital? Has the word of God been put on the back burner in your life?

Take heart, there isn't one of us as a believer who hasn't been through these times, if we are not going through that kind of time right now! Confess your dryness! Admit your need for fresh living water from your Savior and Lord, who is the water of life. Find your time to get alone with the Lord with His word, and pour out your soul to Him. Ask him to make His word live again in your heart! Like the Psalmist, express your need for refreshment from above. Psalm 42:1. *"As the deer pants for the water brooks, so pants my soul for You, O God."*

Showers of Blessing!
(Written in 1883 by Daniel Webster (1840–1901) under the pseudonym of D. W. Whittle.)

There shall be showers of blessing.
This is a promise of love.
There shall be seasons refreshing,
Sent from the Savior above.

(Refrain)
Showers of blessing,
Showers of blessing we need.
Mercy drops round us are falling,
But for the showers we plead.

There shall be showers of blessing,
Precious reviving again.
Over the hills and the valleys,
Sound of abundance of rain.

(Refrain)
Showers of blessing,

Showers of blessing we need.
Mercy drops round us are falling,
But for the showers we plead.

There shall be showers of blessing,
Oh but today they might fall.
Now as to God we're confessing.
Now as on Jesus we call.

(Refrain)
Showers of blessing
Showers of blessing we need.
Mercy drops round us are falling
But for the showers we plead.

Chapter 26
So You Want To Be A Pastor!
Acts 20:13-38

Seminaries report that there is a shift in the profile of the people that are being trained for pastoral ministry. There is a high shift in age as many people do a career change and enter pastoral ministry training. The other thing that is happening with alarming frequency is the shift from pastoral ministry to some other career. Many are the former pastors who are in management, in insurance sales, in car sales or a host of other lines of work. Disillusionment has come to many who have been bashed around by congregations that expect more than any individual can provide. Some may have discovered that they were not called of God and not gifted to be pastors, but a whole host of others have become victims of a market place mentality about ministry.

"Every church ought to grow numerically", we are told, and if it is not growing, someone must be found to blame. Often it is the pastor who takes the brunt of the blame.

Kent and Barb Hughes teamed up to write a very important book, "Liberating Ministry from the Success Syndrome". Kent, a wonderful pastor, was then serving at College Church of Wheaton, Illinois. He had gone through a terrible time of depression and discouragement. Earlier in his ministry he was sent out by his home church, where he had served for several years in youth ministry, as the founding pastor of a daughter church. The mother church sent about 20 committed couples, and $50,000 to aid them in getting started in a prime location. Kent Hughes shares his story.

Here is his account of this experience. "From the start, we had everything going for us. We had the prayers and predictions of our friends who believed a vast, growing work was inevitable.

We had the sophisticated insights of the science of church growth. We had a superb nucleus of believers. And we had me, a young pastor with a good track record who was entering his prime. We expected to grow.

"But to our astonishment and resounding disappointment, we didn't. In fact, after considerable time and incredible labor, we had fewer regular attenders than during the first six months. Our church was shrinking, and the prospects looked bad - really bad. . . . After more than a decade of ministry, I began to lose my equilibrium. My long established world of bright prospects and success had melted around me. I was in the darkest, deepest depression of my life . . .I wanted out."[112]

The modern churches, and their pastors, need to do a lot of rethinking about what the Bible has to say about the nature of the true church and also about this matter of being a pastor. Seminaries and pastoral students need to clearly identify the biblical pattern for serving as a pastor.

As Paul bids a final farewell to his fellow pastors from Ephesus and Asia Minor, we gain great insight into the pastoral call. It is an awesome task and a fearful responsibility to be a pastor.

What Is A Pastor? Acts 20:17, 28.

In our modern high pressure world, companies are down-sizing and expecting more and more from their employees. In churches, we are falling into the trap of expecting more and more of the wrong things from pastors. If the church is not growing numerically and the financial picture getting brighter

---

[112] "Liberating Ministry from the Success Syndrome", Tyndale, Wheaton, 1987, page 18.

and brighter, then we conclude that it is probably the pastor's fault.

The pastor of a certain church was called to go to another church as their new pastor. "The same God who sent me to you," the pastor announced, "is now calling me away." There was a moment's silence, and then the congregation rose and began to sing, "What a Friend We Have in Jesus." We find this humorous, but really, it is no laughing matter.

What is a pastor to be according to Scripture? The word 'pastor' comes from the Latin word, "pascere" meaning 'to feed'. It is the equivalent of the Greek word 'shepherd' in verse 28. It is the picture of a shepherd caring for but primarily feeding his sheep.

As you read verse 17, Paul calls the 'elders' ('presbutyros' in Greek) from the church in Ephesus to come and meet him at the beach at the port of Miletus. Luke gives Paul's reason for bypassing Ephesus in verse 16. He wanted to be in Jerusalem by Pentecost. Study of verse 28 shows that these 'elders' are the same men to whom he refers as 'bishops' or 'overseers (episcopos in Greek). In verse 28, these same people are told to 'shepherd' or 'pastor' the flock.

We must therefore conclude that elders, bishops and pastors in the New Testament are the same people. Peter also verifies this conclusion in 1 Peter 5:1-3 (NIV). *"To the _elders_ among you, I appeal as a _fellow elder_, a witness of Christ's sufferings and one who also will share in the glory to be revealed: Be _shepherds_ of God's flock that is under your care, serving as _overseers_ - not because you must, but because you are willing, as God wants you to be; not greedy for money, but eager to serve; not lording it over those entrusted to you, but being examples to the flock."*

Ignatius makes it clear that the idea of a bishop over other pastors is a second century development. Pastors-teachers are some of the gifted people that God has given to His church. Ephesians 4:11-12. *"And He Himself who gave some to be apostles, some prophets, some evangelists, and some pastors and teachers, for the equipping of the saints for the work of the ministry, for the edifying of the body of Christ. . ."*

It is a humbling thing to be called and equipped by God to be a pastor-teacher in a local church of Jesus Christ. This is why a pastor, a bishop, an elder is to be a mature Christian, so that he will be humbled by God's call, rather than being puffed up or arrogant. Paul's instruction regarding the man who is to be a bishop/elder/pastor is clear in 1 Timothy 3:6-7. Among many other qualifications, he must not be *"a novice, lest being puffed up with pride he fall into the same condemnation as the devil. Moreover he must have a good testimony among those who are outside, lest he fall into reproach and the snare of the devil."*

What Is A Pastor's Chief Responsibility? Acts 20:22-24; 28-31.

Paul testifies to these elders of how he has sought to faithfully discharge his responsibilities as a bishop/elder/pastor called by God. *"And when they had come to him, he said to them: "You know, from the first day that I came to Asia, in what manner I always lived among you, serving the Lord with all humility, with many tears and trials which happened to me by the plotting of the Jews; how I kept back nothing that was helpful, but proclaimed it to you, and taught you publicly and from house to house, testifying to Jews, and also to Greeks, repentance toward God and faith toward our Lord Jesus Christ. And see, now I go bound in the spirit to Jerusalem, not knowing the things that will happen to me there, except that the Holy Spirit testifies in every city, saying that chains and tribulations await me. But none of these things move me; nor do I count my life dear to myself, so that I may finish my race with joy, and the ministry which I received from the Lord Jesus, to testify to the gospel of the grace of God."*

Paul would say that the chief responsibility of the pastor is to be "faithful" to the Lord. 1 Corinthians 4:1-2 says, *"Let a man so consider us, as servants of Christ and stewards of the mysteries of God. Moreover it is required in stewards that one be found faithful."*

Yes, we are also to be fruitful but fruitfulness is the responsibility of the Vine (Christ) and the Vinedresser (the Heavenly Father). We must abide in the Vine. Kent Hughes writes, "As Barbara and I searched the Scriptures, we found no place where it says that God's servants are called to be successful. Rather, we discovered our call is to be faithful."[113]

Leaders in God's kingdom and in the church are to be "servant-leaders". Christ taught His disciples about greatness and it is found in being the servant of all. Mark 10:42-45. Peter made it clear that pastors are to be *"eager to serve, not lording over those entrusted to you. . ."* 1 Peter 5:2-3.

In 1878, when William Booth's Salvation Army was beginning to make its mark, men and women from all over the world began to enlist. One man, who had once dreamed of becoming a bishop, crossed the Atlantic from America to England to enlist. Samuel Brengle left a fine pastorate to join Booth's Army. But at first General Booth accepted his services reluctantly and grudgingly. Booth said to Brengle, "You've been your own boss too long." And in order to instill humility in Brengle, he set him to work cleaning the boots of other trainees. Discouraged, Brengle said to himself, "Have I

---

[113] Kent Hughes, IBID, page 35.

followed my own fancy across the Atlantic in order to black boots?" And then, as in a vision, he saw Jesus bending over the feet of rough, unlettered fishermen. "Lord," he whispered, "you washed their feet; I will black their shoes."[114]

It isn't a good use of a pastor's time to be always cleaning the toilets in the church, but it better not be beneath his dignity to do it. To be faithful shepherds, Paul gives these elders three commands.

1) Feed the flock. Verse 28b. *"Shepherd* [feed] *the church of God which He purchased with His own blood."* In other words, be a shepherd, not a CEO. There is a tremendous load of expectations placed upon pastors today that occupy their time and energy so that it is impossible for them to feed the flock with good expository preaching and teaching. When the shepherd is starving spiritually, the sheep will not be fed. Remember that a homemaker cannot provide a good nutritious meal without the time and energy to prepare it.

2) Guard yourself. Verse 28a. *"Take heed to yourselves . . ."* First, and foremost, as a pastor, one must be authentic. One must walk the walk with Jesus and not just talk the talk. Every pastor must be aware that he is always a target for Satan. All one needs to do is to look around and see the wreckage of pastors who have fallen into gross sin because of lust or greed.

It is imperative to maintain a walk with the Lord that keeps on practicing close fellowship with Christ Jesus. Make certain, as a pastor, that you are applying the word of God to your own life before you preach it to your congregation. Set the example for the flock that you are shepherding as Paul did. Remember his words to the Corinthians about setting the example. 1 Corinthians 10:31–11:1. *"Therefore, whether you eat or drink,*

---

[114] Kent Hughes, IBID, page 45.

or whatever you do, do all to the glory of God. Give no offense, either to the Jews or to the Greeks or to the church of God, just as I also please all men in all things, not seeking my own profit, but the profit of many, that they may be saved. Imitate me, just as I also imitate Christ."

3) Guard the flock. Verse 28a. *"Take heed . . .to all the flock, among which the Holy Spirit has made you overseers . . ."* In verse 29, Paul commands them as pastors to guard against false teachers and against *"savage wolves"* who will come in among them to tear the flock apart. Note the warning that Paul gives about false teachers coming from outside and arising from within the body. Acts 20:29-31a. (The Message paraphrase). *"I know that as soon as I am gone, vicious wolves are going to show up and rip into this flock, men from your very own ranks twisting words so as to seduce disciples into following them instead of Jesus. So stay awake and keep on your guard."* One of the main traits of a false teacher is that he will seduce disciples to follow him or her, rather than Jesus.

What Are The Primary Temptations of a Pastor?

Paul implores the pastors to first of all guard themselves. Let's consider some of the prominent pitfalls that pastors face. These apply to all of us, but especially to pastors.

a. Discouragement because of a wrong measure of success.

If we fall into the trap of measuring the church by the same standards of success as we do businesses, we will miss out on God's kingdom. It is still true that people must enter the narrow gate in order to be on their way to heaven and Jesus taught that only a 'few' would find it. Matthew 7:13-14.

Becoming a large church does not mean necessarily that the message is being compromised. However, neither does the bigness of a local church necessarily mean that it is by the power of the Spirit of God that it has grown. Remember that some false-cults like Mormons and Jehovah's Witnesses are growing well. Some churches have grown to be mega-churches but are preaching a false gospel, promising health and wealth to those who follow the Jesus they preach.

We need to seriously consider such questions as: What is success for a pastor? What is failure for a pastor? Is it possible, in God's sight, to be a success in the ministry and pastor a small church? The answer to that must definitely be 'yes', if we are thinking biblically.

b. Laziness because of a wrong view of pastoral ministry.

Some who are entering ministry somehow have gotten the impression that you can be a pastor and not work hard. I hear of pastors who play golf three or four times a week and I wonder how they can do that with all that is involved in being a dedicated pastor.

Kent Hughes tells of a letter he received from a young pastor with whom he had spent an evening, discussing how "faithfulness not only demands obedience to God's Word, but hard work." Here is Pastor Hughes' response.

"I feel compelled to make the following comments. Most of what I say is to both my surprise and chagrin.

"It seems that in trying to correct some possible pastoral abuses of the past, seminaries are exposing their students to a recurring theme: don't burn out . . . be sure to get your day(s) off . . .marriage first, ministry second." These refrains may all be quite true, but they come with such repetitive force that I fear that the pendulum has swung from those who jeopardized their families in the name of "ministry" to men who think that they have something coming to them because they are "in the ministry." We now have men who are so thoroughly warned of sacrificing their families that they sacrifice nothing!"[115]

Paul's testimony, as he addresses these pastors from Ephesus, makes it crystal clear that hard work, self-denial, fervent commitment and suffering for the sake of Christ and the gospel, are normal fare for one who serves the Lord Jesus in the ranks of His under-shepherds.

c. Pride because of a distorted view of our importance.

Paul did not see himself as indispensable to the success of the Lord's cause, but as one called by the grace of God. He was privileged to be an ambassador and a servant of the Lord whom he once persecuted. Acts 20:18-19. *"And when they had come to him, he said to them: "You know, from the first day that I came to Asia, in what manner I always lived among you, serving the Lord with all humility, with many tears and trials which happened to me by the plotting of the Jews; . . ."* Pride in any shape or form totally destroys our usefulness to the Lord.

d. Compromise because of a need to please everyone.

In verse 20, Paul says, *"I kept back nothing that was helpful, but proclaimed it to you, and taught you publicly and from house to house."* But what is helpful is not always what we want to hear. If someone is getting a divorce for a non-biblical reason, it is not popular to hear your pastor tell you that you are sinning and disobeying God. If you are needing correction when it comes to your priorities, you do not always want to hear warning words from your pastor. Often the loving thing to do, as a pastor, is to warn a person of danger up ahead. If a

---

[115] Kent Hughes, IBID, page 41.

bridge is out in the road ahead, one does not aim to be "well-liked" when warning a driver of impending doom, if he continues down that road.

e. Wrong priorities because of the pressure of expectations.

We have already touched upon this to some extent. It is not easy to carve out the hours of time that are essential for study and time alone with the Lord, in order to be prepared to feed the flock when they gather together. Remember that well-fed flocks of sheep are generally contented sheep.

In the Shepherd's Psalm 23, the Chief Shepherd ('LORD' indicating Yahweh or Jehovah) is my shepherd who meets our needs by making us lie down in green pastures and leading us beside the still waters. If we as under-shepherds do not make the time to discover those green pastures and still waters for ourselves, how can we lead our flock to those green pastures and still waters?

f. Shipwreck because of the rocks of unchecked passions.

This has already been addressed to some extent. However, the sensual passions that lead pastors astray are allowed to fester before they burst out. Absolute tenacious honesty regarding your inner thoughts and motives is essential to living victoriously in Christ. As someone has said, "You can't prevent a bird from landing on your head, but you must prevent it from building a nest in your hair."

Unchecked desires in the areas of sex, wealth and power are signs of impending disaster. Resolute and inflexible discipline of the inner heart is essential to godliness and purity.

Let me close with this challenge to those whom God may be calling to pastoral ministry. Be certain God is calling and it is not just your own personal desires. What is your response when you become a pastor, and you find yourself suffering rejection and abusive criticism when you are seeking to be faithful to the word and to the Lord?

Paul shares his prospects that lie ahead of him as he makes his way to Jerusalem. Acts 20:22-24. *"And see, now I go bound in the spirit to Jerusalem, not knowing the things that will happen to me there, except that the Holy Spirit testifies in every city, saying that chains and tribulations await me. But none of these things move me; nor do I count my life dear to myself, so that I may finish my race with joy, and the ministry which I received from the Lord Jesus, to testify to the gospel of the grace of God."* The NIV says, *"And now, compelled by the Spirit . . ."* I believe it was Spurgeon who said, "if you can do anything else and be a peace about it, do it." This compulsion of his call from God led Paul to write to the Corinthian church, *"For if I preach the gospel, I have nothing to boast of, for necessity is laid upon me; yes, woe is me if I do not preach the gospel! For if I do this willingly, I have a reward; but if against my will, I have been entrusted with a stewardship."* 1 Corinthians 9:16-17.

It's Not An Easy Road!
(Written by John W. Peterson)

It's not an easy road we are travelling to heaven,
For many are the thorns on the way.
It's not an easy road, but the Savior is with us,
His presence gives us joy every day.

(Chorus)
No, no, it's not an easy road.
But Jesus walks beside me and brightens the journey,
And lightens every heavy load.

It's not an easy road; there are trials and troubles,
And many are the dangers we meet.
But Jesus guards and keeps, so that nothing can harm us.
And smooths the rugged path for our feet.

Though I am often footsore and weary from travel;
Though I am often bowed down with care.
A better day is coming when home in the glory,
We'll meet in perfect peace over there.

Chapter 27
When The Authorities Oppose The Grace Revolution!
Acts 22:1 – 26:32

The Apostle Paul's last visit to Jerusalem proved to be one of severe opposition by the powers-that-be in the holy city. When he followed the advice of the church leaders to pursue a vow of purity with four other men in the temple, it led to opposition from the Jewish high priest and his cohorts. Acts 21:27-28 informs us of the attacks upon him as some Jews who had come from Asia stirred up the crowd to physically lay hands on him. Verse 28 states their charges against him. *""Men of Israel, help! This is the man who teaches all men everywhere against the people, the law, and this place; and furthermore he also brought Greeks into the temple and has defiled this holy place."* They *'supposed'* (Verse 29) that Paul had brought a Gentile, Trophimus of Ephesus, into the temple. It was all based on hearsay and presumption rather than on true facts.

As the Jews were intending to kill Paul and were severely beating him, the commander of the garrison in Jerusalem brought soldiers and rescued Paul from this blood-thirsty crowd. Paul was bound in two chains. When the commander, who had misidentified Paul, was informed that he was a Roman citizen, he gave him permission to speak to the people. Acts 21:29-40. Chapter 22 is the account of Paul's defense testimony before this hateful crowd that were stirred up to the point of seeking to murder him.

Around our world, many of our fellow-Christians are experiencing this kind of opposition and persecution. In many cases they are attacked by the religious authorities who oppose Christ and His followers. In other cases, they are opposed by secular government authorities in Communist and other dictatorial socialist countries. In some cases, the secular government and the religious authorities are one and the same, as in Iran and other hostile Islamic regimes.

In chapters 23 through 26 of Acts, we find the record of Paul's interrogation before the Jewish authorities and the Roman authorities ruling in Israel.

Paul's Appearance before Ananias, the High Priest, and the Jewish Council. Acts 22:30 – 23:11.

1) First we examine the details of this historical conflict in Jerusalem.

The Roman military commander in Jerusalem was in a very precarious situation. He had violated Roman law by putting a Roman citizen in chains and he was seeking desperately to quell a riot of the populace of Jerusalem. In Acts 22:30, we find that he *"commanded the chief priests and the council to appear, and brought Paul down and set him before them."* I am certain that Paul was aware of Jesus's promise to those who are dragged before magistrates, and no doubt he was relying on that promise. Luke 12:11-12. *"Now when they bring you to the synagogues and magistrates and authorities, do not worry about how or what you should answer, or what you should say. For the Holy Spirit will teach you in that very hour what you ought to say."* Paul courageously makes his opening statement which is about all he got to say in his defense. Acts 23:1. *"Then Paul, looking earnestly at the council, said, "Men and brethren, I have lived in all good conscience before God until this day."* This prompted the high priest, Ananias[116], to command that

---

[116] Ananias the son of Nedebaeus reigned as high priest from A.D. 48 to 58 or 59 and was known for his avarice and liberal use of violence.

someone in the Council strike Paul on the mouth. This slap in the face was against the law when Paul had not yet been convicted of any crime. Such behavior by the high priest was clear evidence that no justice would come from this tainted court.

Paul calls the high priest a *"whited wall"*, a term used to indicate he was a hypocrite. When Paul is informed by some by-standers that he was reviling the high priest, he apologized, stating that he was unaware that he was speaking to the high priest. John G. Butler says, "Ananias was not the high priest. The true high priest was to be a direct descendant of Aaron and hold the position for a lifetime. But Rome controlled who was the high priest. Therefore Ananias was not the high priest. Biblically, Paul did not revile the high priest but only an imposter."[117] Warren Wiersbe explains that, being this was a more informal meeting of the Council, Ananias was not likely wearing his high priestly robe and may not have been seated in his usual place in the Council.[118]

Paul used a strategy that pitted half the Council against the other half. He perceived that the Council was split between Sadducees and Pharisees and that they had very different beliefs. Acts 23:6-10 tells us the result of the turmoil created as they began debating amongst themselves concerning the resurrection. *"But when Paul perceived that one part were Sadducees and the other Pharisees, he cried out in the council, "Men and brethren, I am a Pharisee, the son of a*

Josephus says he confiscated for himself the tithes given the ordinary priests and gave lavish bribes to Romans and also Jews (cf. Antiq. XX, 205-7 [ix.2], 213 [ix.4]). He was a brutal and scheming man, hated by Jewish nationalists for his pro-Roman policies.

[117] John G. Butler, Analytical Bible Expositor, Volume 12, LBC Publication, Clinton, IA, 2009, page 281.

[118] Warren Wiersbe, The Bible Exposition Commentary, Volume 1, Victor Books, Wheaton, IL, 1989, page 495.

Pharisee; concerning the hope and resurrection of the dead I am being judged!" And when he had said this, a dissension arose between the Pharisees and the Sadducees; and the assembly was divided. For Sadducees say that there is no resurrection - and no angel or spirit; but the Pharisees confess both. Then there arose a loud outcry. And the scribes of the Pharisees' party arose and protested, saying, "We find no evil in this man; but if a spirit or an angel has spoken to him, let us not fight against God." Now when there arose a great dissension, the commander, fearing lest Paul might be pulled to pieces by them, commanded the soldiers to go down and take him by force from among them, and bring him into the barracks." The commander had to rescue Paul from the fighting and argumentation of the Council.

Some commentators believe that Paul made a big mistake in coming to Jerusalem when he had been warned repeatedly that trouble lay ahead of him there. However, this appears to me to be in error. Rather, it was God's will for Paul to go to Rome and this was His way of getting him to Rome. Acts 23:11 indicates clearly that God was with Paul in these trials as he witnessed for Christ Jesus in Jerusalem, and God assures him by appearing to him during the night that he must also bear witness for Christ in Rome.

2) Now let's consider **the inevitable eternal conflict.**

The Old Covenant of Moses had become obsolete and had been fulfilled by the New Covenant. As the writer of Hebrews, inspired by the Holy Spirit, tells us in Hebrews 8, *"Now this is <u>the main point of the things we are saying</u>: We have such a High Priest, who is seated at the right hand of the throne of the Majesty in the heavens, a Minister of the sanctuary and of the true tabernacle which the Lord erected, and not man. For every high priest is appointed to offer both gifts and sacrifices. Therefore it is necessary that this One* *also have something to offer. For if He were on earth, He would not be a priest, since there are priests who offer the gifts according to the law; who serve the copy and shadow of the heavenly things, as Moses was divinely instructed when he was about to make the tabernacle. For He said, "See that you make all things according to the pattern shown you on the mountain." But now He has obtained a more excellent ministry, inasmuch as He is also Mediator of a better covenant, which was established on better promises. For if that first covenant had been faultless, then no place would have been sought for a second."* (Verses 1-7) . . . *"In that He says, "A new covenant," He has made the first obsolete. Now what is becoming obsolete and growing old is ready to vanish away."* (Verse 13).

The Old Covenant and the Law was simply *"the shadow of the good things to come, and not the very image of the things . . ."* Hebrews 10:1ff. Paul was the messenger of Jesus Christ, the Lamb of God, who was the eternal Passover Lamb, who fulfilled the shadows of the hundreds of thousands of lambs that had been sacrificed under the shadow of the Old Covenant. Christ Jesus came as the eternal High Priest, who shed His own blood as the means of justifying sinful man with the Holy and Righteous God. Hebrews 9:12-15 declares, *"Not with the blood of goats and calves, but with His own blood He entered the Most Holy Place once for all, having obtained eternal redemption. For if the blood of bulls and goats and the ashes of a heifer, sprinkling the unclean, sanctifies for the purifying of the flesh, how much more shall the blood of Christ, who through the eternal Spirit offered Himself without spot to God, cleanse your conscience from dead works to serve the living God? And for this reason He is the Mediator of the new covenant, by means of death, for the redemption of the transgressions under the first covenant, that those who are called may receive the promise of the eternal inheritance."*

This corrupt high priest, Ananias, and his Council, were maintaining an old system of sacrifices that had become obsolete through Jesus Christ and His atoning blood. They were seeking to maintain their power and their human control over the people and conflict was unavoidable.

For Christians everywhere, conflict with the world's power systems is also inevitable. Christians everywhere often face hostile authorities who are operating with hateful prejudice against them. Even in our country, over the last few years, some Christians are suffering from the prejudicial decisions of state governments and judges when they do not recognize the revised legal definition of marriage. Our Supreme Court has ruled that marriage includes any two people who want to be married to each other, regardless of sex. God's eternal plan is revealed in Genesis 2:24, *"Therefore a man shall leave his father and his mother and be joined to his wife, and they shall become one flesh."* In the fourth of the Ten Commandments, we are to *"Honor your father and your mother. . ."* - not 'your father and your father' or 'your mother and your mother'. God established the structure of the family forever and governments and courts cannot change the eternal plan of the Creator. Nor can courts and governments change the two sexes, 'male and female' into a new structure of '57 varieties of gender', dependent upon one's feelings.

Alex Swoyer reported in the Washington Times on one case that has been in the courts for a couple of years. "A Christian florist is appealing to the Supreme Court after Washington State's highest court ruled against her for refusing to create floral arrangements for a same-sex wedding on the grounds that doing so would violate her religion.

Barronelle Stutzman, who owns Arlene's Flowers, first asked the Supreme Court to consider her case in 2017, but the justices sent it back to the State to reconsider last year in light of another high court ruling telling Colorado to reconsider penalties against a Christian baker in a similar case.

On Thursday, the Washington Supreme Court again ruled against Ms. Stutzman, saying the record shows she had a fair hearing the first time and was found to have violated the State's public accommodations law, which prohibits discrimination against individuals on the basis of sexual orientation.

"The hostility my State has shown me because of my faith is undeniable and I am confident the U.S. Supreme Court will see that viewpoint," Ms. Stutzman said in announcing her appeal.

The Supreme Court ruled last year for Jack Phillips, a Christian baker, who had refused to create a cake for a same-sex wedding, saying the Colorado Civil Rights Commission had acted with religious animus when investigating the baker's actions."[119] Especially if the leftist socialists succeed in taking over our national government, we as Christians are sure to face increasing removal of our religious freedom. In America today, one wonders how long it may be before Christians will be imprisoned for their stand for their faith and the truth of Scripture.

The same conflict comes for Christians in the matter of abortion. Just because the Supreme Court has declared that a woman has the right to choose to end the life of her baby in her womb does not make God's law obsolete. Murder is

---

[119]Alex Swoyer, The Washington Times, Thursday, June 6, 2019

still murder. No matter how you much lipstick you put on the pig, it is still a pig.

The Conspiracy of the Jews to Murder Paul. Acts 23:12-35.

Forty hostile Jews conspired to kill Paul and they vowed to not eat or drink until they accomplished his demise. Acts 23:12-15. They worked out a scheme with the corrupt chief priests and elders to request another appearance of inquisition the next day. On his way, they had resolved to take his life by attacking him even though Paul would be accompanied from the barracks by Roman soldiers. Just consider the corruption of religious leaders who would concoct a scheme of murder to maintain their control of their obsolete system.

In God's providence, Paul had a nephew, his sister's son, who was in the right place at the right time, a clear indication of God at work in Paul's behalf. He overheard the nefarious plans of these evil men. Verse 16. Paul's nephew secretly reported this scheme to Claudius Lysias, the Roman governor. As a consequence, the governor developed a solid plan to remove Paul from the imminent danger of Jerusalem and he sent him to Caesarea to Governor Felix. Acts 23:23-24 describes the lengths to which Claudius Lysias went to assure Paul's safe arrival in Caesarea. Two hundred soldiers, seventy horsemen and two hundred spearmen left at nine-o'clock at night with Paul on horseback. So Paul arrived safely and was kept in Herod's Praetorium in Caesarea. This stay in Caesarea lasted from 57–59 AD.

The next phase is **Paul's Defense before Felix. Acts 24:1-27.**

Paul's Jewish accusers came down from Jerusalem to present their charges against Paul before Governor Felix who was governor over that territory on the Mediterranean Sea. They even brought along a prominent orator, Tertullus, to argue their case. After Tertullus butters up Governor Felix with praise, he accuses Paul in verses 4-8, *"Nevertheless, not to be tedious to you any further, I beg you to hear, by your courtesy, a few words from us. For we have found this man a plague, a creator of dissension among all the Jews throughout the world, and a ringleader of the sect of the Nazarenes. He even tried to profane the temple, and we seized him, and wanted to judge him according to our law. But the commander Lysias came by and with great violence took him out of our hands, commanding his accusers to come to you. By examining him yourself you may ascertain all these things of which we accuse him."*

Paul gave his reasoned defense before Felix, disputing the charges against him as 'trumped-up' charges that were not the least according to the facts of his appearance in the temple in Jerusalem. Verses 10-21. Felix adjourned the proceedings and promised a decision when Claudius Lysias would come to Caesarea. Felix, who was married to a Jewess, Drusilla, often conversed with Paul about his case, hoping to be offered a bribe so that he might release him. So Paul was given much liberty by Felix and he was bound as a prisoner under Felix for two years, when he was succeeded by Governor Festus. Felix kept Paul in custody *"to do the Jews a favor."* Acts 24:27.

Now we move to the next phase of his legal ordeal; **Paul's defense before Festus. Acts 25:1-12.**

Three days after taking office as governor, Festus went up to Jerusalem, and there met with the high priest and the chief men of the Jews who had accused Paul of wrongdoing. They implored Festus to bring Paul to Jerusalem with the intent of carrying out their death-threat upon Paul while on the way. Festus refused them their request and told them that they should come to Caesarea to bring their charges against Paul.

Ten days later, Festus returned to Caesarea and the Jews who had come from Jerusalem brought their false accusations against Paul, *"which they could not prove."* Verse 7. After Paul defended himself, Festus asked Paul if he was willing to go to Jerusalem. Paul refused, knowing that the Jews had not given up the idea of killing him. He also knew that his destination was Rome, according to God's revelation to him, (Acts 23:11) and the quickest way to get there was to appeal as a Roman citizen to Caesar. Besides, as a prisoner of Rome, the expenses of the trip would be paid by the Roman government. Acts 25:10-12 from 'The Message' paraphrase says, *"Paul answered, "I'm standing at this moment before Caesar's bar of justice, where I have a perfect right to stand. And I'm going to keep standing here. I've done nothing wrong to the Jews, and you know it as well as I do. If I've committed a crime and deserve death, name the day. I can face it. But if there's nothing to their accusations - and you know there isn't - nobody can force me to go along with their nonsense. We've fooled around here long enough. I appeal to Caesar." Festus huddled with his advisors briefly and then gave his verdict: "You've appealed to Caesar; you'll go to Caesar!"*

Finally we come to **King Agrippa's involvement in Paul's case. Acts 25:13 – 26:32.**

King Agrippa and Bernice came to visit the new governor to welcome Festus to his new office and responsibility, probably simply a visit of protocol. They visited for many days and Festus brought up Paul's case, indicating that this was a left-over case from his predecessor, Felix.

Who was this King Agrippa? Who was Bernice? John G. Butler says of these two people, "These were two slimy creatures in character. Agrippa was Herod Agrippa II, a member of the Herodian family. His great-grandfather killed the children in Bethlehem in an attempt to kill Christ. His uncle killed John, the Baptist. His father killed James (Acts 12:2). Bernice was Agrippa's sister. She had married her uncle and lived incestuously with him. When he died, she lived with her brother Agrippa in another incestuous relationship. Some years later, she became the mistress of Titus, the Roman general who destroyed Jerusalem and later became the emperor of Rome. Since this Agrippa had no children, thankfully he was the last of the Herodian family to rule."[120] Felix's wife, Drusilla, was a younger sister of Bernice which gave the new governor, Festus, some concern. He certainly would want to be careful not to say anything too negative to King Agrippa II about his predecessor.

King Agrippa seemed to be intrigued with Paul's case and indicated to Festus that he would like to hear Paul's defense. So with great pomp and circumstance, (verse 23) it was arranged for Paul to come to the auditorium. Festus introduced Paul and declared that he was going to be sent to appear before Caesar Nero in Rome but that he had nothing concrete to write to the emperor about any charges that were legitimate. So Festus is hoping that after this appearance he would know what to write.

Paul shares a detailed testimony as his defense against the charges of the Jews, declaring himself innocent of any wrongdoing. He shared his experience on the road to

---

[120] John G. Butler, Analytical Bible Expositor, Volume 12, LBC Publication, Clinton, IA, 2009, page 307.

Damascus, telling Agrippa, and all that were gathered there, about his conversion from being a persecutor of Christians to being a messenger of the gospel to both Jews and Gentiles. He concluded with a clear statement about the factual resurrection of Jesus. Acts 26:22-23. *"Therefore, having obtained help from God, to this day I stand, witnessing both to small and great, saying no other things than those which the prophets and Moses said would come - that the Christ would suffer, that He would be the first to rise from the dead, and would proclaim light to the Jewish people and to the Gentiles."*

In our witness for Christ and the gospel, we must always be certain to declare the resurrection of Jesus Christ from the dead. It is the fact of Christ's resurrection that is proof positive of Who Jesus really is. Romans 1:4 unequivocally states that Jesus was *"declared to be the Son of God with power according to the Spirit of holiness, by the resurrection from the dead."*

Festus is an unbelieving skeptic and declared, *". . . with a loud voice, Paul, you are beside yourself! Much learning has made you mad."* Acts 26:24. That is the way some will react to the gospel message. They think the message of the cross is foolishness. 1 Corinthians 1:18. Warren Wiersbe comments, "Festus had not interrupted because he really thought Paul was mad. Had that been the case, he would have treated Paul gently and ordered some of his guards to escort him to a place of rest and safety. Furthermore, what official would send a raving madman to be tried by the emperor? No, the governor was only giving evidence of conviction in his heart. Paul's words had found their mark, and Festus was trying to escape."[121]

---

[121] Warren Wiersbe, The Bible Exposition Commentary, Volume 1, Victor Books, Wheaton, IL, 1989, page 506.

However, this rejection by Festus does not deter Paul and he begins to reason with Agrippa, whom he believes is aware of the truth of all these events surrounding Jesus. Agrippa responded with honesty to Paul in verse 28, *"You almost persuade me to become a Christian."* Paul then said to Agrippa, (verse 29), *"I would to God that not only you, but also all who hear me today, might become both almost and altogether such as I am, except for these chains."*

After Agrippa, Bernice and Festus went aside and discussed Paul's case, Agrippa declared, *"This man is doing nothing deserving of death or these chains."* Verse 30. Then he told Festus, *"This man might have been set free if he had not appealed to Caesar."* Verse 31.

Was it a mistake on Paul's part to appeal to Caesar, when he could have been a free man? No, it was God's will for Paul to go to Rome and this was God's way of getting him there. God's ways are beyond our ways and His thoughts are higher than our thoughts. When we trust Him to lead us through the maze of our lives, we will be where He wants us to be. When we follow Him and believe in His goodness, He will make no mistakes in our lives, even when it results in being a prisoner in Rome. Romans 8:28-29 is still in the Bible and it is still true. *"And we know that all things work together for good to those who love God, to those who are the called according to His purpose. For whom He foreknew, He also predestined to be conformed to the image of His Son, that He might be the firstborn among many brethren."* And nothing, absolutely nothing can separate us from His love!

Savior, Like A Shepherd Lead Us!
(Written by Dorothy A. Thrupp - 1836)

Savior, like a shepherd lead us,

Much we need Thy tender care;
In Thy pleasant pastures feed us,
For our use Thy folds prepare:
Blessed Jesus, blessed Jesus,
Thou hast bought us, Thine we are;
Blessed Jesus, blessed Jesus,
Thou hast bought us, Thine we are.

We are Thine, do Thou befriend us,
Be the guardian of our way;
Keep Thy flock, from sin defend us,
Seek us when we go astray:
Blessed Jesus, blessed Jesus,
Hear, O hear us when we pray;
Blessed Jesus, blessed Jesus,
Hear, O hear us when we pray.

Thou hast promised to receive us,
Poor and sinful though we be;
Thou hast mercy to relieve us,
Grace to cleanse, and power to free:
Blessed Jesus, blessed Jesus,
Early let us turn to Thee;
Blessed Jesus, blessed Jesus,
Early let us turn to Thee.

Early let us seek Thy favor,
Early let us do Thy will;
Blessed Lord and only Savior,
With Thy love our bosoms fill:
Blessed Jesus, blessed Jesus,
Thou hast loved us, love us still;
Blessed Jesus, blessed Jesus,
Thou hast loved us, love us still.

Chapter 28
Living Through Your Shipwreck!
Acts 27:1-44

American poet, Henry Wadsworth Longfellow, wrote a famous poem, "The Wreck of the Hesperus". The poem was published in the New World, edited by Park Benjamin, which appeared on January 10, 1840. Longfellow was paid $25 for it, equivalent to $654 in 2015. Longfellow combined fact and fiction to create this poem. His inspiration was the great blizzard of 1839, which ravaged the north-east coast of the United States for 12 hours starting January 6, 1839, destroying 20 ships with a loss of 40 lives. The poem appears to combine two events. Longfellow probably drew for the specifics on the destruction of the Favorite, a ship from Wiscasset, Maine, on the reef of Norman's Woe off the coast of Gloucester, Massachusetts. All aboard were lost, one a woman, who reportedly floated to shore dead but still tied to the mast. The name used in the poem is that of another vessel, lost near Boston. The poem is so well known that the loop road leading close to Norman's Woe from Route 127 is named Hesperus Ave.[122]

It was the schooner Hesperus,
That sailed the wintry sea;
And the skipper had taken his little daughter,
To bear him company.

Blue were her eyes as the fairy-flax,
Her cheeks like the dawn of day,
And her bosom white as the hawthorn buds,
That open in the month of May.

The skipper he stood beside the helm,

---

[122] https://en.wikipedia.org/wiki/The Wreck of the Hesperus.

His pipe was in his mouth,
And he watched how the veering flaw did blow
The smoke now West, now South.

Then up and spake an old Sailor,
Had sailed to the Spanish Main,
"I pray thee, put into yonder port,
For I fear a hurricane.

"Last night, the moon had a golden ring,
And to-night no moon we see!"
The skipper, he blew a whiff from his pipe,
And a scornful laugh laughed he.

Colder and louder blew the wind,
A gale from the Northeast,
The snow fell hissing in the brine,
And the billows frothed like yeast.

Down came the storm, and smote again,
The vessel in its strength;
She shuddered and paused, like a frighted steed,
Then leaped her cable's length.

"Come hither! Come hither! my little daughtèr,
And do not tremble so;
For I can weather the roughest gale
That ever wind did blow."

He wrapped her warm in his seaman's coat
Against the stinging blast;
He cut a rope from a broken spar,
And bound her to the mast.

"O father! I hear the church-bells ring,
Oh say, what may it be?"

"'Tis a fog-bell on a rock-bound coast!" —
And he steered for the open sea.

"O father! I hear the sound of guns,
Oh say, what may it be?"
"Some ship in distress, that cannot live
In such an angry sea!"

"O father! I see a gleaming light,
Oh say, what may it be?"
But the father answered never a word,
A frozen corpse was he.

Lashed to the helm, all stiff and stark,
With his face turned to the skies,
The lantern gleamed through the gleaming snow
On his fixed and glassy eyes.

Then the maiden clasped her hands and prayed
That saved she might be;
And she thought of Christ, who stilled the wave
On the Lake of Galilee.

And fast through the midnight dark and drear,
Through the whistling sleet and snow,
Like a sheeted ghost, the vessel swept
Towards the reef of Norman's Woe.

And ever the fitful gusts between
A sound came from the land;
It was the sound of the trampling surf
On the rocks and the hard sea-sand.

The breakers were right beneath her bows,
She drifted a dreary wreck,
And a whooping billow swept the crew

Like icicles from her deck.

She struck where the white and fleecy waves
Looked soft as carded wool,
But the cruel rocks, they gored her side
Like the horns of an angry bull.

Her rattling shrouds, all sheathed in ice,
With the masts went by the board;
Like a vessel of glass, she stove and sank,
Ho! Ho! The breakers roared!

At daybreak, on the bleak sea-beach,
A fisherman stood aghast,
To see the form of a maiden fair,
Lashed close to a drifting mast.

The salt sea was frozen on her breast,
The salt tears in her eyes;
And he saw her hair, like the brown sea-weed,
On the billows fall and rise.

Such was the wreck of the Hesperus,
In the midnight and the snow!
Christ save us all from a death like this,
On the reef of Norman's Woe!

Paul, as a prisoner, was on his way to Rome, when he and the other 275 passengers are involved in a shipwreck after two weeks at sea in a fierce storm. As you read this 27th chapter of Acts, you can put yourself in the place of these desperate sailors and passengers, traveling on this sailing ship. It was a small craft by our standards, but not just a tiny sailing boat, as it accommodated almost 300 people. When you read Longfellow's poem, as a novice who has not experienced the fury of a terrific storm at sea, you can imagine the experience of being adrift at the mercy of the raging sea.

What do you do in life, when the storm rages on and ultimately your ship goes down or wrecks on the reefs of life? As we read this account, we can gain many insights about the storms of life and how to live through the 'shipwrecks' of life.

Our Reactions To The Storms.

Often one of our reactions, when the storms of life are pounding us is, we **1) Question the severity of the storm. Acts 27:13-20.**

Before you have been a Christian very long, you realize that trusting Christ as your Savior does not exempt you from the storms of life. But when the storm continues for a long period of time, you may question, "Lord, why do the winds continue to blow with such intensity for such a long period of time?"

Paul was within the providential plan of God as he was being taken as a prisoner to Rome. He, along with 275 other passengers, were caught in an intense storm, of hurricane force. In verse 14, we find that they named their hurricanes then as well. This one was called 'Euroclydon', which is a term used for a 'northeasterner', sweeping down from Europe. In Acts 27:13-20, you get a feel of the storm's severity and threat to their safety. *"When the south wind blew softly, supposing that they had obtained their desire, putting out to sea, they sailed close by Crete. But not long after, a tempestuous head wind arose, called Euroclydon. So when the ship was caught, and could not head into the wind, we let her drive. And running under the shelter of an island called Clauda, we secured the skiff with difficulty. When they had taken it on board, they used cables to undergird the ship; and fearing lest they should run aground on the Syrtis Sands, they struck sail and so were driven. And because we were exceedingly tempest-tossed, the next day they lightened the ship. On the third day we threw the ship's tackle overboard with our own hands. Now when neither sun nor stars appeared for many days, and no small tempest beat on us, all hope that we would be saved was finally given up."*

For some the storms of life are of hurricane force and seem to go on indefinitely. Cancer or some other physical affliction strikes your body with destructive force and the treatment seems almost worse than the disease. You experience a job layoff and it seems that God is so slow in answering your prayers about another job. Conflict with a wayward son or daughter ensues that seems to never get resolved. Your mate abandons you and you now struggle with the problems of raising your kids alone. There are many of these storms that come for which there is no clear answer to the question, "Why?" Or, like the Psalmist often asks, "How long, Lord, how long?"

We are like Job who questions God. God says to Job in chapters 38 and 39, "Let me ask you some questions, Job. Job 38:1-13. *"Then the Lord answered Job out of the whirlwind, and said: Who is this who darkens counsel by words without knowledge? Now prepare yourself like a man; I will question you, and you shall answer Me. "Where were you when I laid the foundations of the earth? Tell Me, if you have understanding. Who determined its measurements? Surely you know! Or who stretched the line upon it? To what were its foundations fastened? Or who laid its cornerstone, when the morning stars sang together, and all the sons of God shouted for joy? "Or who shut in the sea with doors, when it burst forth and issued from the womb; when I made the clouds its garment, and thick darkness its swaddling band; when I fixed My limit for it, and set bars and doors; when I said, 'This far you may come, but no farther, and here your proud waves must stop!'* *"Have you commanded the morning since your days began, and caused the dawn to know its place, that it might take hold of the ends of the earth, and the wicked be shaken out of it?"* God continues to question Job, bringing him to the point of humility, recognizing his lack of knowledge and control of all things. Job recognized, as we need to, that "I am not God!"

2) Another reaction is **Depression and despair. Acts 27:20.**

"When neither sun nor stars appeared for many days and no small tempest beat on us, all hope that we would be saved was finally given up." Verse 20

When we get our eyes on the storm instead of on the Master of the storm, like Peter walking on the water toward Jesus, we begin to sink in the ocean of depression and despair. We give up hope and faith is shattered.

What happens to you when you are not only in the storm but your ship is battered on the rocks and it sinks. What is your reaction when you know you are going to die soon because you have terminal cancer? Do you find your hope in the Lord and His wonderful provision for your salvation? Can you face death with confidence that you are saved from God's wrath through the shed blood of Christ on the cross? Can you still sing with the song-writer, "It is well; it is well with my soul?"

It is so difficult to react like the prophet Habakkuk does. *"Though the fig tree does not blossom, nor fruit on the vines, though the labor of the olive may fail, and the fields yield no food; though the flock may be cut off from the fold, and there be no herd in the stalls - yet I will rejoice in the LORD, I will joy in the God of my Salvation. The LORD God is my strength; He will make my feet like deer's feet, and He will make me walk on my high hills."* Habakkuk 3:17-19.

How often we **3) Resort to self-effort to solve the storm. Acts 27:21-32.**

Paul had heard an angel of the Lord regarding the future fate of all aboard. Acts 27:21-26. *"But after long abstinence from food, then Paul stood in the midst of them and said, "Men, you should have listened to me, and not have sailed from Crete and incurred this disaster and loss. And now I urge you to take heart, for there will be no loss of life among you, but only of the ship. For there stood by me this night an angel of the God to whom I belong and whom I serve, saying, 'Do not be afraid, Paul; you must be brought before Caesar; and indeed God has granted you all those who sail with you.' Therefore take heart, men, for I believe God that it will be just as it was told me. However, we must run aground on a certain island."*

However, as they neared the reefs, some sailors attempted to save themselves. Verse 27-32. *"Now when the fourteenth night had come, as we were driven up and down in the Adriatic Sea, about midnight the sailors sensed that they were drawing near some land. And they took soundings and found it to be twenty fathoms; and when they had gone a little farther, they took soundings again and found it to be fifteen fathoms. Then, fearing lest we should run aground on the rocks, they dropped four anchors from the stern, and prayed for day to come. And as the sailors were seeking to escape from the ship, when they had let down the skiff into the sea, under pretense of putting out anchors from the prow, Paul said to the centurion and the soldiers, "Unless these men stay in the ship, you cannot be saved." Then the soldiers cut away the ropes of the skiff and let it fall off."*

Now, we ought to do all that God's word clearly gives us direction to do in solving the problems of storms that have come as a result of our disobedience. If we have sinned, we are to forsake our sin and confess it to the Lord, then accept his forgiveness and cleansing and move on with our lives. 1 John 1:9.

Some storms come to us even when we are obeying our Lord. If you are going through the storm of unemployment, you must be getting out there applying for jobs. PRAY and TRUST the Lord, but don't just sit there and expect God to dump a job in your lap.

Too often, we resort to our own self efforts to extricate ourselves from the storm, which often just result in further problems. We try to escape in our own life boats by our own humanly devised schemes. We face an economic storm and we fall for some get rich scheme by which we are going to solve all our financial problems. We find it is a scam and you end up with a basement full of some 'super' product that you can't sell. You are worse off than you were before.

When it comes to our salvation from sin, are you reverting to your own life boat, your own good works, thinking that you will arrive in heaven? It will never get you there.

Now let's think about **The Reasons for the Storms.**

Often we can never definitively discover why the storm has come to our lives, but there are at least four reasons we discover in Scripture.

1) Sometimes it is Satan's opposition. Acts 27:7-8.

It was God's will for Paul to get to Rome, but he faced great opposition and hindrance in getting there. The storm and the opposing winds were making their progress toward Rome very difficult. The Egyptian ship that was sailing to Rome was boarded by Paul, under the guard of the Roman centurion.

Verses 7-8 speak of this opposition on their journey. *"When we had sailed slowly many days, and arrived with difficulty off Cnidus, the wind not permitting us to proceed, we sailed under the shelter of Crete off Salmone. Passing it with difficulty, we came to a place called Fair Havens, near the city of Lasea."*

Paul speaks of this as he writes in Romans 1:9-10 and 13. *"For God is my witness, whom I serve with my spirit in the gospel of His Son, that without ceasing I make mention of you always in my prayers, making request if, by some means, now at last I may find a way in the will of God to come to you."* . . . *"Now I do not want you to be unaware, brethren, that I often planned to come to you (but was hindered until now), that I might have some fruit among you also, just as among the other Gentiles."*

Storms often come in life when we are doing God's will and obeying Him with fervency of heart. Remember the disciples were sent out by Jesus onto the Sea of Galilee as He ascended the hills to pray. A fierce storm came up on the Sea of Galilee and was threatening their lives. Just because a storm comes in your life, this does not necessarily mean you are sinning and out of God's will. Satan will seek to defeat the plan of God in our lives by sending storms which are providentially allowed by God - a mystery to our finite reason, hidden in the overarching sovereign wisdom of God.

2) Sometimes we are going against God's will. Acts 27:9-12.

Paul gave warning which was godly wisdom given to Paul, not necessarily revelation from God, but his prediction of trouble ahead fit in with good sea sense. This was commonly a very dangerous time of the year, late October and November. The 'fast' referred to in verse 9 was the Day of Atonement commemoration for the Jews that occurred about the time of the autumn equinox or September 21st.[123]

The decision was made by the centurion, on the basis of advice of the ship captain and the owner. According to verse 12, *"the majority advised to set sail. . ."* We live in a democracy, but when it comes to God's revealed will, it isn't up for a vote. When we make decisions contrary to God's revealed will, we are in for some storms of consequence. Just because "everybody's doing it" doesn't make it right. Galatians 6:7 says, *"Do not be deceived, God is not mocked; for whatever a man sows, that he will also reap."*

Sometimes, storms do come because we are sinning and going against God's will. When young people are dabbling around in sexual promiscuity, it often leads to a young girl's pregnancy, and all the resulting stormy consequences. A Christian marries a non-Christian, going against God's command to not be unequally yoked with an unbeliever, and it results in a stormy marriage.

3) Sometimes the storm is to advance our witness. Acts 27:25

How we as Christians react in the midst of the storm will affect our witness for Christ. When we suffer patiently under the mighty hand of God, and still trust our Good Heavenly Father and our loving Savior, others see that there is integrity and reality to our faith.

In this passage, Paul was a strong witness to Julius the centurion, and to the other passengers on board. He shared the word of the Lord boldly and the Lord kept His word. Acts

---

[123] John G. Butler, Analytical Bible Expositor, Volume 12, LBC Publication, Clinton, IA, 2009, page 327.

27:25. *"Therefore take heart, men, for I believe God that it will be just as it was told me."*

Dave Dravecky was a pitcher for the San Francisco Giants, who had his arm break as he was pitching, and they discovered he had cancer in his arm. Dave was a believer and this lead to great opportunities of witness for Jesus Christ. Joni Earickson-Tada, quadriplegic from a teen-age pool accident, has been a powerful tool for Jesus Christ over these many years of her shining faith in Jesus Christ. As the apostle Paul shares in Philippians 1:12-14, *"But I want you to know, brethren, that the things which happened to me have actually turned out for the furtherance of the gospel, so that it has become evident to the whole palace guard, and to all the rest, that my chains are in Christ; and most of the brethren in the Lord, having become confident by my chains, are much more bold to speak the word without fear."*

4) Sometimes storms are used by God to cause us to mature.

Paul had gone through many storms in life and had been shipwrecked three times. He had learned that sufferings are the way to maturity, providing you respond by submitting yourself to the wise and mighty hand of God. We dislike this truth and much of modern Christianity refuses this truth from God's word. The 'word of faith' people and the 'prosperity gospel' people are teaching falsely that if you really trust God, He will always heal you from your diseases and He will always bless you financially. If you accept that false doctrine, then if you are not healed or if you are poor, you will whip yourself or be whipped by the false teachers as they tell you, "You are sinning or you do not have enough faith!"

Listen to Paul's testimony in 2 Corinthians 6:3-10. *"We give no offense in anything, that our ministry may not be blamed.*

But in all things we commend ourselves as ministers of God: in much patience, in tribulations, in needs, in distresses, in stripes, in imprisonments, in tumults, in labors, in sleeplessness, in fastings; by purity, by knowledge, by longsuffering, by kindness, by the Holy Spirit, by sincere love, by the word of truth, by the power of God, by the armor of righteousness on the right hand and on the left, by honor and dishonor, by evil report and good report; as deceivers, and yet true; as unknown, and yet well known; as dying, and behold we live; as chastened, and yet not killed; as sorrowful, yet always rejoicing; as poor, yet making many rich; as having nothing, and yet possessing all things."

1 Peter 1:6-9 also shares the same thoughts about trials leading to maturity in Christ Jesus. *"In this you greatly rejoice, though now for a little while, if need be, you have been grieved by various trials, that the genuineness of your faith, being much more precious than gold that perishes, though it is tested by fire, may be found to praise, honor, and glory at the revelation of Jesus Christ, whom having not seen you love. Though now you do not see Him, yet believing, you rejoice with joy inexpressible and full of glory, receiving the end of your faith - the salvation of your souls."*

Now let's consider **The Results of the Storms.**

We are really already dealing with the results when we talk about God's reason for the storm being to produce maturity in us as His people. But let's address some of the other desired results that come as we respond to God's reasons for the storm.

1) Dependence upon God's presence. Acts 27:23-25.

Paul let the passengers know that God is in their midst. Acts 27:23-25. *"For there stood by me this night an angel of the God to whom I belong and whom I serve, saying, 'Do not be afraid, Paul; you must be brought before Caesar; and indeed God has granted you all those who sail with you.' Therefore take heart, men, for I believe God that it will be just as it was told me."*

Whenever the waves are pounding us and the winds of adversity persist, we are prone to question "Where are you, God?" Satan attacks us as a roaring lion, seeking to devour us! That is the context of what Peter is saying in 1 Peter 5:6-9. *"Therefore humble yourselves under the mighty hand of God, that He may exalt you in due time, casting all your care upon Him, for He cares for you. Be sober; be vigilant; because your adversary the devil walks about like a roaring lion, seeking whom he may devour. Resist him, steadfast in the faith, knowing that the same sufferings are experienced by your brotherhood in the world."*

We have the constant assurance, as believers, that the Master of the storm will never ever abandon us. Matthew 28:20b *". . . surely I am with you always, to the very end of the age."* Hebrews 13:5b also assures us, *". . . God has said, "Never will I leave you; never will I forsake you."*

2) Testing of our faith. Acts 27:25.

Paul speaks of his faith in the midst of the storm Acts 27:25 *"Therefore take heart, men, for I believe God that it will be just as it was told me."* When the storm is howling and persists, or even when your ship sinks, will you still trust in God? Will you believe God?

3) Experience the deliverance of God. Acts 28:1.

God may deliver you from your storm and keep you in this life. Or the time will come when in His wisdom, He takes you home. In the case of the shipwreck on the island of Malta, they all reached shore safely, with no loss of life. Acts 28:1. However our ultimate goal is to arrive home safely on the other side of death. That is the assurance of every true believer, who is saved from his sin by the blood of the Lamb. When we leave this earth, we are going home.

Ultimate healing is being delivered from this frail boat called the physical body and to be home with the Lord. In the time of Christ's return for His redeemed people, all believers will receive their new bodies made like unto his glorious resurrected body.

There is no secure anchor for your soul other than Jesus Christ. He is the Rock of ages, the Solid Rock upon whom we can anchor our lives. He will see you through all the storms of life, no matter how severe they may be. And He will see you through the final storm of death and take you over Jordan to your heavenly home.

The Haven of Rest!
(Henry L. Gilmour, published in 1890)

My soul in sad exile was out on life's sea,
So burdened with sin and distressed,
Till I heard a sweet voice, saying, "Make Me your choice";
And I entered the "Haven of Rest"!

(Refrain)
I've anchored my soul in the "Haven of Rest,"
I'll sail the wide seas no more;
The tempest may sweep over wild, stormy, deep,
In Jesus I'm safe evermore.

I yielded myself to His tender embrace,
In faith taking hold of the Word,

My fetters fell off, and I anchored my soul;
The "Haven of Rest" is my Lord.

The song of my soul, since the Lord made me whole,
Has been the old story so blest,
Of Jesus, who'll save whosoever will have
A home in the "Haven of Rest."

How precious the thought that we all may recline,
Like John, the beloved so blest,
On Jesus' strong arm, where no tempest can harm,
Secure in the "Haven of Rest."

Oh, come to the Savior, He patiently waits
To save by His power divine;
Come, anchor your soul in the "Haven of Rest,"
And say, "My Beloved is mine."

EdenPURE®

GUARANTEE

This product carries a 30-day satisfaction guarantee. If you are not totally satisfied, your purchase price will be refunded if you contact Customer Service to obtain a Return Authorization within thirty (30) days of receipt. Upon receiving Return Authorization, product must be returned within 10 days. The product must be returned in the original packaging to avoid damage to the product during shipping.

LIMITED WARRANTY

The Company warrants this product to the original purchaser to be free from defects in workmanship and materials under normal use and service for 1 year from the date of purchase.

The Limited Warranty is void if any of the following occur: a.) Failure of the product resulting from accident, abuse or misuse; b.) the product has been altered or tampered with in any way, without first contacting Customer Service for authorization; c.) the product was not used correctly or the product was not maintained according to the care instructions.

LIMITATIONS: THE FORGOING LIMITED WARRANTY IS THE SOLE WARRANTY AND THERE ARE NO OTHER WARRANTIES OF ANY KIND, EXPRESS AND/OR IMPLIED. COMPANY HEREBY DISCLAIMS ANY AND ALL OTHER WARRANTIES, EXPRESS AND/OR IMPLIED, INCLUDING, WITHOUT LIMITATION, THE IMPLIED WARRANTIES OF MERCHANTABILITY, NONINFRINGEMENT AND FITNESS OF THE PRODUCT FOR A PARTICULAR PURPOSE. IN NO EVENT WILL COMPANY BE LIABLE FOR ANY SPECIAL, INDIRECT, INCIDENTAL, PUNITIVE, OR CONSEQUENTIAL DAMAGES ARISING FROM, OUT OF OR RELATED TO THE PRODUCT OR YOUR USE THEREOF.

Some jurisdictions do not allow the exclusion or limitation of incidental or consequential damages, so the above limitation or exclusion may not apply to you. The Company will not be responsible for damages or losses, direct or indirect, caused by misuse, abuse, accident, negligence, conditions of transportation or storage, or failure to follow the accompanying written instructions. The Company will not be responsible for any statements that are made or published, written or oral, that are inconsistent with this written warranty, or which are misleading or inconsistent with the facts as published in the literature or specifications by the Company.

LIMITED WARRANTY CLAIM PROCEDURE: During the 1-year Limited Warranty period, a defective product will be repaired or replaced by the Company with the same or similar model without charge. However, return shipping will be at the expense of the consumer. If product has been discontinued and is no longer available and/or cannot be repaired, you will receive a prorated refund of purchase price.

Any consumer returning a defective product for exchange or repair after the 30-day guarantee period will receive a refurbished product in exchange.

PRODUCT MUST BE RETURNED IN THE ORIGINAL BOX AND PACKAGING.

ANY REPAIRED OR REPLACED PRODUCT SHALL BE WARRANTED TO THE ORIGINAL PURCHASER ONLY FOR THE LENGTH OF THE UNEXPIRED PORTION OF THE ORIGINAL LIMITED WARRANTY PERIOD.

For more information, or for assistance, please contact our Customer Service Department at:
Telephone: 1-800-225-6595
E-Mail: custserv@edenpure.com
Website: www.edenpuresupport.com

EdenPURE®

GARANTÍA

Este producto tiene una garantía de satisfacción de 30 días. Si no está totalmente satisfecho, se le devolverá el precio de compra; para ello, comuníquese con el área de Atención a clientes para obtener una autorización de devolución en los treinta (30) días posteriores al recibo. Cuando reciba la autorización de devolución, deberá devolver el producto dentro de un plazo de 10 días. El producto debe devolverse en el empaque original para evitar daños al producto durante el envío.

GARANTÍA LIMITADA

La empresa garantiza al comprador original que este producto está libre de defectos en materiales y mano de obra, en condiciones normales de uso y servicio, por un periodo de 1 año a partir de la fecha de compra.

La garantía limitada no será válida si ocurre algo de lo siguiente: a.) falla del producto que sea consecuencia de un accidente, abuso o mal uso; b.) el producto ha sido alterado o manipulado indebidamente, sin solicitar antes la autorización del área de Atención a clientes; c.) el producto no se usó correctamente o no se le dio mantenimiento de acuerdo con lo que especifican las instrucciones de cuidado.

LIMITACIONES: LA GARANTÍA LIMITADA ANTERIOR ES LA ÚNICA GARANTÍA QUE SE OFRECE Y NO HAY NINGUNA OTRA GARANTÍA DE NINGÚN TIPO, SEA EXPLÍCITA O IMPLÍCITA. LA EMPRESA RECHAZA TODAS Y CADA UNA DE LAS DEMÁS GARANTÍAS, SEAN EXPLÍCITAS O IMPLÍCITAS, INCLUIDAS, ENTRE OTRAS, LAS GARANTÍAS IMPLÍCITAS DE COMERCIABILIDAD, DE NO VULNERACIÓN DE DERECHOS Y DE IDONEIDAD DEL PRODUCTO PARA UN FIN ESPECÍFICO. EN NINGÚN CASO LA EMPRESA SERÁ RESPONSABLE POR DAÑOS ESPECIALES, INDIRECTOS, FORTUITOS, PUNITIVOS O CONSECUENTES QUE SURJAN DE O SE RELACIONEN CON EL PRODUCTO O EL USO DEL MISMO.

Algunas jurisdicciones no permiten la exclusión o limitación de daños fortuitos o consecuentes, por lo que la limitación anterior puede no aplicarse en su caso. La empresa no se hará responsable por daños o pérdidas, directos o indirectos, causados por el mal uso, abuso, accidente, negligencia, condiciones de transporte o almacenamiento, o por no seguir las instrucciones escritas acompañantes. La empresa no se hará responsable por ninguna declaración hecha o publicada, escrita u oral, que sea inconsistente con esta garantía escrita, o que sea engañosa o inconsistente con los hechos publicados en la información impresa o en las especificaciones de la empresa.

PROCEDIMIENTO PARA PRESENTAR UNA RECLAMACIÓN DE GARANTÍA LIMITADA: Durante el período de 1 año de garantía limitada, la empresa reparará el producto defectuoso o lo cambiará por otro igual o de un modelo parecido sin costo alguno. Sin embargo, el embarque de devolución correrá por cuenta del consumidor. Si el producto ha sido discontinuado y ya no está disponible o no puede ser reparado, el usuario recibirá un reembolso prorrateado del precio de compra.
El consumidor que devuelva un producto defectuoso para cambio o reparación después del período de garantía de 30 días recibirá a cambio un producto renovado.

EL PRODUCTO DEBE SER DEVUELTO EN SU CAJA Y EMPAQUE ORIGINALES.

EL PRODUCTO REPARADO O CAMBIADO SE GARANTIZARÁ AL COMPRADOR ORIGINAL ÚNICAMENTE POR EL TIEMPO QUE QUEDE VIGENTE DEL PERÍODO ORIGINAL DE LA GARANTÍA LIMITADA.

Para obtener más información o si necesita ayuda, comuníquese con nuestro
Departamento de Atención a clientes a:
Teléfono: 1-800-225-6595
Correo electrónico: custserv@edenpure.com
Sitio web: www.edenpuresupport.com

Portable 360 Super Fan™
Model: A5982

IMPORTANT:
SAVE THESE
INSTRUCTIONS

To ensure you get the best results
from your Super Fan™, please read
this manual first and keep it for future
reference. For additional information,
please contact your place of purchase
or call 1-800-225-6595

Thank you for choosing EdenPURE®

Your EdenPURE® 360 Super Fan™ cuts your cooling bills over 90%.

Here is why.

The EdenPURE® 360 Super Fan™ cools over 90% less energy than air conditioners.

The EdenPURE® 360 Super Fan™ propels air out over 20 feet with high wind chill cooling. It is an investment that will pay for itself 100 times over.

The EdenPURE® 360 Super Fan™ cools 234% better than a high power ceiling fan. Yet, you can take it to any room. You can then turn the thermostat in your home way up and still be cool and comfortable in the room you are in.

Ceiling fans bring the hottest air from the ceiling down, which is 18° hotter than floor air. The Super Fan takes the coolest air off the floor and moves it 360° around the room. It is a Reverse Ceiling Fan.

The EdenPURE® 360 Super Fan™, in direct position, drops the True Feel Temperature 8 feet from the unit by -17.2°, which is over 243% better cooling than a ceiling fan which only drops it by -7° standing directly under. And, unlike ceiling fans, you can take it anywhere. You can take it room to room, to your porch, patio, garage and camping sites.

The EdenPURE® 360 Super Fan™ in direct position 8 feet away, can change an 87° temperature in an area to a 70° True Feel Temperature in 15 seconds.

The EdenPURE® 360 Super Fan™ provides a much more comfortable and healthy cooling than air conditioning. Air conditioning produces an uncomfortable chill and puts a lot of viruses and black mold bacteria in the air because of condensation.

IMPORTANT INSTRUCTIONS

READ AND SAVE THESE INSTRUCTIONS
BEFORE USING THIS PRODUCT

When using electrical appliances, basic safety precautions should always be followed to reduce the risk of fire, electric shock, and injury to persons, including the following:

- Always operate the product from a power source of the same voltage, frequency and rating as indicated on the product identification plate.

- Remove the unit from its packaging and check to make sure it is in good condition before using.

- Do not let children play with parts of the packaging (such as plastic bags).

- Close supervision is necessary when the product is used by or near children or persons with reduced physical, sensory or mental capabilities. Do not allow children to use it as a toy.

- Do not operate any product with a damaged cord or plug, or after the product malfunctions, or is dropped or appears damaged in any way. Contact Customer Service for repair or replacement.

- Before unplugging the power cord, be sure to turn the power off. When touching the unit, be sure your hands are dry to prevent electrical shock.

- Never install the unit where it is exposed to direct sunlight, excessive moisture/rain, dust and lack of ventilation near any heat sources.

- Avoid making contact with moving parts. Never insert fingers, pencils or any other objects through the guards whenever the power plug is connected, especially while the unit is working.

- Always place the fan on a stable, level surface when operating to prevent the fan from overturning. Do not run the power cord under carpet. Do not cover the power cord with throw rugs or runners. Route the power cord away from walking paths so that nobody can trip over it. The cable should be kept away from heat, sharp edges and oil.

- To reduce the risk of electric shock, do not immerse or expose the product or flexible cord to rain, moisture or any liquid other than those necessary for correct operation of the product.

- This product should not be used in the immediate vicinity of water, such as bathtub, sink, swimming pool etc., where the likelihood of immersion or splashing could occur.

- Switch off and unplug from outlet when not in use, and before cleaning. Remove by grasping the plug - do not pull on the cord.

- Be sure that no other high current appliances are plugged into the same circuit as your fan, as an overload can occur.

- Do not use the appliance for other than its intended use.

- Do not leave the appliance unattended when switched on.

- Do not cover the grill, or operate in close proximity to curtains etc.

- The use of attachments or accessories not recommended or sold by the product distributor may cause personal or property hazards or injuries.

- This product is intended for normal domestic/household use only.

- Never leave a working appliance unattended, even for a short period of time – always switch it off. Please unplug the appliance from the power supply when not in use.

- Use this fan as described in this manual. Any other uses not recommended by the manufacturer may cause fire, electric shock, or injury to persons and may void the warranty.

- This appliance is not intended for use by persons (including children) with reduced physical, sensory or mental capabilities, or lack of experience and knowledge, unless they have been given supervision or instruction concerning the use of the appliance by a person responsible for their safety.

- Children should be supervised to ensure that they do not play with the appliance.

- **WARNING:** If the power cord is damaged, it must be replaced by the manufacturer, its service agent or similarly qualified persons in order to avoid a hazard.

- This product has not been designed for any uses other than those specified in this booklet.

- **CAUTION:** Never insert your fingers or any other objects (hair, clothes, utensils, knives, screw drivers etc.) into the openings of the guard or close to the blade when the appliance is connected to the power supply.

CAUTION: DO NOT COVER the appliance in any way in order to avoid overheating and fire.

CAUTION - RISK OF ELECTRIC SHOCK: To reduce the risk of electric shock do not open this device: there are no serviceable parts for customers. Please contact Customer Service.

BEFORE FIRST USE

Before use, remove all packaging materials and inspect the appliance for any damage. If there appears to be any damage, please take the unit back to place of purchase for a replacement.

Assembly 1
Pressing the buttons on the base

Press the buttons (1) on each side of the base of the fan (A).

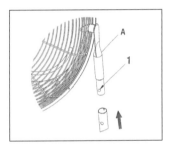

Assembly 2
Connecting the bracket

Insert the fan (A) onto the bracket (B) until the buttons snap into place in the bracket (B).

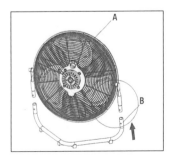

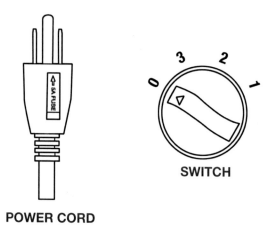

SWITCH

POWER CORD

TURNING THE FAN ON/OFF AND ADJUSTING THE AIRFLOW SETTINGS

1. Plug the power cord into an outlet.
2. Turn the switch to the desired speed. The settings are 0 = Off, 3 = High, 2 = Medium, 1 = Low.

OPERATING INSTRUCTIONS

NOTE: Before inserting the plug into a power outlet, make sure that the correct voltage being used, corresponding to what is indicated on the rating label.

CAUTION: Select a suitable location for the fan. Always choose a safe location in accordance to the safely recommendations outlined.

1. Unpack the fan gently.
2. Remove the protective foam and plastic bag and save it for future use.
3. Place the fan on a dry, firm and level surface.
4. Plug the DC Plug of the adaptor to the DC connector that is located at the fan's base.
5. Turn the switch to the desired speed. 0 = Off, 1 = Low, 2 = Medium, 3 = High
6. To turn the unit OFF, turn the switch to "0".

CAUTION: The fan should always be switched off before moving the unit to a different location.

CARE & CLEANING

NOTE: If the power cord set of this appliance becomes damaged, discontinue use. Repairs should be undertaken only by a qualified technician. Contact Customer Service.

CAUTION:

To avoid of electric shock, you must always switch off and unplug the fan before cleaning.

Do not use harsh detergents, chemical cleaners or solvents as they may damage the surface finish of the plastic components and the finish.

Your appliance must be switched OFF via the main power supply and unplugged, and allow it to cool down before proceeding with any cleaning.

- Clean the product with a damp cloth, a vacuum cleaner or a dusting brush.
- DO NOT use the product in oily or dirty areas (i.e. the kitchen, smoky places, etc), as air vents may become blocked.
- DO NOT use gasoline, paint thinner, solvents or abrasive cleaners on this appliance.
- DO NOT immerse the fan in water or liquid and never allow water to drip into the motor housing.

Store the fan in the original packaging or cover the fan to protect it from dust.

NOTE: If the power cord set of this appliance becomes damaged, discontinue use. Repairs should be undertaken only by a qualified technician. Contact Customer Service.

DISPOSAL
Environmental Protection

Electrical products should not be disposed of with household waste. Please recycle where facilities exist. Check with your Local Authority for recycling advice.

SPECIFICATIONS
Model: A5982
Voltage: 120
Wattage: 157
Amperage: 1.35A

CUSTOMER SERVICE
For repairs or service, please visit your place of purchase, call 1-800-225-6595 or visit www.edenpuresupport.com.

Follow us/Like us

facebook.com/
Edenpure

Instagram.com/
edenpureproducts

twitter.com/
edenpure_

pinterest.com/
Edenpure

<u>WARNING</u>
ANY REQUIRED SERVICE OTHER THAN ROUTINE CLEANING SHOULD ONLY BE PERFORMED BY AN AUTHORIZED SERVICE REPRESENTATIVE

Chapter 29
The Foundations of the Church Completed!
Acts 28:1-31

Luke wraps up his account of the grace revolution with the details of Paul's arrival in Rome and his stay as a prisoner in Rome. Although he was a prisoner awaiting his trial before Emperor Nero, he was given considerable liberty and carried on his witness there in Rome. Acts 28:30-31 tells us, *"Then Paul dwelt two whole years in his own rented house, and received all who came to him, preaching the kingdom of God and teaching the things which concern the Lord Jesus Christ with all confidence, no one forbidding him."*

They had ship-wrecked on the island of Malta and were welcomed warmly by the residents of the island. Acts 28:1-10. Paul was bitten by a poisonous viper that emerged from some sticks that he had gathered to place on the fire that the islanders had started to keep them warm in the cool rainy weather. He was not harmed and the islanders thought him to be a god because of it. Paul healed the father of Publius from dysentery and a fever. Publius was an estate owner on Malta who had hosted them for three days.

After three months, they sailed from Malta on an Alexandrian ship, named Twin Brothers that had wintered at the island because of the inclement weather conditions. They finally made their way to Rome where some Christian brothers had met them. Paul, and other prisoners were delivered to the captain of the guard by the centurion who had escorted them to Rome. Verse 16 tells us that *"Paul was permitted to dwell by himself with the soldier who guarded him."*

Paul, after only three days in Rome, called for the Jewish leaders and began witnessing to them, sharing the facts of his false arrest by the Jewish leaders in Jerusalem. He is persistent in sharing the gospel message with many who came to his dwelling place to discuss *"the kingdom of God, persuading them concerning Jesus from both the Law of Moses and the Prophets, from morning to evening. And some were persuaded by the things that were spoken, and some disbelieved."* Verses 23-24.

Luke ends his record of the grace revolution without any reference to Paul's fate or death. Therefore, we must assume that at the time of Luke's writing, Paul was still alive.

For these two years, (60-62 AD), Paul is chained to a Roman guard, one of several guards who rotated shifts. As a result, over time, many soldiers were converted. Ephesians, Philippians and Colossians are the prison epistles, all written during this time of Paul's confinement in Rome. In Philippians 1:12-14, Paul refers to the success of his witness to the palace guards. *"But I want you to know, brethren, that the things which happened to me have actually turned out for the furtherance of the gospel, so that it has become evident to the whole palace guard, and to all the rest, that my chains are in Christ; and most of the brethren in the Lord, having become confident by my chains, are much more bold to speak the word without fear."*

In spite of the inconvenience of being chained to a guard, Paul carries on his ministry, with many people coming and going. This is how the Acts of the Apostles ends. Paul is in the heart of the Roman Empire, declaring the gospel openly, with the full knowledge of the Roman government, which is a marvelous success.

It is general consensus that Paul was released by Emperor Nero because the Jews that had accused him had not come, over a period of two years, to prosecute their case. Probably Paul was released in 62 AD or early in 63 AD. Little is known of Paul's ministry during this brief time of freedom, but tradition says that he made his way to Spain and other European colonies.

Then an event occurred that had a major impact on the Christian movement, especially in Rome. Rome burned! On the night of July 18-19, 64 AD a fire began in the region of the Roman circus and burned down half the city before it was brought under control after six days. Various rumors circulated about the fire's origin and many held Nero responsible.

Roman historian Tacitus told us that after the fire, Nero brought in food supplies and opened places to accommodate the refugees. Of Rome's fourteen districts only four remained intact. Three were leveled to the ground. The other seven were reduced to a few scorched and mangled ruins.

The great fire of Rome was a terrible tragedy! But then it got blamed on the Christians. According to Roman historian Tacitus (56-120 AD), most of the Roman residents believed that the fire was the result of an order by Nero.

The date of Paul's death is believed to have occurred after the Great Fire of Rome in July of 64 AD, but before the last year of Nero's reign, in 68 AD. According to several Church Fathers and apocryphal books, Paul was beheaded in Rome by orders of Nero, but the exact date is uncertain.

Paul apparently wasn't convicted by accusations of the Jews that brought him to Rome to be tried before Nero about 60-62 AD. But after the terrible fire that consumed much of Rome, anyone considered as a leader of the Christians in Rome was subject to arrest and death, whether or not he was a Roman citizen. We can assume that Paul was arrested once more and was in custody in Rome sometime in 64 or 65 AD.

Tradition tells us that Paul spent his last imprisonment in the infamous Mamertine prison in Rome. There prisoners were lowered through an opening into a lower dungeon. Both St. Peter and St. Paul were imprisoned there, according to tradition.[124]

It is thought by many historians that Paul wrote his second letter to his protégé pastor, Timothy, while in this second imprisonment in the Mamertine dungeon. 2 Timothy 1:16-17 and 2:9 speak of his suffering in chains. It is also likely that Paul also wrote his letter to Titus during this imprisonment. One of the laments of Paul is that no one from the Christian community in Rome stood with him in his trials, but they all abandoned him. 2 Timothy 4:16-17. Paul asks Timothy to come to him, because Demas had forsaken him. He asked Timothy to bring his cloak and the books, especially the parchments. 2 Timothy 4:9-13.

The spreading of the gospel of grace has continued for almost two thousand years. Many have come to be followers of Jesus, the Christ, through the faithful witness of God's servants who have followed in the steps of the apostles. Many have been faithful in discipling others as Paul instructed Timothy to do, in 2 Timothy 2:2. *"And the things you have heard from me among many witnesses, commit to faithful men who will be able to teach others also."*

With the deaths of the apostles Paul and Peter, the foundation of the Church of Jesus Christ was completed. The apostle Paul refers to two aspects of the foundation of the Church of Jesus Christ in his writings.

---

[124] Information from Dr. Ralph F. Wilson is the Director of Joyful Heart Renewal Ministries. Drawn from http://www.jesuswalk.com/paul/10_prison.htm. Also information from other sources such as Wikipedia.

There is one foundation of the Church and that is the Person of Jesus Christ himself. 1 Corinthians 3:10-11 makes this abundantly clear. *"According to the grace of God which was given to me, as a wise master builder I have laid the foundation, and another builds on it. But let each one take heed how he builds on it. For no other foundation can anyone lay than that which is laid, which is Jesus Christ."* Paul taught that he was laying the foundation of the churches on the gospel of Jesus Christ, The gospel and the foundation of the church is Jesus Christ. The foundation is all found in who Jesus is. It is all founded in the incarnation and in the redemptive work of Jesus on the cross. It is all verified by the literal resurrection of Jesus Christ from the grave. There is no salvation apart from Jesus Christ and there is no Church without Jesus, the Messiah.

However, there is a second aspect of that foundation that Paul speaks of in Ephesians 2:19-22. *"Now, therefore, you are no longer strangers and foreigners, but fellow citizens with the saints and members of the household of God, having been built on the foundation of the apostles and prophets, Jesus Christ Himself being the chief cornerstone, in whom the whole building, being fitted together, grows into a holy temple in the Lord, in whom you also are being built together for a dwelling place of God in the Spirit."* This foundation of which Paul speaks to the church of Ephesus is the foundational teachings (doctrines) upon which the Church of Jesus Christ is built. Paul was careful to clarify that Jesus Christ is the 'chief cornerstone' of those foundational teachings.

Much of our New Testament is composed of the writings of Paul, and the other apostles. Some of the four Gospels may have been in existence before the death of the apostles Paul and Peter. Luke wrote his gospel before he wrote the book of Acts, according to Acts 1:1, where he refers to his former account to Theophilus.[125]

How long will the doors of heaven be open to those who repent in godly sorrow and turn to place their faith in the death, burial and resurrection of their Savior? No one knows but the signs of the times are pointing to the soon return of our Savior. If you are not yet a believer, let the Spirit of God convince you as you research the truth about Jesus, the Son of God. Become a recipient of God's grace, providing you with the gift of eternal life. Put your faith in Jesus Christ for there is no *"salvation in any other; for there is no other name under heaven given among men by which we must be saved."* Acts 4:12.

As the apostle John concluded his gospel account, *"Jesus said to him, "Thomas, because you have seen Me, you have believed. Blessed are those who have not seen and yet have believed." And truly Jesus did many other signs in the presence of His disciples, which are not written in this book; but these are written that you may believe that Jesus is the Christ, the Son of God, and that believing you may have life in His name."*

Going Home To My Master
(Written by Norman P. Anderson)

---

[125] From https://evidenceforchristianity.org/what-are-the-dates-when-the-four-gospels-were-first-written-how-do-we-know/
"It is general consensus of conservative scholars puts Mark at about AD 60-65. Some even put Mark in the 50s AD. Matthew and Luke are usually given a date of writing of about AD 60-70 and John AD 70-90. These are obviously rough approximations. Such dates are based on guesses about which authors relied on the others. For instance, it is not unreasonable (though not proven) to think that Mark was a source for Matthew and Luke. Matthew and Luke relate prophecies of the destruction of Jerusalem (which happened in AD 70) which seems to support these books being published before AD 70."

(Refrain)
Going home to my Master, where all is joy and peace.
Going home to my Jesus, where all storms have ceased.
Going home to my Savior where death shall reign no more.
I'm going home, yes, I'm just going home.

The years have been good ones I've lived on this earth.
I have had times of trouble and of mirth.
I have seen the Lord's hand in all His wise ways.
His grace and His mercy have showered my days.
From my sin and my lostness, Jesus rescued me.
He redeemed me and gave me faith to believe
His blood is sufficient to save me from sin,
And give me a home where life shall never end.

(Refrain)
Going home to my Master, where all is joy and peace.
Going home to my Jesus, where all storms have ceased.
Going home to my Savior where death shall reign no more.
I'm going home, yes, I'm just going home.

The cross made the difference, life instead of death.
There is no more fear of my final breath.
I long for the day, to see Him face to face,
When I take my last step at the end of my race.
My heart is longing to hear your loud trumpet call
To meet you in heaven ere sunset shall fall.
By death or the rapture, of which will it be?
Whatever your will, you'll be waiting for me.

(Refrain)
Going home to my Master, where all is joy and peace.
Going home to Jesus, where all storms have ceased.
Going home to my Savior where death shall reign no more.

I'm going home, yes, I'm just going home.

I'll be singing in the choir, perfect harmony,
Bringing glory to God eternally.
With those from all nations, color and of race,
We'll praise our King Jesus, see Him face to face.
There'll be no night there for Jesus will be the Light,
No sickness, no sin, for all then will be right.
I'll see all my loved ones who've gone on before,
Who are saved by His blood, alive ever-more.

(Refrain)
Going home to my Master, where all is joy and peace.
Going home to my Jesus, where all storms have ceased.
Going home to my Savior where death shall reign no more.
I'm going home, yes, I'm just going home.

Made in the USA
San Bernardino, CA
17 January 2020